WOMEN IN CLASS SOCIETY

WOMEN
in Class Society

Heleieth I.B. Saffioti

Translated from the Portuguese
by Michael Vale

Monthly Review Press
New York and London

Library of Congress Cataloging in Publication Data
Saffioti, Heleieth Iara Bongiovani.
    Women in class society.
    Translation of A Mulher na sociedade de classes.
    Bibliography: p. 367
    1. Women—social conditions. 2. Women
—Brazil. I. Title.
HQ1150.S213   301.41'2   77-76170
ISBN 0-85345-415-9

Monthly Review Press
62 West 14th Street, New York, N.Y. 10011
47 Red Lion Street, London WC1R 4PF

Manufactured in the United States of America

10 9 8 7 6 5 4 3 2 1

Contents

Introduction by Eleanor Burke Leacock   ix

Preface to the American Edition   1

Author's Introduction   3

PART I: WOMEN AND CAPITALISM

Chapter 1. Class and Status in Stratified Society   13

Chapter 2. Levels of Consciousness
of the Woman Problem   31

Chapter 3. The Rise of Capitalism
and the Social Position of Women   35

     Aspects of Capitalist Production

     Women and the Birth of Capitalism

     Historical Trends

     Vicissitudes of Female Labor

     Organized Labor and Women

Chapter 4. The Socialist Perspective   74

     The Utopian Socialists

     Marxism

     Views of Women and the Family Structure:
       A Critique

PART II:
THE HISTORY OF WOMEN'S CONDITION IN BRAZIL

*Chapter 5. Some Aspects of the Development
of the Brazilian Economy*   95

    Introduction

    The Slave-Owning Economy

    Abolition of Slavery, 1850

    Wage Labor and Economic Development

Chapter 6. The Social Position of Women   115

    The Broader System of Domination

    The Female Slave and Her Master

    The White Woman of the Manor

    Changes in the Family Structure:
        The Nineteenth-Century Transition

    The Uneven Spread of Urbanization
        and Industrialization

*Chapter 7. Education for Women in Brazil from
the Colonial Period to the Present*   140

    The Eternal View of Women

    Religious Education: The Role of the Convents

    The Imperial Education System

    The Growth of Normal Schools

    Colonialism Defends Its Role in Education

    The Liberal Challenge

    The Education of Women Under the Republic

    Protestant Schools

    Normal Schools Under the Republic:
        The State of São Paulo

    Education After the 1930 Revolution

Chapter 8. The Female Workforce   179
     General Considerations
     Employment of Women in Brazil

Chapter 9. Manifestations of Feminism   197
     Sources and Perspectives
     The Code for Women: Early Struggles
     The Code for Women, 1937
     Left-Wing Movements and Brazilian Feminism
     Conclusions: Feminism and the Feminist Mystique
     Appendix I: Feminist Manifesto,
        Brazilian Federation for Women's Progress, 1928
     Appendix II: Women's Labor Code, May 17, 1932

PART III:
THE FEMININE MYSTIQUE AND THE SCIENTIFIC ERA

Introduction: Rationality and Irrationality   237

*Chapter 10. Psychoanalytic Theory and
     the Feminine Mystique*   240
     Freudian Theory
     Freud and Social Theory
     The Feminine Mystique as a Social Control Myth

Chapter 11. Margaret Mead and Cultural Relativism   263

*Chapter 12. Linkages Between the Occupational Structure
     and the Kinship Structure*   272
     Social Status and Competition
     Socialization and the Category of Sex

*Chapter 13. The Position of Women in
    Dialectical Perspective*   281
    The Social Division of Labor

Conclusion   297

Notes   307

Bibliography   367

INTRODUCTION

by Eleanor Burke Leacock

It is important for English-speaking readers to have Heleieth Saffioti's analysis of women in capitalist society made available. This treatment, written over a decade ago by a Latin American woman and from a Latin American perspective, was a significant pace setter in the effort to define the relations between women's issues and class struggle. Furthermore, the book not only presents a broad theoretical statement on women's oppression and the perpetuation of capitalist relations generally, but deals with women in one country, Brazil, in the kind of historical detail that is much needed for all areas.

At present the maintenance of bourgeois power relies heavily on divisions within the working class, and between it and its potential allies. Nationally, regionally, and locally, people are being pitted against each other according to race, sex, nationality, religion, and increasingly, age as well. A strong international coalition of socialist-oriented women could play a critical role in helping to clarify and overcome these divisions. To build such a coalition, however, requires understanding of variations in women's position in different countries and different classes. Such understanding, in turn, requires for discussion studies that have the scope and rigor of Saffioti's work.

The issues raised in *Women in Class Society* can be grouped under six topics: (1) the economic marginalization of women in capitalist society; (2) functions served by family organization (or kinship, as Saffioti puts it) in capitalist society; (3) relations among sex, race, and class; (4) the organization of women in imperialist and in Third World nations; (5) science and the ideology of the "feminine mystique"; and (6) women and the struggle for socialism. As Saffioti notes in her preface to this edition, a great deal of both empirical and theoretical work on the issue of women has been done in the decade following the first edition of her book. Accordingly, I shall comment on the significance of Saffioti's main points in relation to these six topics, as I understand them, and note some of the directions subsequent analyses have been taking.

The Marginalization of Women in Capitalist Society

Saffioti's central point is that the "marginalization" of women follows from the inability of a capitalist economy to employ all potential workers, and its need for a reserve army of labor that can be utilized or cast aside in accord with economic exigencies. Women's position, then, is not so much based on family demands, as these are commonly conceived, as family structure itself is based on the marginalization of women that is essential to capitalism. This reality is rationalized by the "masculinity complex" and the "feminine mystique," that socialize the sexes for their roles and help to make them acquiesce in the exploitation of their labor. Although struggles to reform women's status have been important, women's full liberation is impossible without their equal participation in production and the concomitant socialization of domestic duties. These goals are only achievable in a collective economy; hence women's liberation is inseparably linked to the emancipation of men. However, Saffioti points out that while women's status has greatly improved in contemporary socialist countries, their full equalization is by no means automatically ensured but requires continued struggle.

In tracing the history of women in Brazil, Saffioti explicates two further points that are relevant to the understanding of women's situation internationally. First, contrary to common assumptions, capitalism has not been responsible for drawing women into production. Instead, as capitalism develops, the formerly productive functions of family units are taken over by factory organization and women are pushed out of public production. Second, Brazil, along with other Latin American countries, cannot be considered comparable to feudal Europe, as an underdeveloped area that is now being "modernized." Brazil can be understood only in terms of the deliberate shaping of underdeveloped capitalist countries by the core countries of the capitalist system. The marginalized position of Brazil has meant that the process whereby women have been pushed out of public production as capitalism has developed has been more extreme than in the controlling countries, and that the ideals of female docility and male authority which were defined with respect to white, upper-class women under the "slavocratic seigneurial order" have been more rigidly maintained.

Saffioti, then, is among those scholars who have emphasized the planned underdevelopment of the neocolonial world, and she has explored the concrete implications of this controlled underdevelopment for the exploitation of women. The undercutting of women's productive activities that takes place as colonial countries are drawn into a fully capitalist economy, and the concomitant constriction of areas in which they exercise a measure of control, has since been documented for other areas besides Brazil.[1] Parallel and contradictory developments that need to be assessed in their specificity in each country are the movement of some women into government bureaucracies, where they may raise issues concerning the equalization of women's social and legal status, and the utilization of women as grossly underpaid labor by multinational corporations.

The Family in Capitalist Society

A kinship structure based on economically independent nuclear family units, in which a male wage earner is supposed to support his wife and growing children, is economically, socially, and ideologically of primary importance to capitalism, and despite much evidence to the contrary, the nuclear family is commonly presented as a "natural" human universal. In the present work and elsewhere,[2] Saffioti discusses the multiple functions served by the capitalist family form. Economically, the family maintains women as a reserve labor force that can be manipulated according to economic exigencies, while drawing on their unpaid labor to add to the productivity of men and to rear and socialize successive generations of workers; socially, it acts as a buffer, mitigating the intense competitiveness of the capitalist system; and ideologically, it mystifies women's economic marginalization through the fiction that family structure flows naturally from the attributes of men and women, and the assumption that the man's wage is sufficient for family maintenance.

Further elucidation of capitalist family organization and the history of its emergence is now being offered by work in various world areas and different periods. A wealth of new data on changes in family function as well as reinterpretations of old data are being produced. Insofar as it is possible to categorize these studies, they pertain to five broad lines of inquiry: (1) analysis of production relations in "primitive communal" society in which multi-family bands or kin groups, rather than nuclear families, are the basic economic and reproductive units; (2) historical reconstruction of the linked processes whereby both class differentiation and patriarchal relations between the sexes developed; (3) study of changes in family function and the economic relations among men, women, and children in the transition to capitalism; (4) interpretation of kinship and family among the most severely exploited workers, both in colonized nations and among racially oppressed peoples in colonizing nations, where the idealized nuclear family form is often less viable than serial polygamy and broad kin networks; and (5) examination of relations among female employment and migration and family function.[3]

In each area, the long overdue attempt to define women's changing position in terms of political economy has led to important discussion and debate. Saffioti's formulation of the multiple functions family organization serves in capitalist society is apparently directed against positions that imply women's full liberation to be achievable through reforms in educational, occupational, or family policies, rather than through fundamental social transformation. She recently has restated her point that it is not the family that keeps women in an inferior position in the labor force and in society, but the need for women's marginalized role as workers and as the unpaid producers and reproducers of the labor force that is responsible for family organization and its social-psychological concomitants. "The institution, family, which has been viewed as the obstacle to developing the female situation in a direction parallel to the development of the economic system of class societies, is merely one of the principal means through which that same economic system can survive."[4]

In another recent article, Saffioti takes explicit issue with Mariarosa Dalla Costa's formulation that the unpaid labor of women in the household *directly* produces surplus value—in precise Marxist terms, Saffioti states, the process is indirect—and also criticizes Ira Gerstein's alternate formulation that the production of labor power by the family is "simple commodity production"—with simple commodity production, people control the distribution of their products. Instead, Saffioti stresses the historical specificity of the capitalist family form as "a social institution which is highly adapted to capitalist production." She also restates the important distinction to be made between possibilities available to women in central capitalist countries, where massive investment in nonproductive areas is possible, and in peripheral countries, where the greater burden of capitalist exploitation is borne.[5]

Relations Among Sex, Race, and Class

Saffioti points out that the natural category of race, like that of sex, is seized upon by capitalism not only to increase profits, but also to obscure the basic class nature of exploitation. Perhaps the most painful contradiction on the contemporary political scene lies in the fact that people who share the same ultimate class interests are so widely and successfully played against each other by virtue of race and sex. A central responsibility for Marxist writers should be to interpret the interrelatedness of oppression by race, class, and sex in whatever situations they are addressing, in order to help achieve the revolutionary potential of common struggle against all three. It is tragic, however, that instead, the recognition of class exploitation as basic commonly has been insisted upon in a mechanical manner that ignores oppression by race and sex and nullifies the power of struggle against it. Elsewhere I have referred to the prevalent tendency to picture capitalism as a largely internal European development centered wholly on the exploitation of people who were white and male.[6] The implication of such a view is that the oppression of nonwhites, however harsh and brutal, is somehow peripheral to the dominant mode of exploitation. Historically, however, it was the uniting of class and racial exploitation on a world scale that made the triumph of the European bourgeoisie possible. Saffioti's historical treatment of Brazilian women reaffirms the further fact that the double oppression of working-class women and the triple oppression of nonwhite working-class women were, and continue to be, fundamental to capitalist exploitation. Readily observable conditions reflect analytic reality.[7]

In Brazil, as in the United States, the relation between oppression by race and that by sex was recognized by those early feminists who spoke out against slavery. However, although feminists in Brazil made important gains for women in educational and legal reforms, as Saffioti shows, most of them did not overcome their ties with their privileged upper-class status. The gap between upper- and lower-class women in colonial Latin America was enormous, not only with regard to standard of living, but also pertaining to family organization and lifestyle. Saffioti describes the polarized positions of white, upper-class women and black slave women as defined by the slavocratic seigneurial order, and Elinor Burkett has recently offered similar data on elite and Indian and black women in colonial Peru.[8]

White women of the seigneurial class in Brazil were married in their teens. They were raised to grace patrimonial estates as mothers of legitimate heirs, and the luxury they enjoyed was restricted to the confines of their cloistered status in strictly patriarchal households. While some few among them rebelliously took lovers or used their energies as resourceful and capable managers (to what extent is a subject that invites further research), most were pressed into the social style of modest dependence, albeit underlaid by seductive manipulativeness that was the accepted pattern for feminine behavior. The restricted position of women in the upper-class family was counterposed against the license of the household head with respect to his female slaves. Since the household head commonly recognized and took some interest in his illegitimate children, the upper-class family was in effect polygynous, although the polygyny was one in which women had no formally recognized voice regarding decisions about their own persons or their children.

The upper-class family structure necessarily presupposed a different family structure among the slaves. Furthermore, such a family structure was an impossibility for poor whites, and Saffioti points out that daughters in poor white families often resorted to prostitution to support themselves. Saffioti refers to the "instability" and common law marriage that became the formal characteristics of the working-class family. The actual structure of working-class family relations, the importance of wide kin ties, the significance of greater personal freedom for women, black-white differences, and changes over time are all important subjects for detailed investigation. The nature of kinship structures in the independent communities of escaped slaves that kept forming on Brazilian frontiers should also be examined, insofar as the sparse data allow, as well as the instances where black women became elevated to leading positions in what were in effect Afro-Indian societies.[9]

Whereas the extreme gap between Brazilian upper- and lower-class women was modified somewhat with an end to slavery and the growth of the urban proletariat and the middle class, the leaders of the developing feminist movement continued to confront contradictions between their interests as part of an elite and their interests as women. These contradictions were and are important throughout the capitalist world. However, I think it is fair to say that there has been a rapidly growing recognition among academic, professional, and other middle-class or elite women that it is not enough to take up women's issues as such; and that if effective organization is to be achieved, ways have to be found to put the knowledge and resources of such women at the service of working-class women in the process of active alliance.

Saffioti writes of the divisiveness in working-class organization that resulted from male bias against working women, especially in the trade unions. Along with women's practical difficulties in finding time beyond job and family, and the effects of their socialization as ideally dependent, Saffioti points out that such negative male attitudes discouraged women from organizing, although they were often militant enough when it came to striking. Like the contradictions in feminist programs, this pattern is also contemporary and widespread. Furthermore, it coexists with the divisiveness caused by institutionalized racial discrimination and attitudes of white superiority.

It is impossible to overstate the importance of such divisions to contemporary capitalism. Workers, men and women the world around, are now being exploited directly by the same network of capitalist enterprises. European capitalism now depends on what United States capitalism has long built upon: mass migrations of labor from Third World countries, which furnish cheap labor, save the social cost of reproducing the national labor force, and can be used to divide the working class politically. Women constitute an important sector of this migrant labor. Concomitantly, multinational corporations based in central capitalist countries are exporting industry to peripheral countries where workers can be grossly underpaid, and these are often women. In sum, a truly international proletariat is being built at a rapid pace, and women are an integral part of it. Given this central fact of the contemporary world, it is little wonder that holders of power use all means at their command to perpetuate strife and discord through structuring competitive relations among workers by race and sex, and to see that these relations are bolstered with ideological assertions of the "natural" dependence of women and the inferiority or undependability of nonwhites.

Feminist Organization

In her sympathetic but critical history of feminist activity in Brazil, Saffioti offers valuable material that is unfamiliar to English-speaking readers. Her discussion of the distinctions between bourgeois feminism and socialist feminism signals an enormously important step in the understanding of women's position economically and its significance for women's organization that was taking place at the time of her writing. In my student days in the 1940s, *feminism* meant *bourgeois feminism* in left-wing terminology, at least in the United States. As I remember it, the assumption was widespread that to organize around women's problems was by its very nature antithetical to organization in the interests of the working class. Nonetheless many Marxist women were convinced that a feminist orientation which is clearly concerned with the vast majority of women and their needs is not only compatible with working-class goals but is essential to their realization. Saffioti's analysis of the significance of women's position in the capitalist family has for the reproduction of capitalist relations is one of the major statements underwriting that conviction.[10]

Not that the definition of socialist or Marxist feminism solves the problem of how to build unity between middle-class (or occasional upper-class) women and working-class women; but it does place the problem in workable perspective. Saffioti's own treatment of class relationships among women is purely historical, stopping short of the contemporary period, and lacks information on contemporary lifestyles and attitudes of working-class women. She has been conducting research on women in domestic and factory work which will fill this gap.[11] At present there is continual writing, debate, and discussion among women of Marxist or radical commitment about questions that are critical for uniting middle-class or elite women and working-class women at local and national levels, and women of capitalist and colonial nations on an international level. Bulletins and working papers, as well as formally published articles, are discussing the relations between oppression by sex and oppression by race (I see the major problem here to be overcoming chauvinistic attitudes among white women and helping them recognize the necessity of respecting the leadership and insights of black and other racially and nationally oppressed women); the different orientations and short-term goals of women in different classes with regard to work and family life; the different understanding of relations between short-term goals and the long-term struggle for socialism in imperialist nations and in nations that must join this fight with that for national liberation; and the relations between taking action against job discrimination in its various forms, against violence and brutality toward women, for decent child care, schools, and housing, and on other immediate issues, and the building of a class-conscious socialist orientation among women.[12]

Science and Ideology

Saffioti draws into a Marxist framework the holistic perspectives of anthropology as well as what she finds useful in Weberian sociological and Freudian psychoanalytic theory in

the analysis of how socialization practices, personality attributes, and ideological systems are shaped in conformity to
the needs of capitalism. Her discussion of science as ideology
illuminates the conscious and unconscious processes whereby
scientific knowledge is used to control rather than to liberate.
Scientific knowledge is used, in effect, for ideological manipulation, and the fragmentation of scientific effort helps
make this possible. Saffioti points out that the influential
formulation of Helene Deutsch on the female personality
should have been impossible in view of the cross-cultural
knowledge anthropologists were making available at the time
Deutsch was writing. The same pattern is being repeated
today: despite clear evidence to the contrary, a new spate of
writings argues that male dominance and female subservience,
together with the double standard for sexual behavior, are
universal and biologically based. Sad to say, many anthropologists are contributing to this line of argument.

Contemporary assertions of male dominance as biologically based and/or universal serve several functions besides that
of directly rationalizing the status quo. They commonly pose
a matriarchal rule of women over men as the alternative to the
patriarchal rule of men over women in the historical past.
Thereby, they obscure the reciprocal nature of sex relations
in egalitarian or "primitive communist" society, and the
image of social organization as necessarily involving structures of dominance and submission is perpetuated. Second,
the image of humans and especially men as basically aggressive and competitive is reinforced. Third, the notion of sexual
equality is presented as Western and foreign to the traditions
of Third World peoples, whereas egalitarian reciprocity between the sexes characterized precolonial life among many of
them.[13]

Two other important lines of ideological attacks on
women require brief mention here. The first, an attack on
black women, was fully formulated by Patrick Moynihan. He

built on Oscar Lewis' culture of poverty concept to argue that the difficulties of black men were in large part caused by the strength of black women. The second, an attack on women's organization generally, has grown apace since Saffioti's book was written. It is epitomized by the media catchword *women's lib,* a phrase that distorts and trivializes the early stages of what will necessary become a central component in the fight against all oppression.

The Struggle for Socialism

As I have indicated several times, the fundamental thrust of Saffioti's analysis is that the fight against women's oppression and the struggle for socialism are inseparable. "Prejudices which on the surface seem to hold back the progress of the capitalist order turn out at bottom to be weighty factors in helping to maintain it," she writes. It will take the joint action of both sexes, as they "become conscious of the contradictions of the age in which they live and of the means for overcoming them," to eradicate private property and the stratification by sex that it underlies. Only in a collective economy it is practicable to socialize mothering.

Saffioti writes of the need for further theoretical development in order to complete the fight against sex oppression in socialist countries. In this regard, I would stress the importance of developing Engels' discussion of how commodity production itself and the family as an economic unit were historically linked. According to his formulation, it would follow that only through the total eradication of both can women's liberation be fully achieved, or, to put it another way, can socialism itself be fully realized. However, while it is important to have some general understanding of why this is so, in order better to comprehend developments in countries politically committed to socialism, our immediate concerns in the United States are otherwise. We have yet to define precisely women's relations to production, attitudes, and goals in different sections of the working class, and in that mix of workers and petty bourgeoisie confusedly lumped as the middle class, in the interest of effective organization and the building of a revolutionary understanding.

NOTES

1. An early study of women's continuing economic activities in a colonial society of West Africa is Niara Sudarkasa, *Where Women Work: A Study of Yoruba Women in the Marketplace and in the Home.* Ann Arbor, Michigan: Anthropological Papers, Museum of Anthropology, University of Michigan, No. 53, 1973. Ester Boserup has documented the colonial policies that push women out of production in farming economies in *Women's Role in Economic Development* (London: Allen and Unwin, 1970). Field studies on how such policies affect women are exemplified by two chapters in Rayna R. Reiter's edited collection, *Toward an Anthropology of Women* (New York: Monthly Review Press, 1975): Anna Rubbo, "The Spread of Capitalism in Rural Colombia: Effects on Poor Women," and Dorothy Remy, "Underdevelopment and the Experience of Women: A Nigerian Case Study." Further studies and discussion on women and capitalist development can be found in two special issues of *Latin American Perspectives* (Riverside, California): "Women and Class Struggle" (4, nos. 1 & 2, Winter-Spring, 1977), and "Population and Imperialism/Women in Revolution" (4, no. 4, Fall, 1977); a special issue of *Signs* (University of Chicago Press); "Women and National Development" (3, no. 1, 1977); and in June Nash, *Certain Aspects of the Integration of Women in the Development Process: A Point of View,* Conference Background Paper, United Nations World Conference of the International Women's Year, Mexico City, 1975; June Nash and Helen Safa, eds., *Sex and Class in Latin America* (New York: Praeger, 1976); and Achola O. Pala, *African Women in Rural Development: Research Trends and Priorities,* Overseas Liaison Committee Paper No. 12, American Council on Education, 1976.

2. Two recent articles by Saffioti in English-language publications are

"Female Labor and Capitalism in the United States and Brazil," in
Ruby Rohrlich-Leavitt, ed., *Women Cross-Culturally, Change and
Challenge* (The Hague: Mouton, 1975); and "Women, Mode of
Production, and Social Formations," *Latin American Perspectives*
(4, nos. 1 & 2, Winter-Spring, 1977). Special issue: "Women and
Class Struggle."

3. It is not possible here to give more than a sampling of the literature
that, in addition to the above-cited works and well-known books
like those of Sheila Rowbotham, will lead the reader to other
recent bibliography, research, and debate. On the first and second
topics, see Mina Davis Caulfield, "Universal Sex Oppression? A
Critique from Marxist Anthropology," *Catalyst*, nos. 10-11 (1977);
Eleanor Leacock, "Women's Status in Egalitarian Society: Implications for Social Evolution," *Current Anthropology* (19, no. 2,
June, 1978); chapters by Leacock and Ruby Rohrlich-Leavitt in
Renate Bridenthal and Claudia Koonz, eds., *Becoming Visible,
Women in European History* (Boston: Houghton Mifflin, 1977);
and Karen Sacks, *Women: Studies Toward Equality* (North
Scituate, Mass.: Duxbury Press, 1978). On the capitalist family in
historical perspective, see Bridenthal and Koonz, eds., *Becoming
Visible*; Wanda Minge-Kalman, "Household Economy During the
Peasant to Worker Transition in the Swiss Alps," *Ethnology* (17,
no. 2, 1978) and "The Industrial Revolution and the European
Family: The Institutionalization of Childhood as a Market for
Family Labor," *Comparative Studies in Society and History* (20,
no. 3, 1978); Joan Scott and Louise Tilly, *Women, Work and the
Family* (New York: Holt, Rinehart and Winston, 1978); and
Eli Zaretsky, "Capitalism, the Family, and Personal Life," *Socialist
Revolution* (3, nos. 1-3, 1973). On kinship in a black working-class
community, see Carol Stack, *All Our Kin* (New York: Harper and
Row, 1974). On migration, see a special issue of the *Anthropological Quarterly on Women and Migration* (49, no. 1, 1976), plus
above-cited material on women and "development."
4. Saffioti, "Female Labor and Capitalism," p. 92.
5. Saffioti, "Women, Mode of Production, and Social Formations,"
pp. 32, 36.
6. Eleanor Leacock, "Class, Commodity, and the Status of Women,"
in Ruby Rohrlich-Leavitt, ed., *Women Cross-Culturally, Change
and Challenge*, pp. 602-04.
7. For black women in the United States, see Frances Beale, "Double

Jeopardy: To Be Black and Female," in Toni Cade, ed., *The Black Woman* (New York: Mentor, 1970).

8. Elinor C. Burkett, "In Dubious Sisterhood: Race and Class in Spanish Colonial South America," *Latin American Perspectives* (4, nos. 1 & 2, Winter-Spring, 1977), Special Issue: "Women and Class Struggle."

9. In addition to the fascinating footnote material Saffioti gives that could be followed up, there are also useful references in C. R. Boxer, *Women in Iberian Expansion Overseas, 1415-1815* (New York: Oxford, 1975) and Ann M. Pescatello, *Power and Pawn, The Female in Iberian Families, Societies, and Cultures* (Westport, Conn.: Greenwood, 1976). For an anthropologist's personalized account of women in twentieth-century Bahia, see Ruth Landes, *The City of Women* (New York: Macmillan, 1947); for source materials on rebel slave communities, see Richard Price, ed., *Maroon Societies* (Garden City, N.Y.: Anchor, 1973); and for reference to black women leaders, see ibid., pp. 196-97.

10. The influence of Mariarosa Dalla Costa's focus on the significance of women's household labor should be noted here (Mariarosa Dalla Costa and Selma James, *The Power of Women and the Subversion of the Community*. Bristol: Falling Wall Press, 1972).

11. Saffioti and Helen Safa are collaborating on a study comparing the backgrounds, attitudes, lifestyles, and family organization of women factory workers in São Paulo, Brazil, and the greater New York City metropolitan area.

12. Articles that should be cited in addition to previously mentioned work are Mina Davis Caulfield, "Imperialism, the Family, and Cultures of Resistance," *Socialist Revolution* (4, no. 20, October 1974); Selma James, "Sex, Race and Working Class Power," *Race Today* (6, no. 1, 1974); Diane K. Lewis, "A Response to Inequality: Black Women, Racism, and Sexism," *Signs* (3, no. 2, Winter 1977); and Helen Safa, "Class Consciousness Among Working Class Women in Latin America: A Case Study in Puerto Rico," in Nash and Safa, eds., *Sex and Class in Latin America.*

13. In addition to some of my previously cited articles, I outline some of these arguments and data in "Society and Gender," in Ethel Tobach and Betty Rossof, eds., *Genes and Gender* (New York: Gordian, 1978).

WOMEN IN CLASS SOCIETY

PREFACE

to the American Edition

This book was written between December 1966 and February 1967. Since then, scientific literature on this question has increased enormously. Feminist movements have also grown substantially. In the United States, in France, in Italy, and in other countries, the women's movement has focused on obtaining passage of laws that would assure them control over their bodies and justice in their situation as workers and in society in general. The areas of struggle have so expanded that they have already led to the appearance in the United States of men's groups, which meet with the objective of discussing male behavior in response to the women's "revolt."

Although their victories are important—the right to vote in Switzerland, legalization of abortion in the United States and in France, passage of a law permitting divorce in Brazil—the analysis remains valid. There are, for example, very few feminist groups with male participation; the male-female division persists. So too does the division between the social classes. Up until now, feminist victories have not gone beyond the limits imposed by the capitalist mode of production. The world economic crisis which we are currently experiencing has ostensibly contradictory consequences for women: liberalization on the sexual terrain—legalization of abortion and generalized use of modern contraceptive techniques—but also rising female unemployment. The present economic recession therefore has special significance in that it demonstrates the real incapacity of monopoly capital to absorb into the labor force these social categories that have been dominated and discriminated against.

The appearance of a great deal of empirical material in the last eleven years tempted me to attempt to bring this book up to date. However, as a basic theoretical interpretation it has not lost its significance, and I have chosen to publish it in English without profound reformulations. Two chapters have been omitted: one on the suffragist movement and another on the Catholic Church. On the former, there is now an extensive body of literature. On the latter, the relevance for a North American public in a book of this nature is limited. Small additions have been made, particularly with reference to legislative advances in various countries. New data have been added, including Table 13 in Chapter 8, and the information provided by the 1970 census has been examined. Taking into account the objective of this work—to deal with a series of problems which had heretofore gone unnoticed or had been dealt with without a theoretical basis—it would in any case have been virtually impossible to bring it totally up to date. The growth of feminist movements in recent years is such that there are now substantial works dealing exclusively with these issues. But since the magnitude of the available empirical material requires specialization, there has been a tendency to narrow the theoretical boundaries in which these facts are located. That is why I decided to publish this book in English with few additions and with very few profound structural changes, in the hope that it will awaken, in both men and women, an interest in studying the subject or that it will at least sharpen the perceptions of all those who witness social discrimination against women. Its ultimate objective is to lead human beings—men and women—to seek for more just forms of shared existence.

Author's Introduction

In this study I shall enquire into the typical ways in which the sex factor operates in class societies to bar large numbers of women from the occupational structure. I shall also try to uncover the underlying causes of this exclusion, justified in the name of a tradition which claims that woman's role lies in the performance of domestic tasks and household functions, or by theories that demonstrate ostensible flaws in the female constitution or personality. Finally, I shall probe into the belief, entertained alike by those defending the present competitive social order and those rejecting it, that women first began to perform economic functions, in the strict sense, under capitalism. I do not intend to take up the special problems women face in precapitalist and socialist societies: I shall therefore refer to the roles assumed by women in these societies only insofar as, by contrast, they may help to clarify and enrich our perception of how women function in a mature or emerging capitalist socioeconomic formation.

This study pursues two ambitions, one of a theoretical, the other of a practical nature. Any attempt to deal theoretically with the problem of how sex and class interact and are interrelated requires a critical review of the major approaches through which feminine problems have traditionally been broached. The reason for this is twofold. First, we should be clear about the assumptions implicit in these approaches and about the particular bias inherent in the interpretations they provide. Second, in analyzing international capitalism as an all-embracing system, the subsystems into which we break it down must be defined in such a way that its more general features are still visible behind the specific forms they may assume in each historically concrete manifestation. The system, in actuality an indivisible whole, may then be reconstructed on a more concrete level by referring to these features in such a way as to bring to light various material and social mechanisms at the core, which give rise to an all-pervasive and uniform way of life.

The choice of advanced capitalist countries and of Brazil (where capitalist industrialization has only just begun) for an examination of feminine roles was dictated by certain goals. In the first place, this allows us to keep track of the general features of capitalism through its various permutations at different times and places in the historical process. Second, it enables us to apprehend certain invariant aspects of the way sex operates socially in the classical capitalist countries as a highly stratificatory factor—either concealing or bringing into relief the class situation—and permits us to pinpoint certain other constants characteristic of today's underdeveloped nations. We shall thus be looking at two forms of capitalism, but in both woman's condition is to be seen as an outgrowth of the interplay between local tradition and the general features of the capitalist mode of production on the one hand, and on the other, of the way in which these general features are modified depending on the degree of autonomy of the particular country—that is, by the way the pattern of international forces is periodically redefined either to maintain the equilibrium of the world capitalist system, or to establish it on a new level. Although capitalism and the competitive social order take various forms at different times and places in history, the basic structure is the same everywhere and at all times, and it is on this general structural level that the condition of woman in class society can best be examined. I shall, of course, make use of empirical data from both advanced and underdeveloped capitalist countries to shed light on the ways particular social structures operate to at once maintain and conceal prejudices against women, and thereby perpetuate their marginal economic status. In dealing with the classical capitalist countries, this use of empirical data will be for the most part restricted to the situation of female labor and various sets of factors directly affecting it, since the purpose is not to describe particular situations in detail, but, through them, to arrive at those general features characteristic of a specific type of social structure. In the case of Brazil, which represents the other form of capitalism with which we shall be dealing, a more generous use of empirical data is in order for two reasons: (1) no historical study of the condition of Brazilian women has yet been made;[1] and (2) all the forces of international capitalism have come together in that country to confine women to domestic patterns of life, even while giving rise to a feminist movement that has made women aware of the necessity for economic emancipation. Since Brazilian society today and always has had a less developed class structure than the countries at the core of the world capitalist system, female roles in Brazil have acquired certain special features which cannot be satisfactorily explained within a narrow national framework.

It is becoming increasingly necessary to see the international capitalist system as a totality, and the national societies as subsystems which, while they retain a modicum of functional autonomy, are fundamentally at one with the overall system and its inner workings. I am not here concerned, however, with abstracting features specific to each of these subsystems, although they themselves may be but variations of a more general theme. Rather, I intend to probe beyond this phenomenal reality to uncover those characteristics of the capitalist system which remain fundamentally the same from one particular historical form of capitalism to the next. The external manifestation of these general features in each of capitalism's various historical forms will vary in a typical fashion, reflecting the particular conditions under which a people must live, so that this external reality is just as much a determinant of the given situation as any of the system's more basic features—indeed, often has an extraordinary power to shape social consciousness. Any analysis, therefore, which purports to get to the root of the feminine question under capitalism *in general* (i.e., beyond the level of the subsystems represented by the national societies) *must be able to apprehend not only the movement of phenomenal reality and the more basic structures underlying it, but also the dialectical interrelationships between these two levels of social being.* The analysis thus leaves off at the same phenomenal level of reality from which it sets out, after ranging through various mediating links, bringing out what is essential to the system and enriching our perception of the whole. Indeed, this new perception of reality, arrived at through analysis and reconstitution of the whole, is an ongoing process of totalization. By examining different partial totalities in turn, the process of ongoing historical totalization[2] enables us to look at all the empirical facts together and discover the connections existing between them. An approach such as this presupposes a theory without which it would be impossible either to apprehend the significance which these facts and partial totalities take on within the organic whole, or to grasp the dialectic of the movement behind them. The Marxist dialectic will be of considerable heuristic value here. It should not only enable us to verify some of the classical formulations, particularly those of Marx himself, but it also should allow us to critically employ theoretical formulations deriving from other conceptions of history by restating their arguments in dialectical terms. Thus, even though it draws on theories methodologically as different as those of Marx and Weber, the approach cannot be called eclectic. Marxist dialectics shall remain the integrating thread of this study, and I shall use it as the basis for reformulating interpretations arrived at by other methodological approaches, as well as those worked out within the tradition of scientific socialism. In the latter case, I shall avoid the analogical line of reasoning that places sex on an equal categorical footing with social class, and instead seek to determine that structural and functional requirements are met by examining the manner in which the sex factor functions socially. The sexes will not be treated as autonomous empirical categories as such, capable by virtue of some intrinsic property of effecting structural change in competitive societies. They will instead be dealt with as social categories that have arisen on a prior basis of fundamental equality, namely, sex in the biological sense. As such they are all-pervasive, cutting across class lines, having conflicting interests in the productive system, and making it all the more difficult to distinguish problems which stem directly from the sex factor and those which derive from the system's need to maintain its pattern of equilibrium. Nevertheless, this difficulty can be partly overcome by comparing woman's condition in different types of social structures. Such comparisons will help to determine to what extent woman's inferior social status derives from a structural necessity of the system, and to what extent it represents merely the persistence of a cultural tradition which sees woman as a submissive creature (or even modifications of this tradition, for example, to keep in the home excess labor power that the dominant system of production is unable to absorb).

Because empirical phenomena are dealt with at various

levels, this analysis occasionally becomes repetitive; the same facts are referred to a number of times in different contexts, and some particularly useful terms will recur for that reason. But it has not been merely for clarity's sake, or because the analysis takes place on different levels that this reiterative method of presentation has been chosen; in fact, certain phenomena do recur on these different levels, that is, in each of the subsystems making up the all-embracing totality of international capitalism, and then again in the system considered as an integrated whole. Therefore, after defining the problems of women in competitive societies in general, and discussing them in light of empirical data from the advanced capitalist countries, I shall go on to discuss the same questions with reference to Brazil, whose economy is still not fully industrialized, yet is based on the same principles as the economies of the developed nations. Finally, I shall reformulate these problems within the broader context of the system as a whole, and offer some theoretical solutions. This final part does not attempt to interpret the empirical data presented in the first two parts, as these already contain an element of interpretation in the sense that they bear the stamp of the overall theoretical approach.

The third part of the book finds an additional justification in the second aim of this study: demystification. Psychoanalysis has had to bear the brunt of some devastating criticisms, all of which leave something to be desired. They either repudiate psychoanalysis without offering any convincing and genuinely scientific theories to replace it, or they reject it only to espouse some of its basic premises—or at least leave room for a certain ambivalence. Further, none of these critical currents has come up with any adequately sound theories of its own to deal with the woman problem. Although many psychoanalytical notions have been theoretically superseded, they continue to serve as a unifying fabric for the feminine mystique. A critique is therefore in order. Science, which on one level is an active factor in social consciousness, can serve to enrich the praxis of the scientist and nonscientist alike, provided it is sufficiently accessible. Specifically, the real or potential mystifying aspects of Margaret Mead's anthropology, with its internal contradictions, seem generally to have been passed over unnoticed by critics; in any case, allusions to these aspects are rare. It therefore deserves to be analyzed to show how concrete science is able to assimilate petty-bourgeois *praxis,* and to show how society reinterprets scientific knowledge so as to render it more compatible with the ends envisaged by the ruling order in class society.

Thus, not only is it possible to demystify the human sciences,[3] but it is also possible to question whether they can be at all useful in solving the social problems generated by capitalism as long as they uphold the status quo, especially when these sciences are used to serve the ends of those who hold the reins in competitive societies. Indeed, it is even questionable whether scientific knowledge can be assimilated uniformly by a people divided into classes. As long as the self-knowledge an individual has is not science, but consciousness,[4] it makes no sense to speak of one social science which upholds the competitive social order and another which rejects it. There is only bourgeois consciousness and proletarian consciousness, and thought will have direct practical implications. Specifically, only proletarian consciousness is in touch with the conditions necessary to put an end to the problems generated by the competitive social order, since it alone is able to seek solutions outside the system to problems which are insoluble within it. But given the reification of the proletariat, "proletarian thought is initially but a theory of *praxis;* little by little, it then transforms itself into a practical theory that subverts reality."[5] As a heuristic tool in a dynamic approach to social reality, the Marxist dialectic offers the broadest perspective since it is also capable of understanding the conservative view "as a social and human phenomenon, and through an immanent critique identify its infrastructure and shed light on its consequences and limitations."[6] Although the Marxist dialectic represents the highest level of consciousness possible in class societies, it must not be regarded as true consciousness. If it were elevated to an absolute, all differences between the subject and object of cognitive action would be eliminated, consciousness would identify itself with humanity in general, and the forward movement of history would come to a halt. As the highest possible consciousness, continually enriched by the action it engenders and hence by its own historical movement, Marxism is capable of revising even its own positions to further its understanding of the process of historical totalization. If this is so, then the truth of theories constructed from the proletarian viewpoint need no longer be regarded as established for all time; they too can be reformulated, through means provided by the Marxist dialectic itself. Objectivity in the social sciences then takes on new dimensions,[7] and it is this objectivity, as distinct from the objectivity of the natural sciences, with which I hope to present this study. But if my desire to come to grips with the woman question in class societies and suggest some ways that it might be solved mars the analysis in any way, I might paraphrase Florestan Fernandes and say that many before me have for different reasons strayed in the opposite direction, into misrepresenting and disparaging woman, who could scarcely be more ill-served by such treatment.[8]

PART I

Women and Capitalism

CHAPTER 1

Class and Status
in Stratified Society

Before looking at the position of women in class society, it will be useful to examine what precisely is meant by such a society, and how it developed historically. Provisionally, we can understand *social class* to refer to a social grouping brought together by processes of cooperation, division of labor, competition, and conflict in the specific domain of production of goods and services, with cooperation predominating in intraclass relations and competition and conflict the rule in relations between classes. The division of labor is a technical division within the same class, whereas between classes it is social in nature.[1] Social class, then, has to do with the relations of production of goods and services, but always within a sociohistorical context, and it is that context which gives the variables of class constitution and class dynamics their specific features. These specific features are crucial, for without them the concept of social class would become extremely general, considering that all historical societies have a system of production of goods and services in which individuals participate in different ways and on which their access to these goods and services depends. The heuristic value of the concept would be greatly reduced by such generality since, although all systems of production have common features which then become generalized in thought, it is only by apprehending the essential features that one can arrive at a full understanding of the specific form that human relations take at a determinate historic moment in production.[2] We can say then that the heuristic value of the term varies in direct proportion to its capacity to maintain a focus on these essential features, for in the last instance it is they that distinguish one real historical mode of production from another equally historical and real, despite other unique qualities each of them may have.

In precapitalist societies, the political, economic, and social spheres are inextricably interwoven, although the units of production are autarkic. But, while the structure these societies present is highly fragmented, especially under feudalism, where the domains of political power, juridical power, and economic power are distinct, there is a complete interlacing of the economic, political, and social spheres. One might say that fragmentation occurs vertically and integration takes place horizontally. However, this must not lead one to assume that under feudalism the units of production maintained close ties of mutual dependency; on the contrary, their autarkic character has already been pointed out. Seen from the point of view of relations between productive units, precapitalist societies were very loosely knit on the horizontal plane as well. I have used the term *horizontal* to indicate the plane on which integration occurs in this type of society; it is meant to characterize a social state in which the tangible realities of political, social, and economic life are played out at the same level. In other words, "the economy had not even objectively reached the stage of 'being-for-itself.'"[3] The organization of production was "implicit," so to speak, in the political organization, such that the state apparatus did not mediate economic domination, but imposed its will directly as political domination. Of course, economic power lay concealed in the bowels of political domination. But since labor was not free, the bare economic bones of productive relations were hidden within and beneath the juridical and religious superstructure. Under such conditions, the social strata that formed in precapitalist societies occupied analogous positions in social, political, and economic life. Whether these strata assumed the form of status groups, or whether they took the more rigid form of castes, the personal qualifications of their members counted alongside their position within the political power structure and their class situation, and were frequently determined by the latter.[4]

The terms *caste* and *status group,* used to designate the social strata of precapitalist society, are comprehensive terms, meant to refer at once to the social, political, and economic aspects of these groupings within the specific historical context in which they exist. In either type of social formation, the economic foundations of society's division into "social classes" remain concealed: in the caste structure, beneath the religious structure which legitimates it; and in the status group structure, under a juridical superstructure.[5]

Two points must be considered. First, the economic basis of a society's division into castes or status groups cannot be perceived by its members. As long as the economic organization continues to be intermingled with religious and/or juridical elements, that is, as long as the economic process has not assumed an autonomous existence, there can be no vantage point from which the society may be apprehended as a totality. The second point, which in a certain sense is contained in the first, is that economic goods are not appropriated as a result of a process of competition—that would bring to the surface the scarcity of these goods and the struggle waged to obtain them—but by virtue of one's belonging either to an ethnic group or privileged status group, or else by violent expropriation, where one ethnic group or the members of a higher status group dominate over others. The technical competence of the individual plays no role in the acquisition of economic status. "Competition" between members of social strata composed of juridically free human beings is conditioned and limited by the "natural" factors that govern status and role ascription. Acquisition of economic status then becomes ascriptive, even in cases where it was decisive in determining an individual's position on the social scale of prestige, and is governed by criteria such as birth, sex, lifestyle, or individual fate, ordained by religion independently of will, etc.

In the final analysis, then, an individual's social status is the result of a process of ascription based on natural characteristics. The fact that an individual may have acquired an economic status which led him or her to learn the ways of the privileged status group and ultimately to assume their style of life, does not come to the surface of the society. Rather, it appears as if it were the individual's personal qualities which had determined and legitimated his or her good fortune. Given these conditions, the links between the different status groups and the different castes take on quite specific features. In both caste and status group, the strata are ranked hierarchically, but not in any dynamic sense that would lead to a struggle between them. The various strata are arranged in a pattern of "composite rank,"[6] in which a number of qualitative factors are combined. Since the economic factor, as a quantitative term, largely determines, or in some cases is determined by, an individual's personal qualifications, when it is mixed with the qualitative variables which determine an individual's position along the scale of social prestige it too takes on a qualitative character at the level of outward appearances. For this reason, the difficult problem of ranking individuals by incommensurable criteria does not arise.

By seeing how political, economic, and social status converge we can see the special way in which integration is effected in societies with caste or status group structures;

because of this convergence we may classify this system of social stratification as a system of composite rank. However, it must be kept in mind that at this point the economic process has not yet acquired the minimum of autonomy necessary to reveal not only its function as a source of status ascription, but also, and especially, as a domain of status acquisition. This is the principal reason why there are no dynamic links between castes or between status groups. A latent conflict between castes and between status groups unquestionably exists, born of the relations of production; but this conflict will never be the product of an awareness of how great a role is played by the economic process in determining how and by whom the available goods, material and nonmaterial, are appropriated and monopolized, nor will it derive from a grasp of the society as a totality. In caste societies, the conflict never fully emerges to the surface because, besides the reasons we have examined, the structure is legitimated in religious terms and its subversion would evoke hierocratic sanctions. In societies organized into status groups, the conflict latent in the relations of production and the mode through which goods are acquired does indeed come to the surface at times, but it remains confined to that aspect of society and does not impugn the existence of the society as a whole.[7]

Thus, in precapitalist societies social status appears outwardly to be entirely the result of social ascription, which is to say that it derives from natural factors that are independent of the individual will. Obviously, to say that social status derives entirely from ascriptive mechanisms only has a valid meaning in the analytical context in which it is made. I have tried to show that, on the one hand, even the domain in which status acquisition is still operative—the economic—is subject to severe limitations imposed by natural factors, as I have referred to them, and on the other hand, that economic status, even when it is acquired, is seen by society as ascribed.

Stratification then assumes the appearance of a natural phenomenon, contested only by conflicts between persons
situated antagonistically in the productive system. These conflicts, however, never go so far as to challenge the social
structure, nor to broaden or deepen such little awareness as
does exist that economic status can be acquired. The criteria
of social stratification remain therefore on the same level.
For example, belonging to a particular ethnic group may,
with religious and/or juridical justification, result in an individual being ranked in terms of the prestige he or she
enjoys on a scale of values so basic to the particular culture
that such a ranking comes to be seen as perfectly natural and
normal. So, too, stratification on the basis of factors which
are also independent of social influence, such as age, sex, etc.,
will also be considered normal.

Since the proviso made above applies to both the economic and educational aspects of the social process, we may
say that stratification in precapitalist societies is essentially
the product of ascription. As we have seen, there is no area of
society where status may in any obvious way be "achieved,"
such that comparisons would lead the social actors to view
status ascription as an arbitrary event. On the contrary, the
identical nature of the factors that determine, at least at the
manifest level of reality, the distribution of individuals
among the different social strata leads at least to the individual's acceptance of society's pattern of stratification, if
not to his or her total adaptation. We therefore find women
viewing their inferior status in the family and society as both
natural and just, legitimated by centuries of tradition. Even
when a woman inherits and becomes the proprietress of an
estate, it is bequeathed to her; she does not appropriate it. It
is men who have access to the potential means for appropriat-
ing material and nonmaterial life chances; for women, these
means exist only indirectly, by a reflex in which the woman
appears only as an extension of the man. Even the fact that

in France, during the period when feudalism was in a state of rapid and advanced decay and commercial capitalism was flourishing, women had full rights to engage in mercantile activities, may be seen in this sense. A woman from the popular masses was free to earn money by becoming a merchant, a person in the legal sense, endowed with rights, because the conduct typically required in the marketplace was incompatible with status honor.[8] A woman had full freedom to enter these new social relations only because the activities involved were held in low esteem by the waning society and the emergent society had not yet established a system of social control to supervise the activities of the sexes with the rigor required by a society that had a fully developed structure. As capitalist society came into being, relations between stratificatory factors acquired more precise contours, and the contradiction emerged, present but not expressed in the structure of precapitalist societies, between the economic and the social processes.

The transformation of the individual's juridical status to one of free citizen not only enabled competition to be extended into more areas of life, but it also laid bare the economic foundations of society's division into classes. The economic process became autonomous, and society shifted its center of gravity from the social sphere in the narrow sense to the production of goods and services. Economic status came to be one of the most important components in the overall status of the individual. The realm of freedom was formally established, and in it individuals were free, theoretically, to compete in the quest for higher economic status without distinctions of color, race, sex, or physical constitution. From a formal viewpoint, a person's upward mobility was limited only by his or her individual competence. Personal success was regarded as attainable by all, contingent only upon individual capacities. Formerly, it had been vouchsafed on the basis of religious, ethnic, or political privileges;

henceforth, it would be something to be achieved through instrumental action, that is, action which is rational in terms of its goals.[9]

Social life, centered on economic activities, underwent a process of intense rationalization.[10] But this rationality was itself the expression of the contradiction residing in the capitalist system. The rationality that marks the internal functioning of capitalist enterprise, yet is at the same time imposed upon by the irrationality, the chaotic character of the system of production as a totality, becomes itself a determinant of that irrationality. This inherent contradiction in the capitalist mode of production is matched by a corresponding contradiction which takes root in the individual personality. To put it another way, the objective contradiction of the overall system of production of goods and services acquires a subjective form by being introjected into the consciousness of the individual. The rationality that so strikes the eye in the professional activities of human actors determines, and is at the same time determined by, the irrationality of their lives outside the context of their jobs. When social stratification became separated from class structure, the stability that had been the crown of the human personality was destroyed at one blow, having been the product of the integrative nature of precapitalist societies. Capitalist societies are held together in a different way. As purely economic categories emerged, the juridical and political forms that provided the outward framework for stratification by status group, in capitalist societies "merely imply the stabilization of purely economic forces so that they frequently adapt themselves in form or content."[11] Henceforth, the state becomes a mediator of economic domination. In capitalist societies economic forces no longer are concealed behind juridical forms which in previous social formations had camouflaged the economic nature of political domination. Social classes, when they existed only in embryonic form, under capitalism become an immediately perceptible reality: "The Asiatic, ancient, feudal and modern bourgeois modes of production may be designated as epochs marking progress in the economic development of society."[12] Class antagonisms, the expression of a dim consciousness in which the economic foundations of the division of society by caste or status appear in disguised form, flare up as purely economic categories, "which express forms of existence and conditions of existence in that particular society."[13]

The development of economic categories and the order in which they have appeared historically must be viewed as a phenomenon subordinate—in terms of understanding society as a totality—to the particular mode of production within which these categories are situated. The positions they then assume may be the expression, within the overall context, of either their subordinate relations or their dominant relations. Thus, the insight that economic categories "express particular conditions of existence" was not gained by abstracting them from the historical-social contexts in which they unfold; nor is the matter at issue "the role which various economic relations have played in the succession of various social formations appearing in the course of history."[14] The question rather is to discover the specific configuration formed by these relations at a real moment in time in the history of production. The purity (abstract precision) of a category shows that its position among the categories operative at a particular moment of history is only a subordinate one; indeed, that is precisely why it is abstract.[15]

Thus, as societies evolve, the higher levels of organization of production always contain, in withered and concealed form, relations rooted in earlier types of societies. Of course, this conservation of previous social structures in caricatured form does not divest the more highly organized structure of its essential characteristics. Their survival means no more than that they have ceded their place to other categories, now dominant, and that they themselves have receded to a subordinate role in the new society. This phenomenon, namely, the survival of social relations typical of concrete forms already superseded, occurs in capitalist societies in two different forms:

(1) The continued existence of "privileged groups whose class situation lacks any immediate economic base,"[16] and whose "status consciousness" tends to give way to class consciousness as it becomes increasingly more adept at transforming its privileges into purely economic forms of control (large landowners, for example).[17]

(2) The effects the continued existence of these privileged groups has on the conditions of social existence of a society's members taken individually.

The meaning of all this may be summed up as follows: whereas in precapitalist societies the class situation of individuals was included, so to speak, in their status, in capitalist societies a person's class situation is separate from his or her status (the economic process becomes relatively autonomous, eluding human control). As noted earlier, in all societies, whatever their system of production, individuals form strata on the basis of the various positions they occupy in the productive system, and with regard to a scale of values. The difference is that in precapitalist social formations this system of values embraces the system of production as well, so that the economic foundations of society's division into castes and status groups remain hidden.

Social classes are antagonistic human groupings, and their struggles express the fundamental contradiction of a productive system, that is, the contradiction between the forces and the relations of production. According to Rodolfo Stavenhagen: "The ruling class, which holds power and controls the means of production, represents the existing relations of production of a society, while the ruled class, whose labor is appropriated by the other, represents the new forces of production, which sooner or later will enter into contradiction with this system of relations."[18] We must bear in mind that the theoretical model—class division—is only an historical tendency; it never acquires the full status of empirical fact. Nonetheless, this class dichotomy has a heuristic value in that it enables us to grasp social classes at once as discrete, complementary totalities which enable the overall socioeconomic capitalist system to function, and as discrete, opposing totalities set off against one another in a relationship of domination and subordination. "Wages and profits are not, as the Keynesians would have us believe, merely two different varieties of income. They are antagonistic forms of income."[19]

Thus, though we may refer to structure as a functional class model, the state of opposition characterizing relations between classes remains undiminished. Each characterization captures the phenomenon at a different level. What defines class as a particular totality of the capitalist socioeconomic formation is not the function that it performs in the society but the fact that it is in structural contradiction with another class. The term *middle class* is therefore misleading; it would be more appropriate to speak of intermediate strata or layers.[20]

Whether we use the term *social stratification* to designate the general process through which individuals, by ascription or achievement, come to occupy social and/or economic statuses, or whether it is reserved for the process whereby they occupy social statuses within a stratificatory schema (stratification here referring to a product, not a process), status must be distinguished from class situation. The distinction between political, social, and economic spheres is not a new one.[21] All individuals are part of the social sphere, but all do not participate in the dominant system of production. If social classes are viewed as human groupings whose position in the system of production places them in a relation of opposition, the concept of social class is relevant just insofar as it enables us to explain the movement of history in terms of the dialectic supersession of the contradictions existing between the forces and relations of production. The *phenomenon* and the *concept* of social class, therefore, are both highly dynamic.[22] To sum up, on the one hand there is a real dynamic class structure; on the other, an analytic concept[23] which, by keeping a clear focus on *praxis,* enables the analyst to grasp the process whereby structures arise and are destroyed.[24]

By contrast, the concept of social stratification is descriptive. Every system of social stratification is made up of a series of strata, each superimposed on the other, and each consisting of individuals of equal or comparable social status. If the stratificatory criteria should be quantitative, the system of social stratification might be represented as a continuum of individual statuses; if they should be qualitative, the picture might be one of a hierarchy of discrete strata. These social categories, that is, strata or layers, are statistical in the sense that they embrace persons who occupy similar status by virtue of possessing a certain set of characteristics, which may or may not be measurable. Generally, members of the same stratum have similar modes of behavior and develop common attitudes. Since in a stratificatory system the unit is the individual, social mobility studies generally describe the upward movement of persons as they leave one status to occupy another within a continuum of social positions, or, in a hierarchical system, as they shift from one status, and hence stratum, to another. Because such studies concentrate only on movement from one status to another and neglect the dynamic of social classes, they are unable to get a picture of the overall social structure, despite the fact that they may start out from the whole of society; moreover, they cannot provide an understanding of the mechanism of historical change. They may be important in their own way, but they are no substitute for an analysis of class structure. Social mobility, as the term is currently used, is hardly a reliable indicator of changes in class structure. Although social stratification and class structure are inter-related phenomena, they retain their fundamental differences, and above all display different degrees of dynamism.[25]

It will be useful to venture a synthesis of the foregoing analysis of social classes by stating that social classes are human groupings which occupy antagonistic structural positions in the system of production of goods and services, that is, groupings whose chief difference lies in the fact that one of them creates, directly or indirectly, the surplus value appropriated by the other. Allowing that the society as a whole has an *economic* infrastructure and an *ideological* superstructure, one may say that the phenomenon of *social class* is properly part of the former, while the phenomenon of *social stratification* belongs to the latter. Just as infra-structure and superstructure mutually determine one another,[26] so there is also action and reaction, back and forth, between class structure and a society's pattern of stratifica-tion. This means that while stratificatory schemata may have their roots in class relations, they are sustained by society's value systems, which in turn camouflage the class structure, rendering it opaque to the understanding of its members and not infrequently even to the purview of the scientist.[27] The class roots of social stratification are not always easy to get at inasmuch as they are almost never directly given.

Furthermore, since stratification is a more stable phenome-non (given the relative inertia of superstructural phenomena) than the relations between classes, it remains more or less the same, although the conditions which shaped it in the first place may have undergone change. How else could one ex-plain the persistence of the ideology of individual success (which presupposes an egalitarian society, without classes, in which an individual's upward mobility from one stratum to the next is contingent on ability alone) in the United States, when it derives from the liberal phase of capitalism and does not at all fit its monopolistic phase? How else, too, can one explain the persistence in Brazil of a racial stratification that accords blacks such a meager amount of prestige, if not by its links with the old slavocratic social structure, in which the black's status was that of an instrument of labor and the embodiment of capital? And in what other way can one explain the fact that in the "open class structure" of the highly advanced capitalist societies, stratification by sex severely limits the participation of women in this structure? What other explanation can be advanced for the fact that Brazilian women have not been absorbed in large numbers into the class structure now taking shape, if not that the continued expansion of the capitalist system of production finds itself fettered by the very factors it employs to justify its own evolution, specifically, that its value systems derive from previous epochs, in which women were condemned to eternal dependency on men? In this respect, a social stratification is at once a superstructural vestige and a rationalization of the status quo. What is important to keep clear is that stratifications do not divide society as does the class structure but, on the contrary, serve as integrating factors in "congealing" the particular socioeconomic structure.[28] In this respect, a society's pattern of stratification is only its outward aspect; its essence must be sought in the social classes into which an historically specific system of production divides its population. Stratification is the immediately given, the tangible fabric from which any scientific analysis starts out. However, the analyst will have to probe more deeply into the social system to determine its essential characteristics and then reconstruct the historical totality (synthesis) so as to bring to light the connections between these more general features (relations of production) and their specific manifestations (social stratification).

From the foregoing it is evident that stratificatory

schemata, based as they are in value systems which claim to be *universal* but in reality are imposed by the dominant class, represent the conservative forces of a society, whereas classes, which evolve their own, sometimes antagonistic, systems of values, represent the dynamic forces of social life. Relations of production, which are transformed more rapidly than stratifications, bring these two processes to historical cross-roads. Thus, in certain periods the ruling class may not be also the upper stratum. In a later phase, through revolution, they will coincide again.

In normal times, a conflict between class relations and stratifications will give rise to a new stratificatory schema which better fits the class structure—or even to a proliferation of stratificatory schemata. But, while several stratifications may coexist in the same society, in each social formation there can be only one class structure. It follows that as stratifications are not mutually exclusive, the same individual can partake in several of them, and there is no person who does not have at least one status. The unit of stratification is the individual. Classes, by contrast, are mutually exclusive; no individual can belong to more than one class at the same time. On the other hand, not all individuals occupy antagonistic structural positions in the productive system; thus, some individuals belong to no class.

It should be stressed that although stratifications are conservative forces in society, they also perform functions that are necessary for the continued existence of the class structure. In other words, stratifications are indispensable because they are the vehicle through which the relations of production find outward expression. Stratifications as such negate production relations, which outwardly appear as a transfigured form of social stratification. Stratification and production relations, therefore, exist at two different levels: the former at the level of manifest reality, and the latter at a deeper, more essential level, at the core of society, although at the same time they find outward expression, and negation, at the manifest level. If, on the one hand, the essential characteristics (relations of production) have no objective empirical form through which they are expressed, on the other hand, it is only in this transfigured form (stratification) that both they and their relations with their outward manifestations can be brought to the light of day and situated meaningfully within their particular historical context. Proceeding from this syncretic view of the social totality, the investigator will be able, through a movement of thought from the abstract to the concrete, to arrive at a reconstruction of *concrete reality* in terms of *concrete concepts.* "The totality as a conceptual entity seen by the intellect is a product of the thinking intellectual which assimilates the world in the only way open to it, a way which differs from the artistic, religious, and practically intelligent assimilation of this world."[29]

Since stratifications express and negate the relations of production, and since the latter do not involve all members of society, stratifications will reflect, at one and the same time, the production relations of the dominant system, the production relations of secondary systems, the social relations existing among individuals who are marginalized from one of the systems of production, and, finally, the relations existing among all individuals with one another.

That is why economic status may reflect equally an individual's class situation transfigured, or his or her marginalization from the class structure. This point is crucial to an understanding of the central problem occupying this study: namely, *sex as a factor of social stratification which at one and the same time expresses and negates the relations of production.* Sex, taken abstractly, has been a stratificatory factor throughout human history; for just that reason, stratification by sex is but an empty characteristic which first becomes relevant to the understanding when situated within the context of its relations with the essential characteristics of the social system as a whole.[30] This serves to justify the marginalization of large numbers of women from the class structure and the absorption of others by this same structure into subordinate positions, while at the same time it reflects the actual workings of a system of relations of production which by its very nature is unable to absorb all the adult, able-bodied members of society. Seen in this light, stratifications, regardless of the immediate criteria on which they are based, are not just "fossilized vestiges of the former class relations in which they were rooted originally";[31] they also represent a discrete aspect of the concrete totality within which they stand in dialectic relation to the deeper lying, essential features of the system that have no empirically discernible, objective form. Interethnic stratifications in Brazil, for example, may be viewed as a superstructural vestige of relations of production that have since been superseded; but they also function as a constitutive factor within the capitalist socioeconomic formation. Of course, a constitutive factor does not function in the latter in the same way as it does in precapitalist social formations. In these, the ideological superstructure does not just obscure perception of relations of production; it in effect totally blocks such perception. In societies with more advanced structures, i.e., in capitalist socioeconomic formations, social stratification may indeed make perception of these relations difficult, but it does not prevent it.

Thus, as the economic process becomes relatively autonomous, society provides its members for the first time the *objective possibility* of discarding the camouflage that social stratification has set up and of penetrating beyond it to the apprehension of the relations of production. In this context —and perhaps only in this context—does Simone de Beauvoir's statement that "women suffer oppression both economically and sexually" have any meaning. Indeed, what capitalist society did was to make explicit a phenomenon present in all human societies: men's domination over women. Yet it has been this same society which gave women a certain degree of economic independence and thereby enabled them to lessen the effects of that domination. This more advanced form of social structure, then, by bringing to the surface the asymmetry existing in relations between the sexes, has exposed them to the direct scrutiny of actors on the social stage as one step on the way toward surmounting them. In precapitalist societies, women are not given the objective possibility of weakening or destroying the structures sustaining their dependent and subordinate status, even after having grasped their situation in its totality. In capitalist society, on the other hand, the horizons of consciousness are extended considerably. The *praxis* of oppressed social groups can collectively bring about the destruction of these structures.

Actual consciousness in capitalist society, however, may not correspond to these extended horizons. Bourgeois feminist movements, for example, reflect a less adequate consciousness than do women's liberation movements which join forces with the proletariat in its revolutionary activity. This is, of course, on no account to identify proletarian class consciousness with consciousness of sex as a social category. But just as various levels of consciousness exist within a class, so too do women's groups present different levels of consciousness of their situation as a social category that is ill-adapted to the capitalist mode of production. The sexes are not social classes, but are embraced by them, either directly or reflexively. At bottom, then, the various feminist movements are but the expression of different levels of class consciousness, whether achieved by women alone or by women and men together.

CHAPTER 2

Levels of Consciousness
of the Woman Problem

The capitalist mode of production, based on the free market, requires juridical equality among individuals. For relative surplus value, created by the labor of the actual producer, to be appropriated in the form of profit there must exist a market on which people are able to sell their labor power as free agents. The obverse side of this formal freedom, however, is the division of society into classes and hence the domination of one class by another. The capitalist mode of production with its internal contradictions is a permanent negation of the juridical freedom which it had created to serve its own needs. The formal equality among human beings thus serves as a framework for the expression of the fundamental contradiction of class society, namely, that permanent contradiction between its productive forces, including the relations of production, and the superstructure to which they give rise. The juridical equality that existed in precapitalist societies concealed the economic basis of the division into castes or status groups; in like manner, the freedom enjoyed by the members of capitalist society camouflages the real import of the natural factors which handicap the individual's capacity as a social being as he or she engages in the social process of competition.

Although the condition of woman in capitalist society has not been linked to previous social structures until recently, it has nevertheless always contained contradictions deriving from these earlier social formations. The persistence of value systems rooted in earlier social structures has permitted class society to utilize female labor power in diverse ways. Woman's labor was freely available, but only insofar as this freedom was the condition *sine qua non* for female labor power to assume the properties of a commodity. Thus, the denial of civil and political rights to woman has limited her field of action, and since the very beginning of capitalism she has been simultaneously a creator of wealth and an obstructionist of social progress. Woman's condition, therefore, reflects more than just the contrast between juridical equality and the inequality created by the division of society into classes; it also reflects the contradiction inherent in the privileged status, *de facto* and *de jure,* enjoyed by men in a society that was ushered in under the banner of equality (at least juridical) for all its members.

In a certain sense, although the condition of woman in capitalist society has not been linked with past social structures until quite recently, the contradictions contained in it have derived from both previous social formations and the capitalist mode of production alike. Female labor power also assumes commodity form in capitalist society. That is the typical means available under capitalism to the individual to achieve objective fulfillment in the outside world, a means to enrich one's self through the acquisition of some objective form of wealth, to broaden the self, to give it a wholeness albeit of a dual nature, as Simmel has pointed out.[1] On the other hand, class society also deprived women of equality with men, discriminating against them both *de facto* and *de jure,* even as it has gone further than any previous society, through the development of technology and machinery, toward eliminating one real disadvantage women suffer with respect to men, namely, that of physical strength.

The processes of industrialization and urbanization concentrated a whole series of problems in urban areas. Among these, the problem of woman has occupied a prominent place. The dissolution of Christian doctrine as a unified body of thought undermined the belief that human institutions obeyed some sort of divine precept; in its place emerged a secularized, if not rigorously scientific, view of things. People were no longer content with the prospect of receiving recompense for their suffering in a life after death, and turned their attention back to earth to find a remedy for their ills. Even as human institutions were being shorn of their mystery, and being made to bear the blame for human misery, woman's condition continued to be viewed as an immutable state of nature. An almost blind faith in the scientific method took shape, and it looked as if it alone were all that was needed to find solutions for all the problems of the age. The desire to act upon society, which was so characteristic of the countries undergoing industrialization in the nineteenth century, gave birth to a myriad of social reforms—but it also spawned a flock of revolutionaries who stood for the total negation of things as they were. The first foundations of social science were laid in an endeavor to alleviate the tensions created by a society in which the poverty, shabby living quarters, miserable food, the cleavage between family life and work, and the utter separation between work and recreative activities all existed side by side. But there was also a radical alternative open to the social sciences: namely, the destruction of the foundations of the old class society and its replacement by another.

Thus, the emergence of capitalism had two important and closely interrelated consequences. Secular ways of looking at the world and explaining events emerged while the holistic outlook of the epoch just past, in which dogma played the preponderant role, progressively disintegrated. The triumph of natural science over theological dogma and metaphysics helped considerably to break down barriers which for centuries had held back the revision of old patterns of thinking; but it was not sufficient to lend these first attempts to construct a social science the prestige and flexibility that was needed to cope with the many special social problems the Industrial Revolution had brought with it. The second consequence of the advent of class society was the emergence of two opposing class viewpoints in the way people looked at things. Once the economic foundations of the class division of society had come to the surface, the outlook of individuals tended to be shaped by their position in the class structure.[2] From the very outset, therefore, social science had to cope with the dichotomy in social life that class society had brought to the surface. This is one reason why the social sciences have never enjoyed the same compelling authority as the natural sciences.[3] Thus, the problems generated by capitalist societies, including the problem of woman which stands out glaringly, are perceived differently by ordinary men and women and by those who endeavor to study these problems scientifically.

CHAPTER 3

The Rise of Capitalism
and the Social Position of Women

Aspects of Capitalist Production

Capitalism brings to a head the contradiction inherent in all previous socioeconomic formations based on private ownership of the means of production and private appropriation of the products of human labor. The empirical saturation of the historical category of *commodity* carries with it an extremely complex social division of labor, and marks the divorce of *use value* of the products of labor from *exchange value*. As long as exchange value does not figure in the social process of production—that is, as long as most items produced go toward the direct satisfaction of the needs of their producers (as in precapitalist societies)—the quantitative aspect of the products of labor is not an essential factor in shaping the labor process or in determining the particular form work may take. But when all or most items produced acquire an exchange value, they assume, as does labor power, the commodity form. And when labor becomes a commodity, dialectical opposition existing objectively between use value and exchange value assumes subjective dimensions as well. One who works no longer produces for personal consumption; he or she now produces goods which have

35

nothing directly to do with his or her needs as an individual. What a worker produces no longer serves—either quantitatively or qualitatively—as the means through which he or she, as immediate producer, produces and reproduces his or her own labor power. Two other processes, also social in essence, intervene between the activity of labor and the products aimed at satisfying the worker's needs—that is, between production, in the strict sense, and consumption. These two processes are distribution and exchange. Hence, the worker appears on the market in two ways: as a buyer of commodities, and as a seller of labor. The latter is in a certain sense logically prior.

For a market economy to function, all individuals must enjoy juridical equality, and the economic factor must become explicit as the distributor of social opportunities. The economic dimension of social relations is no longer concealed behind and obscured by a juridical inequality among individuals (the status of the free citizen versus servant or slave). People enter the market as free agents, possessors of their own labor. But this does not mean that the inner workings of the capitalist mode of production are any more open to view. Outwardly, juridical equality seems to be an adequate gauge of social equality. The freedom enjoyed by each individual on the market creates the illusion that the achievements of each are directly related to his or her own abilities.

When Weber developed the concepts of *class* and *class situation* for the market situation,[1] he was merely attempting to delineate the partial totalities of capitalist society in terms of the ways they behave within one aspect of that society, that less determines than is determined by production in the broad sense. If circulation is exchange considered in its totality, it is, according to Marx, "an intermediate phase between production and distribution which is determined by production and consumption; since consumption is, moreover, itself an aspect of production, the latter obviously comprises also exchange as one of its aspects."[2] Under these circumstances, then, the explanation of the capitalist mode of production, and hence of the division of society into classes, must be sought in the social process of production (production in the strict sense), and in its determining links with other aspects of production in the broad sense.[3]

The manner in which individuals participate in the market, in terms both of labor and goods, is therefore determined by production, yet it also influences the latter in its turn. Commodity circulation and distribution take place within a more basic framework defining the distribution of the instruments of production and hence the distribution of society's members among the different branches of production. If, from one vantage point, distribution appears to constitute an original and natural condition of production, seen from another it appears as the result of the historical development of production itself.

The existence of a market in which the worker as a free agent could offer his or her labor for sale was the *sine qua non* for the emergence of capital.[4] But that said, we must go on to determine the specific way in which the immediate producer's surplus labor is appropriated in every particular sociohistorical formation. In their outward appearance social relations are deceptive: positive factors will appear negative to the observer, and vice-versa. Thus, in all modes of production based on private appropriation of the products of social labor, the worker reproduces what Marx calls his or her own "labor fund,"[5] but also performs surplus labor. The outward form in which surplus labor is appropriated conceals the true relations between different social classes. The slave, the servant, and the wage laborer continually produce and reproduce their own labor power, but at the same time they also create, via surplus labor, a value which is appropriated by the master, feudal lord, or capitalist entrepreneur. In the precapitalist societies, however, the labor fund does not take an objective, empirically discernible form. The slave's labor, or that of the servant, has the form of unremunerated labor, which in part is illusory. That is, that portion of a slave's or servant's labor which procures the means of subsistence needed to maintain and reproduce his or her labor power appears as unremunerated, although actually it is labor paid in kind. On the other hand, wage labor appears outwardly to be fully paid labor when actually it is only partially so. Wages, the monetary compensation for labor, conceal the capitalist's appropriation of the surplus labor of the immediate producer; in one sense, they replace an outmoded juridical justification of the exploitation of one class by another. The use of some universal form, such as money, to pay the immediate producer for his or her labor at once affirms and negates the worker's status as free agent.

As a historical phenomenon, a mode of production evolves; it does not emerge full-fledged. Every mode of production requires some time to mature, depending on social and cultural factors which vary from one society to the next. Yet there are also some discernible invariants. For example, in capitalist societies the absorption of certain population groups into the relations of production is slow, and never complete. The worker's status as free agent, the *sine qua non* for the historical development of the capitalist mode of production,[6] was not bestowed at one stroke upon all members of society. Factors come into play which seem to have nothing to do with the capitalist order (vestiges of old, outmoded social formations) and stand in apparent contradiction to it, not only at its inception, but also during the period of maturity as a flourishing competitive social order. Natural factors—for example, sex and ethnic origin—function as safety valves by speciously easing the social tensions generated by the capitalist mode of production, and by diverting attention away from society's class structure toward the incidental physical traits of certain social groups.

Since class structure is highly restrictive of human potential, beliefs concerning the natural limitations of certain segments of the population must be regularly invigorated—as if the competitive social order were unable to make room for them, and the formal freedom it offers could never become a concrete, tangible reality because of the various handicaps and setbacks with which each group must cope in its struggle for existence. Outwardly, therefore, it is not the class structure which is seen to limit the realization of human potential. Instead, on the surface it seems to be the fault of such social groups themselves, which apparently lack such potential, rendering difficult if not impossible the full realization of the competitive social order. Indeed, whether such social discrimination exists *de facto* or *de jure,* the natural factors invoked to justify it should on no account be regarded as autonomous mechanisms which operate against the interests of the capitalist order. On the contrary, any totalizing perspective of class society cannot fail to see them as factors actively contributing to the historical development of the capitalist system. Just as it is necessary to distinguish between necessary and surplus labor, so it is also necessary to distinguish clearly between (1) acquired status, which in precapitalist societies is concealed behind (2) ascribed status, which in class societies appears to be acquired through competition.

As labor is the form of *praxis* first and foremost responsible for forging the human being's relations with nature and with other human beings, it is also eminently suited for tracing the true status of historical categories within the dialectical totality of capitalist society. Some members of any historically specific society may appear to be marginalized from the relations of production because of race or sex; but why just these traits are singled out as social stigmata is a question the answer to which must be sought in the relations of production themselves. Precisely because they are recurrent, the elementary characteristics or invariants of a society are not in themselves sufficient to explain the totality of which they are a part, the essential attributes of the social system in question, or the way in which these attributes function. As subordinate categories, they function in accordance with the needs and conventions of the system, and will change countenance from one stage of the particular society to the next. Some of the natural traits singled out to function as social handicaps may become ineffective over the course of time; but when this happens, society finds other factors to stigmatize other groups of the population and to justify their place at the base of the social pyramid. Other natural traits, however, cannot be eliminated or their effects blunted: these handicaps are easier to isolate.

No society has yet succeeded in wholly eradicating, once and for all, this social evaluation of natural traits which operate to ease social tensions and hence preserve the class structure. Indeed, it is conceivable even that these immutable traits could come to serve the needs of the system of production to such an overriding extent that as other groups are liberated, remaining handicaps would weigh all the more heavily upon their bearers. With this as a perpetual tendency, sex will operate as a discriminating factor as long as the system of production persists, that is, as long as the means of production are privately owned. Throughout all its particular historical forms, capitalism has shown itself to be quite adaptable: it has permitted and even encouraged institutional reforms which have gone against both tradition and lifestyles, as in the family, for example. However, the flexibility which marks the solutions capitalism finds to deal with its own problems encounters grave limitations within the system itself. It is therefore appropriate to enquire whether that system would be able to provide a full range of opportunities for women's social integration. The redefinition of the labor power of the immediate producer as a commodity is the best index of his or her integration into class society. I have therefore chosen the activity of labor as the central theme in my analysis of the woman problem as it presents itself in competitive societies.

Women and the Birth of Capitalism

In the social strata employed directly in the production of goods and services women have never been estranged from work. At all times and in all places, women have had a hand in providing for their families and in the creation of social wealth. In precapitalist economies, and, more especially, during the period just prior to the agricultural and industrial revolutions, the women of the working strata were always active. They worked in the fields and in the factories, in mines and shops, in markets and workshops; they spun and wove, brewed ale, and performed other domestic tasks. As long as the family existed as a unit of production, the economic role of women and children was fundamental to its existence.

In the boroughs of medieval England, a married woman was permitted to engage in trade independently of her husband, and was legally responsible for her actions. If a woman married a member of a merchant guild, she acquired all her husband's rights and privileges as his partner or assistant, and she shared in the social and religious life of the guild. If her husband died, she inherited the business and had the right to manage it as she saw fit. (The unmarried female apprentice was still rare in the mercantile guilds, which were closed to outsiders. Access to them was difficult for a woman unless she was brought into the trade by a man.) In seventeenth-century England there were married women among the pawnbrokers, moneylenders, stationers, shopowners, booksellers, and clothing contractors for the army and navy. Women held a monopoly in textile spinning, and many engaged in the retail and provisions trades.[7]

In France, too, throughout the *ancien régime,* women enjoyed all the rights necessary for engaging in commercial activities. But in both countries women's freedoms were confined to the sphere of commerce and trade. In all other domains of work or leisure, women were considered inferior and inept beings who required the guardianship of a man— whether as husband or otherwise.

For a woman, personal happiness necessarily meant marriage. Through marriage she secured her social position and guaranteed her economic stability or prosperity. Except for those who remained single and devoted themselves to commercial activities, this effectively meant that women, lacking civil rights of their own, were dependent on their husbands for their very existence. Moreover, this was true of the whole of womanhood, from the leisure classes to the working layers of the population. In the former, women were directly economically dependent on their husbands; in the latter, tradition demanded obedience. In return for the protection a man was duty-bound to provide for woman on account of her fragility, he obtained her help with practical tasks and a submissiveness which patriarchal societies have always considered woman's duty to show toward the head of the family.

However, this tradition of female subjugation and the inequality of rights between the sexes must not be viewed in isolation. As the economic unit of precapitalist societies was typically the family, women in the less privileged strata also worked. Although it cannot be said that women were economically independent (an individualist notion that first emerged with capitalism), work was a family activity, and the economic world was not alien to women. Whether the social position women held by virtue of their economic role adequately compensated for their submissive relation to their husbands, who made all family decisions, is less important for our purposes than another question: namely, whether despite being excluded from decision-making roles, women possessed some means for social integration in precapitalist societies.

How a society produces goods and services constitutes its very essence and defines its structural type. If we understand *mode of production* to mean the concrete framework within which human beings produce their social existence,[8] and each structural type of precapitalist society as a stage in the internally contradictory development of the process of social production toward its culmination in a mature capitalist society,[9] we could say that a woman's chances for social integration vary in inverse proportion to the level of development of society's productive forces.

Although women in precapitalist societies were inferior to men socially, juridically, and politically, they participated in production and hence performed an economic role; however, being less important than man's role, it had a subsidiary status among the various economic functions of the family. As long as the productivity of labor is low (i.e., as long as social wealth is created very slowly) society has no need to exclude women from the system of production. Their labor is still necessary to ensure the leisure of the dominant strata, while their exclusion is clearly foreshadowed in the subsidiary status ascribed to it. On the feudal estates and in the medieval towns (whose economy, in particular, paved the way for the emergence of the manufacturing towns of a later date), employment of women encountered serious obstacles.[10] By barring women, or offering them positions of lower rank and poorer pay, the craft guilds contributed even more than the medieval agrarian economy to the marginalization of women in later, more advanced stages of production.

Thus, the circumstances surrounding the birth of capitalism were extremely inauspicious for women. The process of individualization that commenced with the capitalist mode of production put women at a twofold disadvantage socially. The superstructure traditionally underrated women's capacities, and created myths of male supremacy to justify itself and the existing social order. Secondly, at a more basic level, as the productive forces developed women became progressively more marginal to productive functions, and increasingly peripheral to the system of production.

Women Under Capitalism

The institution of a new mode of production places a great burden on some of society's members. In the transition from the feudal to the capitalist mode of production, this burden fell on the groups of lower status in the old order, and these gradually crystallized into the underprivileged classes of the new. With the advent of the new order, two important characteristics of society came to the surface: it was divided into classes, and one of these classes was economically exploited by the other. The capitalist mode of production not only brought out clearly the nature of the factors responsible for the class division of society; it also appealed to tradition to justify the potential or actual marginalization of certain groups of the population. Sex, a factor which had long been a favorite justification for keeping women down socially, thus came to play a positive role insofar as the evolution of competitive society and the perpetuation of social classes was concerned. The social elaboration of sex, at once a natural and universal characteristic, took on new and unprecedented forms determined by the system of production. Still, it seemed as if physical and mental deficiencies of the members of the female sex were responsible for the continuing flaws in competitive society. Women, therefore, appeared to be an impediment to social development, when in fact it was society which placed obstacles before their full realization. The barriers which class society has placed in the way of women's social integration have nevertheless varied considerably throughout the course of history. In competitive society, these obstacles have been regulated by the needs of the ruling order, not by any need women might have for self-fulfillment through work.

The social opportunities available to different groups of women will vary, then, depending on the stage of society's development, that is, the extent to which it has developed productive forces. The first women to be marginalized from the productive system under capitalism were the wives of prosperous members of the rising bourgeoisie; society was not at the same time able to do without the labor of the women in its lower strata. Indeed, the lowly state in which women had been kept for centuries now made it that much easier to draw vast numbers of women into industrial work. The social disadvantages suffered by women enabled the emerging capitalist society to extract from them a maximum of absolute surplus value by forcing them simultaneously to work at a faster pace, for longer hours, and for lower wages than their male counterparts, and this continued to be the case so long as the relative surplus value obtained from the use of the technology of the day remained insufficient for rapid capital accumulation. The machine unquestionably raised the productivity of human labor, but not enough to sate the bourgeoisie's thirst for more wealth.

The intense urbanization touched off by the Industrial Revolution drove masses of rural workers from the countryside, and undermined the foundations of domestic manufacture and the independent crafts. Gradually, a vast gulf formed between those who possessed their labor and those who possessed the instruments of labor. Ever growing numbers of human masses from the countryside and the towns were forced to sell their labor for wages, while independent work became increasingly limited to a small group of capitalist entrepreneurs.

Although proletarianization (i.e., reduction to the status of wage laborer) doubtless meant a loss of status for the independent producer, there are two important aspects to this which must not be neglected. First, the loss of status affected men and women alike: women's work was reduced to wage labor while men saw their labor power transformed into a saleable commodity. Analyses which deplore the fact that women were forced into working for money fail to see what lies at the heart of the matter inasmuch as they give no thought to the specific form that alienation, which plays such a crucial role in the individual's social integration, takes in each type of society. It is therefore not enough to focus merely on women's labor as the activity or means whereby she must earn her livelihood. One must go further and examine the nature of exploitation when work is performed by a category of human beings which has been subjugated in various ways. Second, the effects of *not* working for wages (i.e., marginalization) must be explored, in terms both of the female personality as well as the organization and structure of society. The acquisition of the status of wage laborer takes place in different ways for men and women, and involves a number of contradictions which are particularly acute in the case of female labor and have repercussions on various substructures of society.

Machinery made sheer muscular strength obsolete, or at least minimized its utility; accordingly, it became possible to employ the labor power of individuals who were either weaker physically than men, or whose bodies had not yet fully developed and yet were quite agile—in short, women and children. Indeed, during the early days of capitalism women and children were hired for factory jobs in such large numbers that Marx was led to observe that "the labor of women and children was the first thing sought for by capitalists who used machinery."[11] On the other hand, the use of machines had other aspects whose consequences varied depending on the stage of development of capitalism and on the periodic crises to which it is subject.

When capitalism was first taking root, the huge arsenal of machinery, which was intended to eliminate human labor, absorbed immense quantitites of the labor power of men, women, and children. Capital accumulation during this early phase eliminates less labor than machines are capable of replacing; it also, however, sometimes eliminates the work of the head of the family—not because the new society subverted the family hierarchy, but because generations of submissiveness make woman a frail creature, unfit for making social demands, and hence more vulnerable to exploitation. Even when it employs all family members, capitalist industry during this phase "spreads the value of a man's labor power over his whole family."[12] Seen from this angle, Mary van Kleeck's assertion that "the employment of women in countries of industrial capitalism has thus been a development arising neither from society's requirement of woman's work in industry nor from woman's inherent need for work, but in the main from the desire of entrepreneurs to utilize cheap labor for profit-making purposes"[13] stands in need of some revision. Society (i.e., capitalist society) constantly, albeit erratically and in a noninstitutionalized fashion, requires female occupations and the occupations of certain other social groups with less prestige. Even though the jobs traditionally done by women can conceivably be done by other underprivileged social groups, society needs the work of women whose income is indispensable for its subsistence. It is a question of survival, for two reasons: first, social stability is undermined if social problems and their disorganizing effects become widespread; and second, women do, after all, comprise half of the human race, and hence are indispensable for its continued existence, even if only as reproducers.

The assertion that women do not have an inherent need

for work is meaningless: there is no specific type of work which could be said to be inherent in, or derived from an inherent need in, either sex. Work, as an activity, in all the forms it has assumed over the course of history, is but the historical result of men's and women's struggle with nature in the social process of producing their existence. Industrial work in capitalist society is, therefore, inherently neither male nor female; it is simply one factor in the historical development of humankind, a specific historical mode in the humanization of nature and the reification of social relations. If we bear in mind that wages do not represent the value created by the immediate producer, and that very often they are not even adequate to meet the needs of producing and reproducing his or her existence, it will be clear that work has always been a means of subsistence for women in the less privileged strata. As society evolves it gives rise to other human needs, which can be met only with the means obtained from some paid employment. The particular forms taken by work in capitalist society are not needed by either men or women for self-fulfillment, although this may be less apparent in the case of men, given the habit of work society has instilled in them.

Of course, these qualifications by no means impugn the general truth of Mary van Kleeck's statement that the capitalist entrepreneur can increase profits by employing more women in industrial jobs. But it is somewhat one-sided, in that it detracts from the importance of other factors which determine the status of female labor in class society. In fact, we might go one step further and say that it becomes false if it implies that the capitalist's greed for profit is the driving force behind the entrance of female labor power onto the labor market. In precapitalist societies the entrepreneurial spirit for profits did not exist, yet women still worked. Granting that the thirst for profit is one of the components of the exploitation of women's labor, one must remember

that is is also one of the factors responsible for expelling
women from the productive system as a whole.

The expenditure of capital generates surplus value, the
proportion of which (or degree of exploitation) is determined
in relation to variable capital (expended on labor power).
This means that the empirical expression of surplus value—
profit—is greater the fewer the number of paid workers
employed or the lower their wages. The realization of this
law of capitalist production is abetted immeasurably by keeping women down socially. Whether by the direct use of
female labor power, or by marginalizing women in productive
functions, the organic composition of capital can always be
altered by reducing its variable part. Feminine meekness,
assiduously cultivated by society over the centuries, helped
enormously to increase the sum of her surplus labor. The
bourgeois male's consciousness of woman's situation has also
played a notable role in sustaining such a system of exploitation. We need only recall the many accounts and descriptions
of the conditions under which women worked in England
during the past century:

> Mr. E., a manufacturer, informs me that he employed females
> exclusively at his power looms . . . and gives a decided preference
> to married females, especially those who have families at home
> dependent on them for support; they are attentive and docile,
> more so than unmarried females, and are compelled to use their
> utmost exertions to procure the necessaries of life.[14]
>
> Girls are employed in the mines from 1s up to 1s 6d a day
> where a man at the rate of 2s 6d would have to be employed.[15]

Thus, work should not be viewed as abstractly contributing to the degradation of female labor. Rather, we should
ascertain what historically specific forms of work have contributed to the objective unfolding of the human personality,
and what other factors have degraded the social being of men
and women. In class society, work is an alienated activity,
but it also is productive of a value which does not accrue

directly to the individual man or woman performing it. However, women appropriate an even smaller amount of the products of their labor than do men, and hence are clearly more directly affected by the private appropriation of the fruits of social labor. Yet it would be an illusion to think that the greater exploitation to which women are subject works directly to men's advantage. Unlike religious or ethnic minorities, the sexes are not even marginally autonomous categories. They complement each other in their reproductive functions, and each is part of the family unit of consumption. Thus, in terms of the gain obtained by the family from the work of husband and wife, respectively, it is wrong to speak of competition between the sexes, or to claim that men suffer any deleterious effects from women's penetration into the labor market. By deluding himself that masculinity implied authority, man condoned, in effect, unequal competition to women's disadvantage, and so helped enormously to bolster a reifying status quo. Seen in this light, Simone de Beauvoir's comment that "the woman problem has always been a problem of men"[16] assumes a new dimension. As active contributors to the mystification of women, men—bourgeois and proletarian alike, but above all the intermediate strata—perform a colossal service for the ruling class.

Men tend to see women as competitors on the labor market, and hence fail to see that women's situation, as well as their own, is determined by the broader historical reality of which both are a part. Allowing themselves to be mystified by the prestige they enjoy if they receive enough wages for their labor to permit them to keep their wives away from productive employment, men do not see that an unemployed woman may constitute a threat to their own jobs. She could become a worker at any time, and the unpaid work she performs in the home helps to maintain the labor power of both men and women, and "lessens the charge upon industry for the minimum subsistence wage which capital must pay for labor power." [17] In other words, incapable of analyzing woman's situation as determined by capitalism as a historical social formation, and failing to perceive how the partial structures of the social whole operate as mediating factors, men abstract not only women but also themselves from the alienating circumstances surrounding them. In a broad sense, "to liberate woman from her alienation is at the same time to liberate man from his fetishes." [18]

Thus, a favorable male attitude toward female labor would be a step toward discrediting the myths which justify woman's inferior social position. It would, moreover, challenge the notion that the capitalist mode of production is adaptable enough to solve its own problems, and in the last instance would lay bare the structural limitations of the system itself. Although this level of awareness of the woman problem has existed before in the history of capitalist societies, women have often been the victims of a backlash from men, who, lacking an overall perspective on society, mistakenly see female labor as the cause of male unemployment.

What had already taken place in England was repeated on a mass scale in France during the last half of the nineteenth century, when women began to enter industry in large numbers (this occurred much later in France than in England because of the persistence of domestic manufacture). Again, male labor was replaced by female labor at lower wages. Those segments of the labor force for whom the hiring of women constituted an immediate threat displayed a varying grasp of the problem that women, as sellers of labor power, represented. During this period French workers in the graphic arts industry went on strike every time a woman was hired by a printing shop. They called for the outright abolition of female labor, and invoked the slogan, "Keeper of the hearth," which was how Proudhon defined woman's role. Just as in the Luddite demonstrations in the early nineteenth century, when English factory workers destroyed machinery they believed to be directly responsible for their unemployment, so French workers in mid-century wrongly directed their hostility against women. Lacking a comprehensive view of society as a coherent whole, workers were driven to single out one factor among all the complex manifestations of social life, to shoulder the blame for what they experienced as intolerable change in the conditions of their existence. Indeed, the Luddites and the negative reactions to female labor were both indicative of a lack of awareness of the true foundations of class society and its tendency to eliminate manual labor.

By contrast, workers in the French food industries saw woman's labor and hence their own as determined in all its many aspects by the overall situation in capitalist society. They accordingly saw women as victims of the capitalist mode of production, not as usurpers of male jobs, and directed their hostility not against working women, but against the system which exploited the labor power of others, and in which women, by virtue of their sex, were the most exploited. Although they considered paid factory work by women one of the evils of class society, they called for equal pay for equal work at their second congress[19] without seeing that the preparation of large numbers of women for gainful employment meant placing a strain on the labor market and effectively hamstringing the ability of the productive system to cope with the problem of unemployment. However, this attempt to place women workers on an equal footing with men did not imply a belief that the prejudices against female labor could be eliminated within capitalist society or that women could achieve their independence from men. It signified merely the use of democratic means to reduce the exploitation of female labor at a historically necessary stage on the way toward the complete emancipation of women in a future society, where the working day would be much shorter and entrepreneurial profits would no longer exist.

Historical Trends

Unfortunately, a positive attitude toward female labor remained limited to groups influenced by Marxist thought, and, in general, did not become widespread. Thus, just as in the past, men continue to play a major role in maintaining woman's twofold determination as member of a class and as a member of a sexual category. But, if women are doubly determined, male consciousness is doubly contradictory. In justifying and supporting the expulsion of women from the class structure on the basis of their sex, men reinforce their own determination as members of one partial totality opposed to another, yet at the same time conceal this determination by maintaining structures in which they continue to reign supreme (e.g., the family). By maintaining a dominant role in the family unit, men turned the family into a shackle on society's economic growth when, in reality, it had served merely to mediate and camouflage the relations of production.

Leaving aside for the moment the differences between how industrialization is proceeding in today's developing countries and how it took place in countries where capitalism originated, statistics show that industrialization of a nation's economy has always made use of both the male and female workforce. In 1866, women comprised 30 percent of the total workforce in French industry.[20] Although the female segment has tended to rise as industrialization has advanced, history shows that not only may we expect the relative proportion of women workers to stabilize, but that it will also fluctuate with wars and economic crises, especially overproduction. The proportion of women among the total working population in the most industrialized countries has been relatively stable in recent years. In the 1950s, it was 38 percent in Austria, 31 percent in Great Britain, 25 percent in Italy, 24 percent in Belgium, 31.2 percent in the United States, and 33 percent in France (where there was actually a decrease in 1954 from 36 percent in 1931).[21] In France, the proportion of working women has hardly altered since the century began, being 22 percent of the total female population in 1906 and 21.9 percent in 1946,[22] although within this period there were some considerable fluctuations. During World War I, the proportion of employed French women rose sharply, from 30 percent to 40 percent of the total workforce in the graphics industry, 39 percent to 50 percent in the paper and pulp industry, 60 percent to 70 percent in the textile industry, and 33 percent to 42 percent in the hides and leather industry. Finally, in the arms industry, where women had not amounted to even 5 percent of the total workforce before the war, their proportion rose to almost 25 percent of the total number employed in that industry. A survey carried out in the middle of 1918 disclosed the following range of figures for the number of women gainfully employed in 41,475 French enterprises: 179,000 in August 1914; 352,000 in July 1915; 489,000 in July 1916; 550,000 in mid-1917; and 433,500 in July 1918.[23] But this increase was not permanent. After the war employment fell to its prewar levels.

During World War II, female employment in England rose to 40 percent: 5,094,000 in 1939; 5,572,000 in 1940; 6,110,000 in 1941; 6,915,000 in 1942; 7,253,000 in 1943; 7,107,000 in 1944; and 6,768,000 in 1945. In 1943 and 1944, employed women numbered practically one-half of the total number of male workers (15,032,000 men in 1943 and 14,901,000 men in 1944).[24] The exigencies of war took the upper hand in determining the movement of the female workforce. Women were urged to take on at least part-time employment, which was a considerable encouragement to employers to hire married women.

Services such as canteens and day nurseries were set up to draw into employment married women with preschool-aged children. But when hostilities ceased, firms showed themselves less prepared to organize shifts, and many wartime nurseries were closed down. An analysis of a survey carried out in 228 British factories in 1945 showed that about two-thirds of the 2000 women interviewed expressed a desire to go on working, with the highest percentages in the older age groups.[25] However, aside from the cutbacks in the facilities offered to married women and mothers, another factor also appears to have been decisive in encouraging women to return to the home and devote themselves exclusively to domestic work once again. This was the feeling that if the number of jobs was lower than the number of persons qualified to do them, men ought to be given priority.

The decline in female employment lasted for several years after the war, but an upswing began again around 1950 in connection with the British government's rearmament. In 1962, women accounted for approximately one-third of the working population in England.

Perhaps the most interesting change in employment patterns among women is the marked rise in the percentage of gainfully employed married women in a number of countries, beginning in the early fifties and continuing in recent years. In Canada, the percentage of married women in the workforce went from 30 percent in 1950 to 38.6 percent in 1956, and to almost 50 percent by the end of 1958. In the United States, the corresponding figures were 25 percent in 1950 to 31 percent in 1955; in Australia, 19 percent in 1947 to 34 percent in 1954; and in England 40 percent in 1950 to 49 percent in 1956.[26] This trend has continued in more recent years, at least in the United States: from 1971 to 1975 the increased participation of married women accounted for 75 percent of the participation changes, continuing a trend noted for the 1967–1971 period.[27] In the fifties and sixties this was partly explained by the fact that many women found themselves with nothing to do within the family unit after their children grew up and left home. Many had had paying jobs when they were single, and when their household functions decreased they had to choose between a job and total isolation at home. Often, they would find that their particular job skill had become obsolete or was in short demand, and when this was the case they were forced to accept lower and poorly paid positions. This is true even for younger women; as male participation in the workforce declines, women provide a new reservoir of labor for the increasing numbers of "poorly paid, menial, and 'supplementary' occupations."[28] In the period 1971-1975, the greatest increases in female workforce participation occurred among married women with children under the age of 6, reflecting a need in increasing numbers of families for two incomes, as well as the capacity of these occupations to absorb lower paid workers. Another change in the 1971–1975 period over the five-year period which preceded it is the shift in age group among women entering the workforce: while for 1967–1971 over half the increase was among women over 35, continuing a trend observable for the period 1947–1971, the big increases are now occurring among women under 35.[29]

These changes no doubt reflect shifting career ambitions as well. Even by the early 1960s, most American women who worked had no intention of pursuing a career. They took temporary employment as salesgirls or secretaries for extra income to enable their husbands or children to pay off debts or complete their studies. Even in those occupations which had traditionally been reserved for women (e.g., nurse, teacher, or social worker), the number of women was steadily decreasing.[30] The prospect of marriage, the fact that they are often obliged to stop working, and the circumstances surrounding an eventual return to the labor force after a long period of professional inactivity were weighty factors in channeling women into lower-ranked occupations entailing fewer responsibilities.

While many middle-class women have begun to change

their goals, however, some realities about women's jobs are harder to change. Not only are the jobs held by women in industry much less rewarding in terms of prestige, and tend to involve repetitive and unrelated tasks, but women are also paid less and rank lower than men even when the professional levels of their jobs are the same. Men's greater physical strength has often been used as an argument to justify this discrepancy, but this argument holds little water in jobs which require no physical strength or when, for example, the male worker whose job does require physical effort finds himself working side by side with a woman under more or less the same conditions. It is then that racial or sexual prejudices come into play to maintain white male dominance and to support the accumulation of capital.

Although many underdeveloped countries employ a high proportion of female labor, many of these women are in nonproductive jobs (e.g., paid domestic services) and hence remain marginal to the productive system in class society. As a country becomes industrialized and the economy grows, more and more female labor is absorbed into the secondary and tertiary sectors of the dominant system of production. In Japan, for example, where female participation in the economy has risen steadily (54.5 percent of women above the age of fourteen worked in 1957), in 1955 the majority of women workers (55.1 percent) still carried out unpaid tasks. This compared with only 14.3 percent of the male workforce engaged in family tasks for which they received no wages. Two facts are almost wholly responsible for these figures: first, the exodus from the countryside with the onset of industrialization involved far more men than women, and second, agriculture had not yet been mechanized to any great extent. In 1955, farm work, forestry, fishing, and other industries of this type employed 33 percent of the working male population and 51.8 percent of the female workforce.[31] In the urban centers, World War II drove many women to take on paid jobs outside the home. After the war, reconstruction and industrialization absorbed even larger amounts of urban workers. As elsewhere, the percentage of married women among the total number of female workers increased, from 9 percent in 1948 to 17.4 percent in 1957.

In the past few years, there has been a marked tendency for female labor to gravitate to the tertiary sector of the occupational structure in highly developed countries. In the United States, 55 percent of the female workforce was employed in the tertiary sector in 1909 as compared with 70 percent in 1950. This percentage rose from 52 percent in 1930 to 68 percent in 1950 in Sweden; and from 28 percent in 1921 to 47 percent in 1957 in France; in 1968 40 percent of girls leaving school in Britain went into clerical work.[32] A number of factors have been responsible for this increased concentration. As a nation's economy grows, the tertiary sector expands enormously, absorbing ever larger numbers of the workforce; at the same time, expanding educational opportunities for middle-class women equip them for clerical work.[33]

The large concentration of female labor in the tertiary sector of the occupational structure by no means signifies an unmixed victory for women, despite the step upward from manual to nonmanual labor. The organizations representing the white-collar positions are at a much less advantageous bargaining position than industrial unions, because of the constant dread of losing status under which their members live. Also, there are more part-time jobs in the tertiary sector, precisely the type of jobs which are most vulnerable during times of economic crisis. Indeed, during normal periods, these part-time jobs are good indicators of concealed unemployment, commanding as they do the lowest wages.

Vicissitudes of Female Labor

Many scholars have viewed woman's condition in class society as the result of a convergence of factors stemming from two different orders of things, natural and social. One of the most important factors of the former is the fact that woman's ability to work diminishes drastically during the last months of pregnancy and the immediate post-natal period. The mother is irreplaceable as a source of nourishment for the infant. Such biological facts are often used to justify keeping woman unemployed throughout her entire lifetime, and sometimes have disastrous consequences for both the stability of the female personality and for childraising, to say nothing of marital relations.[34]

It is a truism that motherhood creates serious problems for female labor in competitive societies. It remains to be seen, however, whether practical measures that have been taken will constitute adequate solutions with respect not only to personality stability and childrearing, but to the stability of society itself. Since civilization transforms natural problems into social problems, their solutions are also social. Motherhood must therefore not be seen as exclusively a woman's burden. Indeed, since the survival of society is contingent on the birth and rearing of new generations, it should bear at least part of the cost of motherhood, or find satisfactory solutions to the occupational problems that maternity creates for women. Class societies have instituted some measures to enable women to hold down jobs; paid leaves of absence, for example, before and after childbirth, are a positive step in this direction. But this is no more than a partial solution, although a necessary one. The break in a woman's employment caused by childbirth is one of the arguments employers use to justify keeping women in lower positions in the job hierarchy, and the preference they give men over women for the responsible positions on which the prosperity of a business depends. This "peripheral integration" of female labor into the productive system is therefore legitimate from the employer's viewpoint: how often has a firm undertaken to train its female employees in more skilled occupations at its own expense, only to have them quit to get married or become mothers? The firm's investment is then lost, and it is left with no choice but to draw on its male employees when trained personnel are needed. In an economy based on private enterprise, the profit motive necessitates greater investment efficiency.

The problem of female absenteeism is subject to the same considerations. Here again, natural factors are subtly intermingled with factors of social origin. Surveys have shown that women remain away from work for mild illnesses more often than men. To further aggravate the problem, when man or child falls ill, the woman does not show up for work either, since she is expected to care for her family. These factors contribute to a far higher rate of absenteeism among women.[35] Yet absenteeism is quite clearly not determined solely by the idiosyncracies of the female organism and the woman's family situation; it is also linked to her lower occupational status. Women are much more rarely absent when the work is pleasant, entails responsibility, and is adequately paid.

All of this serves to illustrate the way in which the secularization of thought is subordinate to the interests of the ruling order in class societies. The prejudices which on the surface seem to hold back the progress of the capitalist order turn out at bottom to be weighty factors in helping to maintain it. Through the skillful use of stereotyped notions limits are imposed on the degree and extent of integration of certain social categories into the productive system; this serves to shield the system from potential jolts to its equilibrium and to maintain the tensions it generates at tolerable levels.

The vicissitudes of the female labor force also have been

seen as stemming from the secularization of attitudes, changes in family structure, etc. One might say that if women are ever to be able to enjoy the same latitude of choice and action in the domain of production as men, changes will have to be made in both their reproductive and childrearing function.[36] Whether working or unemployed, these functions serve to discriminate against women socially on the basis of sex by excluding them from class structures or allowing only a "peripheral integration." But to say that the stage of family structure lags behind the economic structure of society, and thereby blocks women's entrance into positions in production, is to fly in the face of the facts.

In Sweden, women enjoy considerable sexual freedom. Illegitimacy of offspring has been abolished; single mothers have elaborate measures of security and protection at their disposal; and the use of contraceptives is widespread. Yet there are fewer women in the occupational structure than in other European countries, such as France, where the family structure is more rigid, where the advertisement and sale of contraceptives was prohibited until 1969, and where until recently only men could get a divorce on grounds of adultery.[37] (Indeed, the percentages of women gainfully employed, between the ages of 15 and 60 years, were 52 percent in England in 1951; 31.4 percent in the United States in 1950; 52 percent in France in 1946; and 23.4 percent in Sweden in 1950.)[38] The high proportion of the Swedish population engaged in agriculture does not explain the small percentage of women in paid employment, since the number of women engaged in agriculture fell from 27 percent of the total number of working women in 1960 to 6 percent in 1950.[39] The rather low Swedish figure is probably due to the fact that a large number of women carry out economic tasks as unpaid members of the family, and therefore were not classified as employed in the census returns.

The example of Sweden shows that a country's economic

structure has a much more decisive effect on the employment of women in paid occupations than does the degree of sexual and reproductive freedom, or the number of child care facilities available to mothers. Birth control and the setting up of canteen services and daycare centers may create the preconditions enabling women to take jobs outside the home, but the decisive factor remains the occupational structure's capacity to absorb labor power. The efforts made by the British government during the last war to allow married women to work outside the home show that the social facilities that create the conditions for women to work will vary in countries with an excess labor force as a function of the needs of the economic structure.

The persistence of vestiges of outmoded productive systems in certain capitalist economies marginalized more women than men from the dominant system of production. The French clothing industry illustrates this form of marginalization well. It relies on work done in the home, which is difficult for the authorities to control and is hence a type of labor whose exploitation knows no strict bounds. Since fine needlework does not lend itself to mass production, production costs would be extremely high if wages were calculated on the basis of labor time. Other types of women's clothing as well are rarely made in large lots, and almost never exceed one hundred pieces for patterns intended for the mass public and never more than twenty for those intended for the elegant set.[40] Moreover, since clothing is a seasonal industry and subject to changes in style, labor power needs vary depending on the time of year. If an employer were to maintain a permanent staff of factory workers it would mean paying for labor that was kept idle for long periods each year, and that is obviously unprofitable. The women's clothing industry maintains large numbers of women in a state of hidden underemployment, and by keeping wages low exploits to the maximum the absolute surplus value produced by its female workers. There has been no decrease in domestic labor in the woman's clothing industry, in contrast to what has occurred in other productive sectors of the French economy. In the mid-fifties approximately 70 percent of the female labor employed in the production of women's clothing was domestic labor, according to a survey by Guilbert and Isambert-Jamati.[41]

Since work in the home is the most compatible with the traditional functions of mother, one might expect that many if not most of such woman workers would also have family tasks. Surprisingly enough, however, the same survey showed that although the majority of women who worked at home were indeed married (62 percent), 80.5 percent of the total had no children, 13.5 percent had only one, 3 percent had two, and 3 percent had three or more.[42] Thus, except in a very few cases children are not the determining factor in the women's decision to take on work in the home. Indeed, only 23 percent claimed family responsibilities as the reason; 9.7 percent stated the desire to work alone; 13.3 percent were forced to take such work by conditions on the labor market (they could get no outside jobs); and 40.5 percent stated that the home was where a woman should be. The feminine mystique plays an important role in justifying the channeling of female labor into jobs which are poorly paid, lacking in prestige, and difficult to bring under the control of labor laws. The French Ministry of Labor keeps no statistics on women working in the home—a practice which is not only to the liking of employers, but is also, in the short run, in the interests of the worker herself, who thus does not lose her family subsidy from the government.[43]

The family's present stage of development—more specifically, the way in which a woman carries out her sexual, reproductive, and childrearing functions—certainly has a considerable influence on female labor. But aside from periods of rapid economic growth and war, society is unable to cope, either systematically or constantly, with the problems these functions generate, since in the final analysis it is the nation's basic economic structure which exercises rational control over female roles. In this respect, the feminine mystique, whatever its degree of sophistication or subtlety, serves consciously or unconsciously the interests of the ruling order in class societies. Mystification, along with other fetishes, works in many subtle and circuitous ways, not always obvious to the casual glance. When capitalism was in its infancy the women of the petty bourgeoisie were faced with rather cheerless alternatives: they could either resign themselves to being deprived of their economic function and remain in the home, or they could accept the few occupations available on the labor market—for example, seamstress or governess— occupations which were both poorly paid and meant a step down socially.

With the growth of capitalism, however, the quest for prestige had to give ground to the worship of wealth; prestige came to be measured, at least in part, by the amount of leisure a man could afford to give his wife. Nevertheless, middle-class women (mainly single, but married ones as well) threw themselves into the rush for paid jobs. The notion that a woman's mission in life was to marry and bear children was not particularly conducive to creating a skillful female workforce. Rather, it led to a kind of specialization that channeled middle-class women into second-rate, poorly paid jobs with no prospects for advancement. Proletarian families in their turn adopted as much of the ruling class ideology as they could: a woman was to be mistress of the home and guardian of the hearth, and no more. The self-conception of the vast majority of women consigns them to a fate wholly defined by sex. Not only do employers justify women's lower wages on sexual grounds, but women themselves set their goals very low. They cannot, after all, feel secure in a world in which they make no decisions and figure as no more than objects to be manipulated. Unconscious fear of failure dampens a woman's aspirations and reduces her incentive to achieve. Hence, women will ordinarily seek to enter the class structure along the paths of least resistance, in areas deemed befitting her sex and in occupations which offer little prospect for the future, are poorly paid, confer little prestige, and are considered unsuited for men. In this respect, competition between men and women is quite different from competition among men alone, and perhaps should not even be considered competition at all. When men enter the fray, they may be handicapped by differences of race, education, political power, and religion (i.e., by class differences) that are marked and difficult to overcome. But women not only must grapple with characteristics which set sexually neutral (i.e., composed of both sexes) groups against one another; they must also bear the additional burden of their sex.

Organized Labor and Women

For a woman, holding a job means much more than receiving a wage, although she may not always be directly conscious of this. It means to participate in social life and to have a hand in shaping it; to leave a natural state to enjoy the fruits of culture; and to feel less insecure. In a very real sense, an occupation is a source of stability for a woman, to which her role in the family is a necessary complement under capitalism. In the one her labor is a commodity to be exchanged on the market; in the other, it is a mere use value in the home, although there it still retains a link to the market through the commodity aspect of her husband's labor. However, whatever the frame of reference (in the family or on the job) aspects of these two roles will be clearly incompatible. Class society does not provide a framework within which women's roles can be appreciated and assimilated; in a society based on class, a woman's life is patently contradictory. Women have a subjective, and often even an objective, need (although in the former case not always conscious) to become full-fledged members of class society, yet they also have both a subjective and ·objective need to be concerned with their families.

The difficulty of finding the proper balance has led many women to forego a potential professional career in favor of a fuller (and in the short term, less trying) integration within the family unit. Indeed, the way to integration into the family is much more clearly laid out than is integration into the occupational structure, not only because of objective factors surrounding the two structures, but also because of the nature of women's education. Women thus come to rank the functions of job and family in order of importance, with the latter taking precedence. In reality both should be on an equal footing as far as integration into society is concerned. Any hierarchical ranking of women's functions in capitalist societies only compounds the difficulties women have with social integration—yet under capitalism this seems the only way.

Such ranking also seems to have played a role in the inadequate use women have made of the traditional means by which the working class defends itself in capitalist society: trade unions. Although male workers have often fought against the unionization of women, the attitudes of women themselves have been mainly responsible for the weaker showing of their union organizations. Since a woman's occupation is of secondary importance in her life, she has neither the motivation nor the time to concentrate effectively on improving her bargaining status on the labor market through union activities.

The high point in female union membership in Austria and Germany was reached prior to the advent of National Socialism. The number of women in German unions rose from

15,000 in 1896 to 230,000 in 1913, or from less than 5 percent of total union membership to 9 percent. Women members numbered 1.2 million in 1919, and 1.7 million the next year or 21 percent of the membership of the free unions.[44] In 1920 there were, in addition, 215,000 women in the Christian unions and 21,000 in the liberal unions. After 1921 the number of women in the free unions declined considerably, and in 1931 it was 14 percent of the total membership. In occupations filled mainly by women, the number of female union members approximated very nearly the percentage of women in the total workforce employed in these sectors. In the textile industry, for example, in which women comprised 58.7 percent of the total workforce, they comprised 56.7 percent of the total union membership. This was also true, although to a lesser degree, of women in the clothing, bookbinding, and tobacco industries.

In England, female union membership was much lower. The first serious attempt to unionize British women was led by Emma Paterson between 1874 and 1886. The movement to open unions to women was supported from the outset by the trade boards in the sweated industries, and received another strong impetus from the National Federation of Women Workers, formed in 1906. The Women's Trade Union fought to increase female union membership, which reached a peak in 1918, when 18.5 percent of working women were organized.

In the United States, the organization of women workers into unions was urged both by the National Labor Union, in the 1860s, and by the Knights of Labor. The predominantly craft character of the unions in the American Federation of Labor was less favorable to organizing women, however, and indeed no mass movement aimed at unionizing women workers ever really emerged in the United States, even under the influence of the socialists at the beginning of this century. During the period from 1910 to 1920, female union membership grew considerably, but even at the peak of organization women made up only 8 percent of the total (a small but significant increase from the figure of 3.5 percent ten years previously). This increase took place almost entirely in the occupations in which women constituted a majority, notably the clothing industry, where female union membership rose from 11.2 percent in 1910 to 46 percent in 1920. In the 1920s this trend reversed itself, and by the end of the decade female union membership had suffered a drastic decline. The cause is to be sought partly in the fact that protective legislation for female labor, long a fundamental concern of American unionism, had by this time largely been achieved. In 1963 only 3 million American women were union members.

In contrast to this sorry showing of woman working-class organization, by the turn of the century bourgeois and middle-class women across the country flocked to the women's clubs, a type of organization considered both chic and educational. Concerned with a broad range of welfare and reform issues, representatives of these organizations, which in some cases were nationwide, functioned as congressional lobbyists, and joined forces with members of Congress to push through desired legislation or amendments. Through these clubs, the women of the privileged social strata commanded respect for their demands.[45]

French women proved even more difficult to organize. Unionized women represented only 5.7 percent of the female labor force in 1900, 7.8 percent in 1908, and 9.7 percent in 1911. In 1965, women were a majority in the textile unions and communications unions, although female representation in leadership positions was negligible. Even in the National Teacher's Union, to which 50 percent of all female teachers belonged in the early sixties, women held no positions of general responsibility, and there were only two women on the national board.[46]

Compared to the USSR, female unionization in the so-called free world is insignificant. In 1929, women constituted 33.3 percent of the working force in the USSR, and 29.7 percent of total union membership. By 1932, 83.3 percent of all women workers belonged to unions.

There are two sets of factors that explain the marginal female union membership in capitalist countries: (1) the basic features of this segment of the labor force, which finds itself split between household work and wage labor; and (2) the attitudes of society and of women themselves toward female labor.

The union movement grew rapidly in the older industrialized countries, although it embraced only skilled workers. In most of these countries, it was more than half a century before semi-skilled and unskilled workers became the targets of union organizing. Female labor was completely unskilled during the early period of capitalism, and even today is only marginally skilled. The marginalization of women from the trade unions thus initially proceeded along the same path as male unionism. Until quite recently, the female workforce in the industrialized nations has been on the average much younger than the male workforce,[47] and the relative youth of women workers has hardly been conducive to speedy successes in union organizing. In addition, the smaller numbers of working women are a definite handicap. Considered by men as competitors, they rarely receive help from men in organizing, although such help could well be invaluable. Thus, the immaturity, inferior numbers, and segregation of women workers are all undeniable factors in low female union membership.

A still more persuasive explanation of this phenomenon is the difficulty women have in adapting to the roles they must assume under capitalism, and the general attitudes held toward female labor. Indeed, the normal view is that female labor is a subsidiary quantity, and a woman's wages merely bolster the family income. Since unions are essentially concerned with improving the workers' material situation, for which they periodically battle for wage hikes and social security benefits, and since both jobs and wages enjoy only a subsidiary status for women, unionism comes to appear somewhat incongruous with female labor in the eyes of society. The potential political power of organized women would itself be sufficient incentive for society to discourage unionization or, worse, active union leadership by women.

But the poor union showing of women obviously cannot be held completely responsible for—or even as a decisive factor in—the generally low pay women receive. In class society, a woman's work is performed under complex conditions which do not allow much latitude in selling their labor power. In this respect, poor union representation is merely a particular expression of the general paucity of opportunities women have to realize labor demands. Despite equal pay legislation, women's wages are still lower than men's. Nonetheless, it is noteworthy that the wage gap between the sexes narrows when women are organized, although this has occurred only in occupations filled predominantly by women.

Although the general restriction of women to unskilled jobs makes comparisons difficult, enough evidence exists to indicate that discriminatory standards have historically been applied to give women lower wages for comparable work. In 1935, American women in the cotton textile industry received 28 percent less than men doing the same work; in the shoe industry, the differential was 36 percent. In the period 1922-1930, a woman's average earnings ranged from 45 percent to 84 percent of the earnings of men, with an average of 70 percent for three-quarters of the cases. These figures show that in predominantly female occupations, wages will vary to the extent to which women are organized, although complete pay equality has never been achieved. In the second decade of this century, the most poorly paid factory trades were in the candy, textile, and tobacco industries, in which union organization was weak; whereas in the clothing industry, wages were highest and the women were comparably well organized.

In the twenties women's wages were around 30 percent lower than men's in Germany. When the British civil service introduced equal wages in the early sixties, they were to be achieved in installments stretching over a period of seven years,[48] and in 1970 equal pay in all occupations was scheduled to come into force five years later, in 1975.

In France, women's earnings were 31.1 percent lower, on the average, than men's in 1920, with this difference steadily decreasing to 9.4 percent in 1964.[49] In Japan no comparable decline occurred: female wages were 43 percent of male wages in 1948 and 41.4 percent in 1957.[50] Even in the Soviet Union, the only country where total wage equality has been achieved, there were still some wage differences between 1920 and 1930, although these were minor. In the printing and machine tool industries women's wages were 81.8 percent and 93.9 percent of men's. In the textile industry, where women took over some of the skilled tasks formerly performed by men, wages were even then the same.[51]

Although women in the United States increased their wages during World War I, even during this period, total wage equality was not achieved in the skilled professions. But once hostilities had ceased women's earnings declined sharply, although the principle of equal wages for equal work was ostensibly still in effect. The spreading notion that a male worker's wages should be adequate to meet the expenses of his entire family signified that female labor was no longer required by the American economy, at least in the same measure as during the war. The notion also aimed at keeping women from taking the men's jobs, which would have meant an enormous rise in business profits, and at the same time increased financial hardship for working-class families. Working women (even the few who were organized) realized that they were not strong enough to defend their rights and that to persist in replacing men in paying jobs would have meant lowering family incomes and giving a valuable boost to capital. Women thus supported the principle that a man should earn enough to support all the members of the family. Because they had not learned that the issue at stake was more than just a question of which type of labor, male or female, was to be used in the dominant system of production, women had no choice but to concur in the view that their own labor was unnecessary. They therefore had a direct hand in sustaining those mechanisms through which society maintains a large force of reserve labor.

The behavior of women's labor unions reflects the duality of women's position in competitive societies. The sexual hierarchy in the family, which prevents or at least makes difficult women's active participation in union work, serves in the end to reinforce the discrimination practiced against her. The expulsion of women from the occupational structure alleviates the tensions generated by a surplus of labor on the market; thus large numbers of women are kept unemployed, although society could mobilize them at any instant. The marginalization of women from the class structure, rationalized through the "masculinity complex" and the "feminine mystique," makes both men and women more or less unconscious vehicles for the exploitation of their own labor in class society.

Perhaps neither unionism nor labor legislation are sufficient to abolish woman's marginal status as a worker in capitalist societies whose hallmarks are insecurity and recurrent crises. This consideration adds a new dimension to the assertion that "emancipation of women requires its convergence with concomitant emancipation of men."[52] The problems which confront women in competitive societies are beyond solution in such societies; because they are class problems which merely manifest themselves differently for men and women, they must be attacked jointly by men and women. Action by either sex in isolation will be a double-edged sword: it may achieve beneficial results over the short term, but at the price of indefinite submission to a status quo that holds back the realization of human potential. The conditions for the utilization of the labor power of both men and women will be created only through the joint action of both sexes. That action, in turn, will depend on the development of society's productive forces, and on the degree to which men and women become conscious of the contradictions of the age in which they live and of the means available for overcoming them.

CHAPTER 4

The Socialist Perspective

The Utopian Socialists

Socialism, both utopian and scientific, has historically endeavored to show women the way to their liberation. Saint-Simon undertook a defense of women, if only a timid one, in *Exposition de la doctrine*. He believed the liberation of women to be a natural outgrowth of the evolution of society, and could not imagine future society without a corresponding emancipation of women. Unlike later socialist writers, however, Saint-Simon did not attack marriage as a typical form of female servitude. On the contrary, he proposed to establish equality between the sexes within marriage.[1]

Actually, utopian socialists, represented principally by Saint-Simon, F. M. Fourier, and Robert Owen, were much more concerned with humankind as a whole than with any particular social group. They did not see themselves as saviors of the oppressed proletariat except insofar as it was a part of humanity, which they intended to redeem by instituting the Reign of Reason. Condemning both the bourgeois and feudal worlds for their irrationality, utopian socialists proposed to resolve society's problems through Reason, and for this it "was necessary, then, to discover a new and more perfect system of social order and to impose this upon society from without by propaganda, and, wherever it was possible, by the example of model experiments. These new social systems were foredoomed."[2]

Fourier went much further than Saint-Simon, and in his *Théories des quatre mouvements et des destinées générales*, written in 1808, he proposed that society should provide men and women with the same education, and free women once and for all from household chores by setting up communal kitchens and nurseries for the children. Contemplating the advent of an era in which geniuses would vie freely with one another, he excluded women from none of the functions of society. Fourier denounced equally women's submissiveness and men's alienation.[3] However, since the liberation of women remained for Fourier contingent upon the establishment of his ideal society, it was never more than the expression of utopian consciousness negating the status quo.[4]

Marxism

With the advent of scientific socialism, the solution to the woman problem shifted terrain: it was held to lie in the total destruction of the capitalist system and its replacement by socialist society. Marx expounded his first ideas on the subject of marriage and the social situation of women in his articles in the *Rheinische Zeitung* in 1842. In his criticism of the proposed Prussian law on divorce,[5] he rejected the Hegelian view that marriage was indissoluble. To marriage as a concept Marx opposed marriage as a social fact, and as such, he argued, it cannot be indissoluble because social facts undergo change, perish, and are replaced by others. When the conjugal union is dissolved *de facto*, divorce is no more than a juridical acknowledgment of a marriage in reality already in a shambles.

Contrary to what is frequently claimed, Marx did not propose the abolition of the family. He denounced the incompatibility of the family, such as he observed it, with the woman working outside the home. He deplored the consequences of the hard life of the working woman for rearing her children, for parental authority, and for family morality. But he certainly did not consider the European family as it existed at that time to be the only possible form of conjugal union. Indeed, what was harmful for children and parents alike was the destruction of the family without any new structure being offered in its place. Even in its most depressing aspects, therefore, capitalism represented an important step forward toward a new type of family:

> However terrible and disgusting, therefore, the dissolution, under the capitalist system, of the old family ties may appear, nevertheless, modern industry, by assigning as it does an important part in the process of production outside the domestic sphere to women, to young persons, and to children of both sexes, creates a new economic foundation for a higher form of the family and of the relations between the sexes.[6]

As a social institution, the family is not immutable; there are major differences between the ancient family in its Greek or Oriental form and the Christian Germanic form, for example. However, there is also a thread of historical continuity.

Marx was far from preaching anarchic sexual freedom; for him, that would have meant making woman even more the mere object of man's pleasure than she was already. He rejected that vulgar communism which contemplated the establishment of a community of women.[7] Reifying woman reifies man as well, for he who obtains gratification from an object, who has no need to enter into relations with another human being, loses all humanity. Thus, for Marx the genuine liberation of woman was part of the more general process of humanization of the entire species. The relationship that exists between man and woman is a good indication of the state of human essence.

Since Marx never considered the woman problem as something isolated from society, whatever its structural type, he steadfastly refused to accept any palliative measure that proposed to protect women or provide a sugar coating for their real sufferings. It was rather the root causes of the degradation of women which he sought.[8] He saw bourgeois institutions as pharisaic to the core: the bourgeois made the laws for others to observe. The transgression of laws was the bourgeois' special talent: he violated the laws of marriage, family, and property, yet these institutions remained intact and formed the very foundation of class society. Since the only real ties existing within the bourgeois family were those of bordeom, money, and adultery, an infraction of its outward juridical form was in fact of no importance. On the contrary, it was one of the ways by which the bourgeois family was maintained as it existed in fact, not as it appeared within the juridical superstructure. This was the line Marx took in countering the charge that communists wanted to introduce a community of women. Since for the bourgeois, he explained, woman is a mere instrument of production, and the communists propose to introduce common ownership of the instruments of production, they conclude from this that communists want to introduce a community of women. But for the bourgeoisie, such a community already existed. "Our bourgeois," he went on, "not content with having the wives and daughters of the proletarians at their disposal . . . take the greatest pleasure in seducing each other's wives."[9]

Thus, for Marx the determining factors of woman's social existence derived from a system of production premised upon the oppression of man by man—a system which alienated and corrupted the body as well as the mind. The solution, then, lay in the supersedure of this phase of the historical (or prehistorical) development of humankind. Henceforth the idea that woman, like man, would only attain true freedom under a socialist system would become a permanent feature of every socialist theory claiming to be scientific.

Although Marx never undertook a detailed analysis of

woman's condition in capitalist societies, and often seemed to give the question short shrift, what he did write on the subject indicates he was aware of the complexity of the problem. Once the family and woman's situation in it and in society at large were placed within a historical context, it was evident that they were tied to the mode of production, not merely to property.[10]

Engels, in his turn, derived monogamy directly from private property, but at the same time held that the monogamous family renders the conjugal bond more solid and unilateral. According to him, monogamy is based on the supremacy of man, "the express purpose being to produce children of undisputed paternity . . . because these children are later to come into their father's property as his natural heirs."[11] Engels considered property, whether of things or persons or both, responsible for the oppression to which women are subject in the monogamous family.[12]

Engels resorted to analogy in his description of the relations between the sexes, and in his enquiry into the root causes of the dominance of one sex by the other. He elaborated on the statement he and Marx made in *The German Ideology* that "the division of labor was originally nothing but the division of labor in the sexual act"[13] with the comment:

> The first class opposition that appears in history coincides with the development of the antagonism between man and woman in monogamous marriage, and the first class oppression coincides with that of the female sex by the male. Monogamous marriage was a great historical step forward; nevertheless, together with slavery and private wealth it opens the period that has lasted until today in which every step forward is also a relative step backwards, in which prosperity and development for some is won through the misery and frustration of others. It is the cellular form of civilized society, in which the nature of oppositions and contradictions fully active in that society can be already studied.[14]

Views of Women and the
Family Structure: A Critique

One may concede that the monogamous family has close ties with private property (or, better, with the capitalist mode of production), especially in its reproductive aspect, that is, the right of inheritance. But it would be too much of an oversimplification to claim that private property was alone responsible for woman's inferior social status, and even more debatable that relations between man and woman are of the same order as relations between social classes.[15] Biological and racial criteria may have been useful for justifying the class structure of competitive society, but they are surely not its cornerstone. Social classes—as partial totalities—possess, at least with regard to reproduction, sufficient autonomy to ensure their continued physical existence. The complementary reproductive functions of the two sexes are certainly important, and should be taken into account in analyzing woman's condition in class society. The categories of sex, however, do not by themselves have the minimum degree of autonomy to ensure continued existence; indeed, individually the sexes are capable only of producing their labor power, not reproducing it.

Engels let himself be misled by the one feature which relations between the sexes and relations between social classes had in common: domination. However, this phenomenon is much broader in its ramifications than the phenomenon of property. Property may well be the determining factor in certain forms of domination, and one might even say that in normal times economic domination decides people's fates in competitive society. At the same time, there are other forms of domination which do not derive directly from private property. For example, the dominance of the adult generation exists by virtue of society's need to transmit to youth its cultural products—when by culture we mean that which sets the standards for social interaction, as well as the effective result of the various ways that people have adapted to the natural world around them.

Property is no more than one, although perhaps the most crucial, element in this process, especially as regards the individual's participation. But adult domination (the socio-cultural dimension of the socializing process) is aimed at preparing individuals to occupy social roles determined by class. Socialization is hence always guided by the individual's actual or potential chance of functioning in some realm of capitalism. As long as it is dominated by class interests and takes place largely within one and the same class, relations of adult domination cannot be considered analogous to class relations. Of course, the socializing process may well contain components which reinforce the class structure, but this merely confirms the assertion that there are forms of domination which do not stem directly from private property. In the socialist countries, where private property has been replaced by collective ownership, political power continues to be exercised, and domination by bureaucracy is in effect.

Not only do age and sex constitute groups of a different order than social classes; their interrelations are fundamentally different from those which characterize interaction between groups occupying antagonistic positions in the social structure. Since they are universal factors (although dependent), they serve more to conceal class antagonism than to sharpen it. When domination is a factor between overlapping social categories, the most acute contradictions may be forced into the background. Man's domination over woman does not mystify masculine consciousness; it encourages men to adopt an attitude opposing women's integration into society, and in this way favors the continued existence of a system of production in which women are sometimes in critical demand—because their employment increases the rate of surplus value or because of a shortage of male labor. Here, the domination of man over woman, while not directly related to the economic structure of society, ends up subserving the interests of those holding the economic power. Men of the subjugated class perform a mediating role in the marginalization of women of their own class from the occupational structure. In this context, the generic characteristic of sex lends a particular twist to historical consciousness, in that both suffer from the effects of the "feminine mystique."

Neither under these circumstances, in which the relations of production are seen behind the scenes,[16] so to speak, nor in situations in which individuals are fully conscious of the true nature of relations between the social classes, is solidarity among all women a realistic hope, as some believe.[17] In class society, the universal characteristic of sex expresses a subordinate relationship which tells us nothing about the workings of the social system. To uncover the root causes of how, specifically, one of the sexes has come to be victimized, one must look to the primary or essential characteristics of the system. But one must also bear in mind that between a system of production, and the marginalization of one sex from it, there is a mediating family structure in which women fulfill their natural functions, as well as their household and childraising functions.

Neither Marx nor Engels made an effort to analyze the specific functions that women fulfill in the family; thus neither was able to come up with even a theoretical solution to the woman problem; nor were they able to resist entirely the notion that the family structure in some way lagged behind the economic structure of capitalist society. The idea that the structure of the family somehow hinders the capitalist system from achieving its full potential is quite widespread, and further compounded by the belief that a new type of family will emerge in class societies when certain prejudices have been overcome. According to this line of reasoning, the compatibility of the family with the capitalist system is progressively increasing, that is, the family is being transformed in a way that will permit the institutionalization of gainful employment for women outside the home. There is some truth to this view. Electric household appliances, semi-prepared foods, birth control, the fact that children begin their formal schooling earlier (in nursery schools and, especially, kindergartens), and many other benefits of modern civilization have certainly relieved women from fatiguing and tedious chores. But there are two considerations which, if they do not completely nullify the conveniences of modern female life, nevertheless serve to keep women bound to the home.

First, modern conveniences exist on the market like any other commodity; they therefore have an exchange value. They cannot always be afforded by families in which the woman works, in particular, in working class families who need them most. Free daycare centers are notoriously inadequate in every country of the world, even the socialist countries, where much effort goes into setting up such services. Access to contraceptives is also at least partly dependent on individual finances, to say nothing about legal and religious factors which complicate their use. (The People's Republic of China has made great strides in this area: it was one of the first countries in the world to officially authorize the use of contraceptives.) Other products of modern industry (semi-prepared foods, household appliances) are not available, irrespective of income, to all. The most lauded advantages of modern living thus simply do not exist for a large number of working women, and for many others who must go to work to augment their family's income—despite a developed system of sales and credit.

But is it really the shortage of these conveniences that prevents women from having an occupation in class society? To be sure, the job of watching over and caring for children is hard enough to keep women from taking outside jobs, or to oblige them to quit such jobs temporarily if they have them. The absence or unavailability of other conveniences has not prevented women from working productively, but it has made integration into society more difficult and burdensome. Furthermore, access to such conveniences is not a sufficient condition to steer women onto the labor market or even reduce the time they spend doing housework.[18] The second important consideration, therefore, is that consumption, above all the use of electric household appliances, far from freeing women from nonproductive tasks and enabling them to engage in more satisfying activities in paid jobs outside the home, is in fact becoming increasingly a substitute for the feminine personality. Adroitly manipulated by the propaganda put out by the manufacturers of domestic articles, many American women find in the purchase and possession of these articles a palliative for the malaise caused by the cribbed and barren lives they lead. In 1945, 75 percent of the purchasing power in the United States was in the hands of women,[19] with the result that their possessive cravings have swelled, to the detriment of satisfying involvement in social, political, and economic issues.

Can it be concluded from this that the changes effected in the family structure have reduced the incompatibility between the roles that a woman fills at home and her functions on the job as a working woman? If one takes the position that the family is the key, the determining structure, in women's economic emancipation, two consequences emerge: (1) for society as a whole, no distinction would then exist between the sex factor and reproduction, and the socialization of the young would remain unresolved; (2) if the problems that surround the family were soluble without a radical transformation of the economic structure, it would become even more incompatible with the system of production upon which the competitive order is based.

Unwanted maternity makes the element of chance important in determining life, but beyond that it is also a real obstacle to female employment under capitalism, and a rationalization used to keep women out of the class structure. Would not therefore the incompatibility between family structure and women's outside work be necessary to the maintenance of the capitalist system of production itself? And would not family planning make those two structures even more incompatible? Even if women were liberated from unwanted maternity and children were reared in an organized way by specifically qualified people instead of in the home, would this liberation have any purpose if the occupational structure were unable to absorb the female workforce that would thereby become available? If the class structure is to be maintained, other natural characteristics will have to be found which can function as stigmas to justify the marginalization of other social groups. In light of these considerations, the emancipation of women is inconceivable without the concomitant liberation of men.

However, it would be an illusion to suppose that the mere economic emancipation of women is sufficient to liberate them from all the prejudices and preconceived notions that discriminate against them. The emergence of societies with collective economies has shown that although economic liberation may be the *sine qua non* of woman's full liberation, it does not constitute the whole picture.[20]

Not all institutions are amenable to change, and rational intervention is necessary if there exists real desire to further the cause of women's emancipation. Engels' view was not only economic, it was remarkably close to being mechanistic. He asked whether monogamy, "having arisen from economic causes will . . . disappear when these causes disappear,"[21] and concluded that prostitution will disappear once the means of production have been collectivized, and that monogamy will become a reality for men and women, but one rooted in individual love based on reciprocity. Although prostitution certainly is closely related to woman's economic condition in private enterprise economies, it forms habits which can persist independently of the economic structure of society. Moreover, the social discrimination suffered by the prostitute makes her integration difficult in all societies, whether their economy is based on private property or socialized property. In China, where prostitution flourished on an alarming scale before the revolution, the social rehabilitation of prostitutes has been long and laborious.

Collectivization of the economy, therefore, does not mean the automatic elimination of prostitution, which has been one of the conditions enabling the legally constituted monogamous family to exist. Obviously, socialization of the means of production and the enactment of legislation barring discrimination between the sexes in the family, in employment, in politics, or even in cultural matters, as have occurred in the USSR and China, are absolute prerequisites for raising the social status of women. Yet society must go further and take measures to eradicate old habits of thinking that serve to keep women down.[22] This is a complicated task, and the work of not one but several generations, but it will be made easier as the cultural, social, and economic development already achieved in the major urban centers becomes more uniform and widespread. One can expect that the modernizing process, which also implies the development of a positive attitude toward woman's liberation, will make less rapid headway in Soviet Lithuania, which is essentially an agricultural republic, than it has in Moscow or Leningrad. In the West, too, women enjoy much more obvious freedom in countries and regions that are socially and economically developed.

Whereas under capitalism serious structural limitations are imposed on women's liberation, their increasing emancipation in socialist countries appears to be contingent on the continuation of the process of economic development. Cultural factors sometimes hold back the process. The success achieved in the social rehabilitation and reintegration of the prostitute in the Soviet Union and in the People's Republic of China is a hopeful sign that the age-old tradition of female inferiority is slowly but surely giving way to a social climate more conducive to sexual equality.

History has thus far not provided a concrete example of how to destroy all the partial structures of a society at the same time.[23] The development of capitalism and socialism show that certain cultural habits molded by old structures may persist long into the new in an uneven pattern of change that has challenged the validity of certain theories. In the USSR, post-revolutionary puritanism revived the legal, monogamous family, which previously had been regarded as a bourgeois institution destined to disappear.

So long as socialist theory persists in seeing the factors that bear on woman's condition as deriving solely from the economic structure, it will lose sight of the partial autonomy that other structures tend to have, and will hence never be able to appreciate adequately the uniqueness of the feminine condition, nor the social opportunities that central planning creates. Engels fell victim to his own economism, although he did recognize that the partial structures of society tended to develop unevenly.[24]

Auguste Bebel, who also saw the woman question as part of the larger social question, likewise saw "many points of similarity between the situation of women and that of the worker," but recognized that the analogy breaks down with the dual determination to which woman's condition is subject. In his words, "woman was the first human being to be subjected to servitude. She was a slave before even the slave was."[25] Moreover, he realized that the past is so deeply rooted in woman's being that conditions which are ultimately contingent appear to her as the natural state of things. Difficult as it may be to make the worker aware of how competitive society works, it is even more difficult to bring women to a consciousness of all factors determining their lives.[26] On top of this, he noted, class division (semi-autonomous partial totalities) is an effective obstacle to achieving universal solidarity among women. Bebel's observation that the inferior social position of women is not in itself a sufficient motivating factor for the creation of a unified feminist movement[27] shows that he was basically able to resist confusing sex and class (although he never explicitly and clearly said as much), and that Engels' likening relations between the sexes to class relations never received a sympathetic response, even within the currents of socialist thought. It could not have been otherwise: to make the feminine question into the most fundamental contradiction of capitalist society would have undermined socialist thought not only as a system, but also as a method.

Class consciousness thus supersedes any consciousness the individual may achieve of his or her situation as a member of the male or female sex. Although women of the ruling class have never dominated the men of their class, they have, in real terms, had free command over the labor of men and women. Thus, though sex may be at issue, solidarity will crystallize first along class lines. Relations between the sexes are at least partly determined by the social class to which the individual belongs. This is especially true in the domain of production, where class differences in the relations between the sexes are quite clear-cut. Among men and women of the bourgeoisie, class solidarity is total; nothing will undermine its cohesiveness. The woman benefits from her husband's appropriation of the surplus value created by the labor of the actual producer. In the working class, solidarity is sometimes shaken by partial competition between the sexes.[28] Working-class and middle-class women vie with men of their own class for positions that will enable them to earn a living.

More than once Engels' confusion of class structures with

sexual differences mars his argument. Class considerations are
responsible, not only for competition at the base of the social
pyramid, but for solidarity between the sexes in the upper
strata of society. Socialists have not come up with a clear
definition of precisely what constitutes sex as a category, nor
of the properties of class. As a consequence, even as they
attack capitalism, they sometimes end up playing to its tune.
In viewing motherhood as a job in the economic sense, Paul
Lafargue provided arguments justifying the marginalization
of women from the class structure.[29] Motherhood is toilsome
—there is no doubt of that—but that it is a job is debatable. A
woman seeks employment as her circumstances require it,
and in the last instance these are determined by the laws
inherent to the particular mode of production. They may
allow her to realize her full potential, but they can also
prevent it. Employment does less outrage to women than
involuntary maternity. A job enables a woman to earn a
living; in maternity she risks life itself. Society can demand
from each according to his or her abilities and make work
obligatory for each of its members, but it cannot require
them to reproduce. Work can be made more efficient, and
organized to increase its productivity; sexuality is by its very
nature resistant to control. Society retains the power to
restrict woman to situations in which she has no alternative
but motherhood, however, and in this way force her to breed
cannon fodder—this was the way of Nazism. By substituting
woman's reproductive function for her productive function,
society shifts emphasis to her identity as a sexual being and
thereby widens the social gap between men and women. This
is why woman's freedom is so closely tied to her freedom to
choose whether or not to have children. An active sexual life
independent of reproduction is not merely a question of
society's level of technological development; it is also dependent on ideological—above all, religious and demographic
—policy. Even the socialist countries have adopted popula-

tion control measures that reflect different expectations with regard to the behavior of women. The USSR legalized abortion by decree in 1920, then abolished this decree in 1936 (instead developing oral contraceptives), then legalized abortion again.[30] Soviet policy on divorce also has shifted back and forth since the 1917 revolution. But the payment of wages for motherhood has never been considered.[31]

Female emancipation is a complex problem whose solution goes beyond the economic dimension. Even an economically independent woman suffers, just by being a woman, from the impact of national and international developments. Everything ideological, including the development of the pharmaceutical industry, has repercussions on the female condition. No socialist ethic can afford, therefore, to lose sight of the unique circumstances surrounding woman's existence. Lafargue, Engels, and Bebel did not ask themselves how woman's unique conditions would enter into the thinking of those who struggled for socialism. Yet this is a challenging question. To accuse the socialists of spreading ideas against the family as an institution and for free love is unfair and unproductive. Lenin rejected the notion that the satisfaction of sexual desires as well as of the need for love is as simple as drinking a glass of water; he considered this to be both non-Marxist and antisocial. For him, the social aspect of sexual life was important, calling into play the individual's cultural past, in which physiology and emotion go hand in hand. Whereas "the drinking of water is really an individual matter . . . it takes two people to make love and a third person, a new life, is likely to come into being. This deed has a social complexion, and constitutes a duty to the community."[32]

Lenin viewed a communist society as one in which sex should bring joy and life, but should not be indulged in without discipline. Divorce in this context should function to give legal force to irremediable separations, giving women as well as men the right to disentangle themselves. Divorce is a fundamental issue in a program for raising women to the status of full-fledged members of society alongside of men. The great task of socialism with regard to women, according to Lenin, is to eliminate the double oppression they suffer in bourgeois society—oppression by capital and oppression of housework. These shackles on woman's development can only be eliminated by the abolition of private property and the replacement of the individual domestic household by a socialized domestic household.

Today, the Soviet government realizes that in addition to legislating equal rights it must create the concrete conditions for women's equality. Although women have equal rights with men, their duties are unquestionably more numerous. Despite massive efforts by the Soviet government, there are still too few nurseries to care for all the children whose mothers have productive jobs, especially in Lithuania, Armenia, Latvia, and Estonia.[33] The traditional practice of nonworking members of the family looking after the children is still one of the major means employed by Soviet families. Moreover, the USSR concentrated its main efforts on developing heavy industry at the expense of the household appliance and foodstuffs industries, whose products are a significant asset to the working woman; it is only now that these industries are being given more attention. In this respect it may be said that women will achieve their freedom only as the economy grows. But on the other hand, it must be acknowledged that Soviet men help their wives in households much less than do their English or American counterparts. Sexual equality in terms of rights and duties, which is after all the socialist aspiration, necessarily implies a more equitable division of household duties. A change in men's attitudes is an absolute prerequisite for equalizing the burdens of both sexes. But a change in women's attitudes is needed too: they must accept their husbands' help and gradually eradicate the stereotyped notion of the emasculated man in apronstrings.[34]

The Soviet experience demonstrates that although woman's liberation, and hence her full integration into society, has not been complete under a socialist regime, it has progressed further. It should also be clear that to regard maternity as a social task is practicable only in societies with collective economies. Birth control, on the other hand, will always be a matter of demographic policy.

PART II

The History of Women's Condition in Brazil

CHAPTER 5

Some Aspects of the Development of the Brazilian Economy

Introduction

The limitations placed by a capitalist social structure on woman's full realization, either as a laborer or as a member of the underprivileged category of the female sex, appear as invariants within any particular historical manifestation of the capitalist mode of production. The essential properties of this mode of production combine in various ways with the features common to all societies to define woman and woman's role. It is through this double determination that society operates to keep the conflicts generated by the competitive behavior characteristic of class societies from becoming excessively acute. As we have seen, there have been only brief periods during which the female labor force has enjoyed a relatively high level of employment, and even this by no means solved the woman question. It rather represented purely a device whereby class societies attempted to maintain their own pattern of stability by defining this stability in new terms. In efforts to maintain an unstable equilibrium, capitalist societies not only utilize the sex factor by giving it a social twist; they also make use of all the possibilities offered by relations of domination and subordination between nations.

At the center of the world capitalist system, international relations provide an outlet for relieving the tensions generated by the class structure of these societies, thereby diminishing the need to utilize the sex factor socially as a means to marginalize the female labor force from the economy. By contrast, in countries at the periphery of the world system, even such a partial solution to the woman question is not so easy to find. In countries with dependent economies, therefore, we find another factor added to those already typical of a market economy. An analysis of woman's predicament in Brazilian society, past and present, might prove useful in understanding woman's special roles in capitalist societies; it should also bring to light the special features that mark the formation of Brazilian class society, whose economy has always been dependent on decisions taken at the center of the bloc of nations comprising the Western democracies.

A full understanding of the social roles of Brazilian women and the history of their evolution from the nation's social beginnings to the present is directly dependent on an analysis of the socioeconomic formation which has been evolving for more than four centuries. Distorted interpretations, transformed mechanically into abstract models devoid even of heuristic value, such as have been produced for Brazilian society,[1] tempt the student to see similarities between women's condition in Brazil and that in medieval Europe, and hence to explain the former in terms of a feudal society. Even writers who limit their enquiry to the present condition of Brazilian women interpret that condition as representative of some stage along the way from a feudal economy. However much they may protest it, they reduce, at least partially, the situation of women in Brazil to that of European women in the Middle Ages. Olga Werneck, for example, given her view that the underdeveloped countries are subsystems peripherally integrated into the international capitalist system, could have come up with a totally new perspective on the woman problem. Nevertheless, she develops her argument in such a way as to explain the female condition in today's Brazil as a function of modernization of certain areas of the country (establishment of capitalist production relations) and of the backwardness of certain others (continued existence of alleged feudal production relations).[2] For this reason, although she sees the social process in terms of the configuration of forces in the capitalist "free world," her argument is vitiated by a theoretical model that assumes every social formation must necessarily pass through the historical stages of slavery, feudalism, and capitalism, in that order. By categorizing the nation's social past as feudal, she obscures the full comprehension of women's social roles in Brazilian society at any given moment, including the present.[3] In order to avoid a similar pitfall, it is important to examine, however briefly, the principal stages of the historical formation of Brazilian society.

The Slave-Owning Economy

Even if we accept the hypothesis that the different modes of production in precapitalist societies which are based on private ownership of the means of production constitute stages of a single socioeconomic formation whose ultimate expression is fully developed capitalist society,[4] this by no means implies that each particular social system seen as a whole must necessarily and in fact go through each of these stages. The dynamics of the capitalist system in all its phases —mercantile, industrial, financial—led the countries in the most advanced stages of this system to establish an economic structure in the new world that would not hamper the further development of capitalism in the old. Thus, the colonization of Brazil was an attempt not to implant a feudal economy but to establish a dependent colonial economy consonant with the interests of the flourishing mercantile capitalism of Europe. In that epoch, the Brazilian sugar industry provided a powerful stimulus to the Portuguese and Flemish economies. When the colonization of Brazil began, the feudal structures of the trading nations of Europe were already in an advanced stage of disintegration, and "trade found itself in fundamental opposition to the rigorous feudal system and the rigid forms of the feudal hierarchy."[5] In this regard, it is futile to look for any intention on the part of sixteenth-century powers to establish feudal economies in the colonies, and even less so in later centuries.

As Celso Furtado and Caio Prado Jr. have pointed out,[6] the Brazilian slave-owning economy, both as a colony and under the empire, was geared primarily to the export of raw materials, farm products, and minerals. These goods brought considerable profit to foreign mercantile capitalists at the time, and the Brazilian economy was later to afford numerous advantages to European industrial capitalism. Thus the Brazilian colonial economy which arose under the aegis of commercial capitalism assumed, with a few minor qualifications, a rather well-defined role in the grand scheme of international capitalism that was just beginning to emerge. That is, it was an economy that exported primary materials and was permanently dependent (its colonial status is of no relevance in this respect) on the dominant nation or nations of the international system.

The system of large-scale agriculture established in the colony was oriented toward external trade. Profit, of course, was an objective, and in this respect the system was profoundly incompatible with a feudal structure. Except in rare instances, it would be wrong to think that the quest for profit, as a motive common to both the ruling stratum of a colony (or country at the periphery, although still part of the international capitalist system) and the commercial or industrial bourgeoisie of the metropolis (or the hegemonic country or countries of the system), would lead to a conflict of interests between these two social groups. The Brazilian economy has always been determined from without, and hence has subserved the interests of a bourgeoisie which historically was first Portuguese and Dutch, then Portuguese and English, then only English, and finally American, French, English, German, Canadian, etc., yet at the same time always Brazilian (from the time a whole generation of Brazilians reached adulthood). This said, however, there has essentially always been but one international bourgeoisie, whose economic activities recognized no political and administrative boundaries. Brazil's colonial status merely made it easier for the metropolis and its financiers or political caretakers to conduct their business; political independence was not accompanied by economic independence. The history of the Brazilian economy is the history of a continual redefinition of shifting ties with the international economic system, although the international division of labor has always kept Brazil in a somewhat accessory position.

Although, as Weber makes clear, a feudal structure is not incompatible with a money economy, it is incompatible with lively external trade and with the notion of profit by exploitation, since "tariffs, fees, and revenue-yielding territorial rights, among them especially judicial powers, were also granted as fiefs."[7] Both these phenomena determined the broader features of Brazil's economy.

The nature of slave labor in Brazil has been largely, if not exclusively, responsible for raising a veil of illusion around the true nature of the Brazilian economy. In likening Brazilian slavery to the slavery of antiquity, various authors have overlooked the fact that the employment of black slaves was a highly rational means to accumulate capital.[8] Indeed, modern slavery did not function at all in the same way as slavery in antiquity.[9] Then, slaves were primarily the spoils of war, and although trade in captives also took place, it was never established on a regular basis for purposes of capitalist exploitation. By contrast, under modern commercial capitalism the slave was not only a commodity capable of mobilizing large amounts of commercial capital, he or she also embodied fixed capital, and was therefore effectively a means of production for the large plantations engaged in capital accumulation. Of course, slave labor was not the best means of accumulation, for reasons we shall examine more closely later.

Two important factors must be considered here: the demographic resources of the colonizing country, and the availability of free labor. Portugal did not have a sufficiently large population to colonize its South American colony with free labor. Even England, which for various reasons—including demographic ones—exported large numbers of its population to its colonies, was unable to supply its American colonies with sufficient labor to meet the needs of capital accumulation. Moreover, where abundant free or cheap land existed, where everyone was free to dispose of his or her own labor power as they saw fit, and where anyone could obtain a piece of land to cultivate, it is not surprising that wage laborers should be scarce, and where they were available that the worker's share in the product of his or her own labor would be very high. Under these circumstances, juridical equality was bound to place serious obstacles in the way of capitalist accumulation, so that the use of slave labor in the colonies proved to be an effective means for furthering the process of primitive accumulation.

Slave labor is unable to advance capitalism beyond a certain stage. Because money fulfills an important function in commodity circulation, capitalism requires wage labor to develop its full potential. There must be sufficient currency to ensure a smooth and continuous turnover of commodities. In turn, workers exchange their wages, which make up the greater part of the money in circulation, for their means of subsistence. Thus the capitalist, after paying out wages to the workers, recovers this money in the form of surplus value.[10] But "in the slave system, the money-capital invested in the purchase of labour-power plays the role of the money-form of the fixed capital, which is but gradually replaced as the active period of the slave's life expires."[11]

Thus, when acquiring a slave a capitalist pays a certain amount as fixed capital, but the slave only gradually transfers value to the product. The capitalist has to reckon the advanced payment of wages as a production factor, in the sense that the transformation of the value of the labor power into commodity and then into money form takes place slowly and piecemeal. But the distinction between fixed and circulating capital introduced to describe the capitalist's recovery of the money paid out and the value embodied in the product hinders an understanding of how surplus value is formed and how capitalism operates. In purchasing a slave, one purchased his or her total future labor; this is certainly one of the reasons this type of labor was so costly in terms of initial investment. The capital so invested, however, yielded a high return.[12]

But commodities were also exchanged for money on external markets, and in that regard the slave constituted an obstacle to the unfettered development of the capitalist system of production in Brazil, whose major industries—sugar, cotton, cacao, coffee, and gold—were based on slave labor. As the slave did not participate in the consumer market, he or she came to be more and more of an impediment to the development of the nation's productive forces, and in particular, hindered the redefinition of the capitalist subsystems made necessary by the advance of English industrialism. The profitability of slave-worked agriculture began to diminish as the capitalist mode of production assumed new characteristics at the ruling center. The period of black slavery lasted roughly three centuries in Brazil, and left its mark on an economic structure which at later stages was to assume more of the features of capitalism.

Generally speaking, we may say that in Brazil slave labor was remunerated (in means of subsistence, not money) when it was used in the production of items necessary to the subsistence of the laborer and his or her dependents, and was unpaid when it was used in the exporting sector. Of course, we are not here referring to every individual slave, nor are we claiming that the subsistence economy existing within the large-scale agriculture was geared solely to the slaves' consumption needs. The important point is that both slave labor and free labor are only partially remunerated, and hence both generate surplus labor, which constitutes the source of surplus value—the secret of capitalist accumulation. In these terms, it is perfectly possible—and indeed it actually happened in Brazil—for a partial capitalist economy to develop (that is, an economy geared to profits), producing an absolute surplus value through the mass use of slave labor. With respect to rationality, both the use of slaves and the extensive farming that developed in Brazil served the ends of capitalist accumulation.

Since capital was scarce, land plentiful, and technology rudimentary, rationality for the exporting planter was measured not so much in terms of increasing the physical productivity of the land or of the slave labor, as in expanding the area of tilled land and the amount of labor mobilized per unit of capital. Since slave labor is incompatible with the employment of advanced technology, it must be considered more expensive than wage labor (even disregarding the fact that slave labor also represents fixed capital) if it is unable to create relative surplus value, which is the means whereby industrial capital increases its rate of surplus value. Given the particular conditions under which Brazil's exporting agricultural enterprises developed, however, it is not useful to pose the question in these terms. If the two types of labor are compared abstractly, wage labor will obviously appear cheaper than slave labor, since purchase of the latter requires a large initial investment, which then remains partially immobilized for years, and because a slave does not produce relative surplus value. Under the concrete historical condition in which the Brazilian exporting agricultural industry developed (scarce capital, abundant land, rudimentary technology), however, the "African slave was a much more profitable venture for the large-scale capitalist" than the import of labor for a temporary term of servitude.[13] To be sure, over the long term slavery was to become a serious obstacle to industrial development, not just for the reasons enumerated above, but also because of the close ties that evolved between the bourgeoisie of economies exporting raw materials and the ruling centers of the international capitalist system. On the other hand, in colonies whose economies were based on imported labor under conditions of temporary servitude, a "national bourgeoisie" arose whose interests came into conflict with those of the bourgeoisie of the metropolis, as was the case with the southern colonies of North America.

Abolition of Slavery, 1850

The international division of labor imposed by European commercial capitalism was a significant and crucial factor in determining what specific features capitalism as a socioeconomic formation would assume as it developed historically concrete forms.[14] Prado Jr. states that the countries of Latin America were from the beginning—their discovery and colonization by European nations—part of the same capitalist system that gave rise to imperialism. Hence their economic and social structure evolved within this system. As Luiz Pereira has shown so well, the first stage in the development of the Brazilian capitalist economy was consummated in the estab-

lishment of one of the two poles delimiting capitalist production relations. The slave's master was "more an agrarian
entrepreneur than a Brazilianized or tropical version of the
European nobleman who happened to be engaged in the
management of production factors, one of which was slave
labor."[15] With abolition, then, capitalist production relations truly achieved maturity, so to speak, since wage labor
became universal.

Just as occurred during the gold epoch in the eighteenth
century, the universalization of wage labor in Brazil effected
a redefinition of the type of link between the ruling center of
the world capitalist system and the dependent economies.
The abolition of slavery in Brazil must be seen within the
international historical context out of which modern slavery
emerged and evolved, and in the contradictory relationships
that developed both internally and externally over the three
and a half centuries during which slave labor was used in the
dependent type of economy established in Brazil. In the
eighteenth century, gold mining caused the Brazilian population to swell with Europeans, and in the process slaves
became a numerical minority. It also stimulated the development of manufactures in England, with the result that England became the most important financial center in Europe.
Because of Portugal's subsidiary status as a mere waystation
for colonial products, England was able to move into a
privileged position of power with respect to the young Brazilian nation, a position it retained through the nineteenth
century, even after Brazil had proclaimed its independence
from the Portuguese metropolis.[16]

Although the reasons which led Brazilians to support or
condemn slavery were linked to the motives the English had
for adopting the same positions, the roots of the attitudes
were different in the two cases. Internally, although the
employment of slave labor was a key factor in the establishment of the large-scale exporting agrarian enterprise, which

played such a vital role in the growth of international mercantile capitalism, slavery came increasingly into conflict with capitalist production relations and began to negatively influence the one pole of these production relations that had already been constituted, namely, the large rural estate. It is true that "miscegenation and the pecuniary foundations of slavery were two factors upsetting the harmony and stability of the ties between master and slave."[17] Even aside from that, production based on slave labor was becoming increasingly more expensive than wage labor, which made economic exploitation more profitable in that it was capable of assimilating the latest advances in technology and did not immobilize capital.

However, the abolitionist campaign did not invariably and in all cases reflect a forward-looking consciousness which keenly perceived that wage labor was a positive step forward in Brazil's advance toward capitalism. Abolitionist practice varied over a wide range, from simple adherence to emancipatory ideas out of a realization that the process once begun was irreversible, to positions evincing a richer and more comprehensive view of the Brazilian socioeconomic formation within the international system. Yet, even those who took the latter position were apparently unable to go beyond the relatively short-term perspective of achieving the status of free-citizen for blacks. As for the liberals, in retrospect it seems that their activities were determined principally by their ties with political parties.[18] Regardless of the level of consciousness achieved by this or that social group with regard to the necessity of abolishing slavery, it is valid to say that "in fighting for the abolition of slave labor, the whites were fighting for their own interests." The main import lies not, as has been claimed, "in the transformation of the slave into a citizen, but in the transformation of the slave laborer into a wage laborer."[19]

Actually, abolition marked the culmination of the long

process of social disintegration of the slavocratic seigneurial social order, but with respect to the development of capital it was only the first step.[20]

Outside the country there was also no uniform opinion as to whether slavery should be maintained in nations at the periphery of international capitalism; the different perspectives rather represented the divergent economic interests of different English groups. Official English policy upheld alternately the interests of groups with ties to the Brazilian export sector, for whom colonialism was a source of revenue, and who were therefore in favor of maintaining slavery and the slave trade, and the interests of British industries, whose objectives were to expand the market for their manufactures. For the latter, slavery was obviously an obstacle, and they fought energetically for its abolition. The history of Britain's actual practice with regard to slavery in Brazil shows the interests of the mercantile bourgeoisie gradually ceding to those of the industrialists, and by 1850, when the slave trade was outlawed, the process of liberation became irreversible.[21] Indeed, with the exception of those whose interests were directly committed in the African slave trade, the interests of other groups came increasingly to be tied in with the question of wage labor, whether they were aware of it or not. The use of slave labor, on which the high level of profit extracted from Brazil's agrarian economy had essentially depended for three centuries, in the end became an obstacle to the development of productive forces and the expansion of consumer markets to feed the growth of British industry already quite advanced.

Thus, however we view the question—from the perspective of the ruling economic center of the international capitalist system, on whose fortunes the vitality of the system as a whole depended, or in the light of the internal contradictions within Brazil's slave economy—wage labor was the order of the day.[22] It was instituted gradually through a series of legislative measures, but also as a result of steps taken by slave-owners themselves, who were threatened by frequent revolts.

The significance of abolition has been underplayed insofar as it did not immediately bring about any substantial changes in the collective attitudes sustaining the asymmetrical relations between whites and slaves, or result in any mass influx of blacks into the labor market as wage laborers.[23] Actually, the formal emancipation of blacks marked the watershed between two processes—the disintegration of the slavocratic order, and the attainment of the second stage in the evolution of class society—both of which were slow and difficult processes, to a large extent determined by external factors. The absorption of the ex-slaves into the wage-labor system depended, it seems, much more on the relative vitality of the various sectors of the economy and on the possibilities of importing a more highly skilled work force, than on the blacks' ability to adapt to their new conditions of work.

Wage Labor and Economic Development

Contrary to what is often supposed, there is no reason to suppose that the institution of wage labor necessarily brought with it a better utilization of the labor force. The internal logic of a wage-labor economy requires that it always maintain some labor power as free agents on a permanent or temporary basis, whereas a slave economy must during certain periods pay the costs of idle or unproductive labor power. In concrete terms, any change in the degree of utilization of labor power brought about by the transition from a slave to a wage-labor economy will depend on a series of factors, such as the level of technology and the possibility of marketing the items produced. In the case of the dependent economies at the periphery of the world capitalist system, the marketability of items produced for foreign consumption is, indeed, undeniably of short-term importance. The Brazilian sugar industry, for instance, had benefited from technical innovations introduced by English capital under the protection afforded it by the law of 1875, yet sugar encountered export difficulties when Cuba became independent and the supply of available labor power declined. In the coffee sector, which was growing, the import of European labor power resulted in underemployment of the newly emancipated labor force. By themselves, the ex-slaves were incapable of putting through any far-reaching economic changes. Their aspirations were very low, and for the most part they were still enmeshed in a subsistence economy. With the advent of wage labor an internal market emerged, providing fresh stimulus to the nation's economy.

The governments of the first Republic shifted back and forth between the leading strata of the exporting sector and the industrial sector, and took turns devaluing the Brazilian currency to distribute losses socially, and adopting a protective policy toward industry. Nevertheless, industrialization was able to move forward despite these erratic shifts.[24] Although the protective policy toward industry and the perspectives of the industrial elite were unrealistic, the country's economy did acquire some muscle, especially during World War I, when the unavailability of some imports forced it to find replacements domestically. By 1920, the working-class population had almost doubled relative to 1907,[25] and was henceforth capable of applying significant organized pressure to raise wages, whose real value had decreased when the national currency was devaluated. The collapse of the international division of labor in the wake of the crash, which had been brewing domestically for three decades in the form of a crisis in the coffee-exporting sector, faced Brazil for the first time with the historical possibility of industrialization for the internal market. Large segments of the urban population mobilized to this end and managed to achieve a greater degree of autonomy for the national economy through the structural expansion of capitalism, although this autonomy remained precarious.

The revolutionary movement of 1930 embodied the aspirations and nationalist ideas that had been in the air since the end of the empire. But an industrial base able to dispense with the importation of goods and capital was not achieved, and the government policy that emerged from the 1930 revolution had long-lasting adverse effects on the nation's economy, despite the short-term advantages it was able to produce by stimulating the domestic economy enough to surmount the export crisis. Of course, one cannot blame the revolutionary government for the scars its protectionist policy toward the coffee industry left on the Brazilian economy, nor for the periods of stagnation the economy was to suffer on that account in the future.[26] Any thrust toward industrialization in a country with a dependent, essentially agricultural economy will encounter outside obstacles, and the success of attempts to surmount these obstacles will depend on how the international division of labor happens to be structured at the moment. Brazil's long period of economic stagnation, from 1937 through 1942, shows how precarious countries on the periphery of the world capitalist system were as soon as the world system showed signs of recovery. Thus, any progress Brazil made toward development depended on seizing the opportunity provided by good times on the international economic front to turn attention to the internal pressures exerted by the urban masses (for whom the structural expansion of Brazilian capitalism meant increasing opportunities to raise their levels of consumption of material and nonmaterial goods).

The showcase effect of the high standard of living in the advanced countries, which raised consumer aspirations among broad segments of the population in the peripheral countries—in particular in the urban and suburban areas—meant that capital accumulation could not precede mass consumption in Brazil. In fact, both these social impulses have been present simultaneously, especially since the 1920s, and as a result the balance between imports and exports, and between production and consumption, have rendered difficult the establishment of both an internal power structure and international relations.

Two sets of factors are relevant here. The policy of trying to simultaneously accommodate the industrial and the agrarian bourgeoisie by reducing both the sales tax and the customs duties, a policy that dates from the very first days of the Republic and is current today,[27] has permitted and even favored the persistence of shocking inequalities in the standard of living between town and country. Nevertheless, despite the constancy with which government authorities have insisted on the need to absorb the most disadvantaged segments of the Brazilian population into the capitalist system (i.e., to move to a higher stage of capitalist production relations), vestiges of the slavocratic order that still exist in the agrarian sector have permitted industry to grow at a relatively greater pace, and large segments of the urban population to retain a higher level of wages than the countryside.

The "multidimensionality" of Brazilian business interests[28] has enabled economic groups to make some concessions to urban wage laborers (whose increased consumer aspirations impel them to demand higher wages) so long as capitalist accumulation could rely on the exploitation of an agrarian labor force that is obliged to work under conditions that are either marginally legal or conceal widespread unemployment.[29] Thus, the agrarian sector of the Brazilian economy, in particular the coffee sector, at least partially finances the expansion of the nation's industry, which results in a partial fusion of interests of the agrarian and industrial bourgeoisie.

The Brazilian bourgeoisie *qua* industrial bourgeoisie can

afford to be relatively generous in distributing the products of labor (albeit always at the expense of the rural laborer) whenever pressures from the urban population mount. Nevertheless, the national industry has been incapable of maintaining a balance between the production of consumer goods and the level of consumption desired by ever growing numbers of people. The step-up in migration from the countryside to the city, especially from 1930 onward, is testimony to the fact that Brazilian industrialization may have made for a more closely knit national economy, but it has never been able to mold that economy into a unified, balanced system. Areas in economic decline continue to pour vast numbers of people in search of a livelihood into the booming sections, in particular the urban industrial centers. Since the secondary sector has been unable to absorb the available labor power, the idle workforce thereby created functions as a reserve army to hold wages at a level below what would be justly proportionate to the productivity of labor. Since urbanization is proceeding at a more rapid pace than industrialization, the imbalances and disproportions in the nation's system of production, distribution, and consumption will grow more acute as the urban industrial centers are unable to provide full employment for their growing population and the less advanced sectors of the nation's economy are unable to produce consumer goods in quantities sufficient to meet urban needs.[30] Even in the period from 1949 to 1959, when the Brazilian economy grew by leaps and bounds, the absorption of labor power by the secondary sector barely reached 50 percent of the demographic growth.[31] At the population's present growth rate, the country would have to create 1.3 million new jobs annually, which would require liquid investments of approximately $1.5 billion per year.

The dislocations and disparities in the domestic system of production, distribution, and consumption derive from capitalism's inherent—and historically demonstrated—inability to achieve full employment, and are aggravated by the disadvantageous position occupied by the "free world's" peripheral nations relative to the ruling center. The most serious internal consequence of Brazil's peripheral position among the Western democracies is the imbalance it causes among the factors of production. There is a natural tendency to appropriate the technology of the more advanced countries, and this artificially inflates wages in the secondary sector. This in turn only encourages further over-mechanization of industries, which reinforces the wage differential between city and country, and at the same time helps maintain low levels of employment. The absorption of foreign technology through the import of machinery and equipment explains why the job structure of the population did not change in the decade 1949-1959, despite the enormous investments made during that period.[32]

One might think that in the new phase inaugurated with the government that came to power in the wake of the 1964 revolution Brazil should be able, within the limits set by its peripheral status, to achieve a relative balance among the different sectors of its domestic production, since these sectors are just different aspects of a single economy that has now entered the urban industrial phase of its development. However, since Brazil's latest reintegration into the capitalist system placed it clearly at a disadvantage, capitalism in Brazil will most surely be constrained to pass through its various constitutive stages at a level below that at which this historical process took place in the highly developed countries.

The economic and political events of the three years following the 1964 revolution indicate that the government had resolved to promote the functional concentration of the national income in state and private enterprises, thereby placing an extreme burden on wage earners. The political complexion of the revolutionary government made it easy to purchase machinery and equipment from abroad and to concentrate property in the hands of the large enterprises, thereby cutting down even more on the cost of labor power. The effect was to aggravate already chronic underemployment. The continued growth in the average level of consumption was thus made dependent on the importation of advanced technology and the necessity to accumulate capital, while the amount of capital accumulated was directly linked to the sum of the surplus value carried off to the center of the world capitalist system.

The way political power is distributed within Brazil, and the argument most frequently evoked to justify that distribution—the specter of communism—suggest that Brazil's progress toward becoming a mass consumption society is dependent on decisions made at the ruling center of the "free world." The Brazilian government's pledge to promote social and economic development is, of course, highly important in that it redefined the functions of the state as a body capable of incorporating the general public's aspirations to a higher level of consumption. But the instruments of economic planning lose much of their efficacy when adopted in countries like Brazil, whose economies do not permit a very balanced internal structure. However, the machinery of a government which aspires to be technocratic is able, much more now than in the past, to conceal Brazil's economic, political, and military dependence on the "senior partners" of the international capitalist system, and thereby reinforce the belief that the development of the Brazilian economy depends exclusively on internal factors.

Within this context, unemployment, supposedly just a part of a passing phase, receives its justification, and the right of the workers to advance their claims for a higher level of consumption is ruled out *a priori.* Since capitalist development need not mean the extension of mass consumption to the whole population,[33] Brazil will be able to aim for development while keeping certain segments marginal to its benefits.

Those who see Brazil as a country which combines feudal

with capitalist relations of production are wont to interpret the 1930 revolution as a bourgeois revolution that was only partially victorious, or even to believe that the "bourgeois revolution," which would enable independent economic development to begin in earnest, is still to come. From its very beginnings, however, capitalist society in Brazil has developed within a context of dependency and within limits imposed by the international power structure. Any understanding of the social roles men and women have had to fulfill in Brazilian society since its inception must begin with an awareness of this dependency and these limitations. In looking at the changes female roles in the family and the economy have undergone over time, together with the level of skills the female workforce has attained as the economy has evolved, we shall at each point attempt to relate the analysis to the development of the nation's productive forces, to the particular forms authority has assumed as Brazilian society has acquired more and more of the basic features of capitalism, and finally, to the levels of consciousness attained with respect to the problems of women.

CHAPTER 6

The Social Position of Women

The Broader System of Domination

Relations between the sexes, and thus woman's position in the family and in the society at large, fit into a broader system of domination. In order to understand the problem reflected in the title of this chapter, therefore, we must first examine the way in which power was organized and distributed during the slavocratic period of Brazil's history, inasmuch as some of the patterns and attitudes, today justified in the name of tradition, were first formed at that time. I shall refer to that tradition in an attempt to shed light on the origins of the myths and preconceptions which present-day society uses to justify barring women from certain jobs and confining them almost exclusively to the performance of social roles and occupations assigned by convention.

Initially, Portugal's purpose in colonizing America was to extract wealth; later, it was to produce articles in its colony that would contribute to the development of European mercantile capitalism. Essentially, the form this colonization took amounted to an attempt to transplant a patrimonial structure of domination to Brazil.[1] Since the person of the king, his functionaries, and thus the Royal Treasury[2] were central to the distribution of power and to securing economic advantages, the power structure in Brazilian colonial society may be described, following Weber, as a state patrimony.[3]

However, the colony was vast and communication problems were many; it was therefore difficult to watch over the royal officialdom. The exercise of arbitrary power was an easy matter for those to whom the king's favoritism had brought riches and the advantages of social position. Thus in practice, the workings of the colonial state patrimony clashed with a patriarchal order. The latter was represented by people who, although they had ready access to the royal coffers, were mindful of their official duties as administrators of the royal patrimony while others sought to draw personal advantages from their position at the expense of the patrimonial state.[4] European mercantile capitalism at this time was approaching the fullness of its development and beginning to shift its course toward industrial capitalism. This process, together with the economic and power structures that had evolved in the colony, prompted the Crown to transfer its interests from the royal functionaries to individuals whose power was based on property and its exploitation for profit. As the heads of families accumulated more and more economic power, the Crown found itself increasingly constrained to seek their support to safeguard its interests. To ensure their continuing prestige and authority, the civil and military representatives of the patrimonial state found themselves obliged to become entrepreneurs in economic ventures.

It was not long before the conflict of interest emerged between this new entrepreneurial group and the patrimonial state. By the beginning of the nineteenth century, the family heads had consolidated their power into a structure of domination that might in rough terms be described as a "patriarchal patrimony." Indeed, from its roots, Brazilian society had been developing in that direction since the very first days of colonization. The colonial economy, geared to foreign

markets, had been developing along a path more conducive to
the emergence of a patriarchal rather than a state form of
patrimonialism (i.e., a patron-client form of domination,
based on personal relationships, rather than the more institutionalized form). This would have created major obstacles for
the development of capitalist productive relations, already in
formation. By contrast with feudalism, the limiting case of
the patrimonial structure is that in it relations between lord
and vassal became institutionalized and fixed,[5] and the patri-
monialistic power structure proved to be eminently compatible with capitalism in its first stages of development.[6]
Although functions and responsibilities in colonial Brazil did
tend to become institutionalized and concentrated in the
hands of a few people, this tendency was not strong enough
to cause the colonial society to develop all of the attributes
of a state. Never a dominant social relation, patrimony increasingly came to be rooted in the exploitation of landed
property for profit.

Since Brazil was colonized to bring profits to commercial
capitalism, its social structure during the slavocratic period
and the colonial epoch in general had the appearance of an
exotic edifice that had retained some rather faded traces of
European feudal structures, combined with an emergent
patrimonial structure favorable to external trade and the
exploitation of slave labor. Under these circumstances, the
caste system that took root presented grave cultural inconsistencies. It rested on a pecuniary as well as an economic basis;
freedom itself became a negotiable item. For this reason the
Brazilian caste system allowed for upward social mobility,
even if only in terms of formal status, and in this respect it
was different from typical caste societies. Nevertheless, the
rigid asymmetry of relations between lord and slave, the
pecuniary foundation of slavery, and miscegenation gradually
undermined these relations. The purely formal measures on
which the dominant stratum relied to protect its position—

for example, prohibiting interracial marriage but not miscegenation—show that the caste division of the population
had economic and not racial roots. The absence of any
feelings of mutual repugnance among the various strata of the
slavocratic society produced a peculiar type of caste stratification in which color, and hence race, were merely outward
signs signaling the individual's economic condition. With respect to female roles, this cultural discrepancy in the Brazilian caste system had diverse consequences.

The Female Slave and Her Master

The production relations of slavocratic society and the
cultural inconsistencies of the caste system were major determinants of women's roles in both castes of Brazil society of
the seventeenth, eighteenth, and nineteenth centuries, but,
seen from either perspective, the role of the black woman
subverted the social order. Florestan Fernandes' statement
that "the social alienation of the black initially transpired as
the social alienation of the slave as an individual"[7] must be
examined very carefully in the case of female slaves. Differences in economic position among individuals were often
matched by differences in social position, the latter determined by race and color.[8] Accordingly, for the black, being a
slave meant being an instrument of labor, with no rights
whatsoever; in other words, precisely the social status of an
object. Still, reification of blacks was not total. Although
whites had always denied blacks human status, both subjectively and objectively, some of the black population, mostly
craft groups, actually did receive relatively humane treatment
from whites, by virtue of the value placed on their particular
functions in the productive process. To be sure, if the slave
crafts worker was held in higher esteem, it was less a real
bond and more because such regard was adapted to the

economic ends of the master. However, true motives often remain concealed in the action itself, and although it may indeed have been a more refined way to exploit their labor power, the better treatment accorded the black slave appeared to be the very opposite of reification. Of course, merely partial reification of the slave in terms of attitudes and behavior did not impede the appropriation of surplus value, nor for that matter the functioning of a system of production already partially capitalist, nor did it in any way jeopardize the continued existence of the system of caste stratification. It merely added to it one more inconsistency, which, together with all the other cultural discrepancies of the caste system in Brazil, helped to expose the true nature of the emerging society. The contradiction between the white master's economic interests as capitalist entrepreneur and the more refined treatment accorded some types of slave progressively undermined the credibility of all the sustaining myths of Brazil's slavocratic order. A number of situations, though only peripherally related to the system of production, shed light on these inconsistencies in the caste society, such as, for example, the gifts "house children" sometimes received by virtue of their living in the same quarters, or even because of affective ties, sometimes strong enough to motivate manumission.

The most serious discrepancy of all, however, emerges in a review of the various things the black woman was called upon to do. In addition to her functions in the productive system, the female slave also had a sexual role to perform. This sexual exploitation augmented her reification, but at the same time helped to expose the true foundations of the caste society. She was a mere tool of her master's sexual pleasures and nothing indicated that this relation between slave and master ever went beyond "the primitive and purely animal level of sexual contact."[9] Yet its issue, the mulatto offspring, became a dynamic point of ferment for social and cultural tensions.

By demanding the female slave administer to his sexual needs, the master was treating her at once as an object and as a human being. The sexual act became for her a process of reification, while her role as a *thing* (i.e., an instrument of labor) assumed human aspects. The characteristic of sex, whose mode of operation is basically determined by the mode of production, came to have a weighty influence over the mode of production itself.

The belief that miscegenation, provided it occurred outside the legal family, would not have any consequences on the relative social positions of the two races betrayed a striking lack of awareness of the degree to which the continued existence of the slavocratic order depended on the ethnic composition of the population. The number of people of mixed origin continued to grow, and this, combined with the inability of the slave population to expand in sufficient numbers to meet the requirements of production (mortality in the slave quarters was high), constituted a permanent threat to the established order. Although the lives led by male and female slaves were basically similar as far as bare existence was concerned, the functions they were called upon to perform were different, and these differences determined the magnitude of the role they played in eroding the foundations of the social order. Neither the gentler treatment accorded the slave craftsworker in consonance with the master's economic interests, nor the master's use of the female slave as an instrument for sexual gratification (directly, when used by the master himself, and indirectly, in a classic example of economic exploitation, when he hired her out to other whites) were enough to bring the slaves to a general awareness of their lot and impel them to undertake some form of resistance.

Whereas the white woman's role was that of wife and mother of legitimate children, the black woman's function remained confined to satisfying sexual needs. The different social fates that awaited a woman depended on her place in the caste system. This was not conducive to maintaining a stratification system that separated people into strata rigorously defined by differences in juridical status and the individual's role in the productive process; nor did it protect the white patriarchal family from the influences of the slave population. The belief that a young black virgin was the most effective physic for the white syphilitic male was not only a convenient excuse for sexual intemperance; it also meant that black women became carriers of the disease and transmitted it to new generations of whites as wet nurses.

At the other extreme, the white mistresses were not immune to jealousy provoked by their husbands' love affairs, although the woman's subordinate position prevented that jealousy from developing into a constant source of conjugal friction.[10] It did, however, create snags in the work setup and in the morality demanded of life in the manor, at least with respect to white women's conduct. Judging from accounts of foreign chroniclers, it seems that some women simply flouted the rules that were supposed to govern a white woman's behavior and had love affairs with other men of their caste or even with male slaves.[11] This illustrates one element in the discrimination against woman independent of socioeconomic condition. Since a child's social status was determined by the juridical status of the mother, one might expect that the son of a female slave and white master would inherit the slave status of his black mother, and that the issue of a union between a white mother and a black father would be fully accepted into the seigneurial class as free persons. However, the frequent manumissions of the offspring of these free unions indicated that in fact paternal filiation determined rights of inheritance and juridical status. The emancipation of these mestizo progeny was, of course, not in itself sufficient to permit their immediate integration into the seigneurial stratum—for this they would have had to lose many of their physical traits as well—but it was unquestionably a crucial step in that process, since it at least gave the mestizo formal equality. Less-than-total social rejection of mestizo offspring became not only total, but even extended to the father, in the rare case where the mother was white, despite the principle of *partus sequitur ventrem*. Since amorous relations between women of the ruling stratum and black slaves were rare, they obviously do not provide the key to why so few persons were incorporated into a family structure.

A number of factors contributed to the sexual liberty that became a part of life in slavocratic Brazil. In addition to the fact that the white master regarded the sexual services of the black woman as a function intrinsic to her condition as slave, the way in which colonization took place was also an important element promoting sexual license. The colonizers very rarely arrived in families. Usually there were lone individuals, who in some cases had left their families behind, awaiting the fortune they were going to amass in the new world. But with a contingent of submissive women of lower social rank readily available to gratify their sexual needs, many a colonizer's family had to wait a long time before he finally returned to Europe, if he ever returned at all. Outside the narrow and marginally organized family structure of the ruling stratum, license was the rule. Indeed, the organization of the white family presupposed a lack of family structure among the slaves. So long as white women were raised for the roles of mistress of the house and mother of a legitimate family, there had to be a class of women with whom the young white males could indulge in the art of lovemaking before marriage. Thus, slavery met not only the needs of the productive system, but also those relative to colonization and family structure.

The White Woman of the Manor

The white woman of the slavocratic epoch had the basic traits required for unquestioning submission to patriarchal authority: she combined ignorance with woeful immaturity. She usually married so young that a girl still single at the age of twenty was considered practically a spinster.[12] It was normal to find a fifteen-year-old girl married and already a mother, and there were many who became mothers as young as thirteen. Brought up in a rigidly patriarchal environment, these child-mothers escaped their father's rule only to fall under the rule of a husband. Foreign chroniclers have given us accounts of the cruelty with which single and married women were treated when there was even the slightest suspicion that they had indulged in amorous flirtations behind the backs of fathers or husbands.[13] Of course, there were some who, aided by their female slaves, did manage to consummate these flirtations. But the difficulties were not to be taken lightly: a thousand eyes were watching them, and the loyalty of the female slave could falter at any moment. As G. Freyre stated wryly, in describing the circle that grew up around the white woman of the manor: it may have been relatively easy to have the eyes of the busybody male and female slaves put out, but it was not so easy to do the same with the eyes of priests and mothers-in-law.[14]

Added to this, the woman of the ruling stratum rarely went out of the house, and then only to go to church, which she never did unaccompanied. Stifled by the rigorous upbringing, uneducated, and broken by a steady string of maternities, she yielded submissively to father or husband. Although some became respectable matrons and enjoyed considerable sway over the domestic servants, their sphere of authority was kept clearly demarcated from that of the patriarch. Given her inferior status in the patriarchal family, the woman often had to shoulder the burdens issuing from the man's sexual excesses. Alcântara Machado refers to wills in which he found husbands enjoining their wives to personally take charge of the upbringing of their natural children.[15] In other cases, the white woman took it upon herself to raise or free the illegitimate children. These situations were especially frequent in the south of the country, where economic poverty sometimes equalized differential status based on sex.

Marriage remained practically the only course of life open to women. True, a girl could always choose the alternative of a secluded life in a convent to escape subjection to father or husband; but even this course seems to have been taken more frequently on the men's initiative. It was not rare to find single girls interned in convents because their fathers suspected misconduct, and husbands were also known to send troublesome wives off to the cloisters, although this was less frequent. Convent life seems to have been held out as a constant threat to single and married women alike. This is one more indication that the white woman of the manor bore little responsibility for the restriction of family structure to the ruling stratum. It is not difficult to see that the chastity of the vast majority of women of the seigneurial class was made possible by the prostitution of others. Daughters of poor whites, without inheritance and surrounded by scruples against work, earned their livelihood with their own bodies. Prostitution blighted not only the cities but the villages.[16] It was the lot of a good number of women in that economically unstable segment of the population who lived from hand to mouth or by their wits.

These economic factors worked against an organized family structure among this layer of the population, as did the fees demanded by the clergy to perform a marriage. The unprejudiced acceptance of extra-legal marriages among the poorer segments of Brazil's population during the slavocratic period has persisted, at least vestigially.

The white woman of the manor usually played an important role in the management and supervision of activities in the home, but we should remember that those activities covered a much wider range than what we think of as domestic chores. The mistress did not only oversee the work of the slaves in the kitchen; she watched over the spinning, weaving, and sewing; she inspected the lacemaking and embroidery, supervised the preparation of meals, the tending of the orchards and garden, and the care of the children and domestic animals. She was in complete charge of arrangements for the celebration of the big social events that convoked family and relatives.[17]

There are other indications, however, that a good number of the women of the dominant class led an idle life. Incapable of commanding discipline from their household slaves or their children, they lolled about in the hammocks, sloppily dressed and unkempt, hushed to sleep by their black slaves' soft songs. This image of the indolent woman, passively looking on as her husband cavorted with the female slaves, seems to have been more frequent in the sugar-growing Northeast, although it was by no means rare in the South. Some authors have even regarded cases where the white women of the ruling strata personally took charge of certain activities as genuine exceptions.[18]

Prudence tells us not to exaggerate the frequency of either of the two types. By all indications, they existed side by side in the dominant class, and both roles were possible to an equal degree. Quite apart from whether a woman performed a useful function or whether she led an idle life, what was universal in the slavocratic society of Brazil was her acceptance of the man's total supremacy within the family and the society at large. Every aspect of a young girl's upbringing was keyed to this submissiveness. "The young girl was denied anything that smacked of independence, even raising her voice in the presence of elders. The saucy and forward little girl was abhorred and punished, while shy bashful ones were adored."[19] Raised to marry a man chosen by her father, usually older than she, the Brazilian woman's expectations of married life were quite realistic, and in this respect she fulfilled social expectations.

It is quite true that many women, oppressed by their husbands or fathers, went against the grain and indulged in sexual irregularities through which they sought to requite desires and feelings denied expression within the confines of the patriarchal family, and in colonial times it was not rare for single girls to become mothers.[20] This was insufficient, however, to work any deep change in society's attitudes toward female virginity and chastity, which remained unbending, nor enough to weaken the upper hand of men. Maternal filiation, then, notwithstanding the illusions it has fostered, neither derived from rank held by the woman nor made for any change in her social status. Girls more often than not received their mother's family name indifferently. The relations of production and the prestige attached to different positions within the productive system often came into conflict with traditions regarding the inheritance of the family name.

Matrilinear descent, the purpose of which was to maintain, at least nominally, the purity of the stock, was created and sustained by miscegeny and hypogamic (interracial) marriages. The marriage of a poor mulatto student or soldier with the miss of the manor required maternal filiation in order to preserve at least the illustrious names, even at a time when the social order was already in a state of rapid decline. Thus, the women Castelo Branco, Albuquerque e Melo, Holanda Cavalcanti, Silva Prado, etc., gave their names to their sons. Matrilinear filiation was an attempt at conciliation: the most drastic solution was for the judge or priest, even in the epoch before Brazil became independent, to refuse to perform interracial marriages, or for the white girl's father to send her off to a convent. The expedient of matrilinear descent, designed to mollify the white race's anxieties about its continued dominance, did in fact represent a clear breach in the rigor with which the seigneurial layer had defended its social supremacy. As for woman, despite the fact that no deep change had been wrought in her social condition or in her position in the home, she began to demand a say in the choice of her mate. Thus commenced a long process of transformation of relations between parents and children and, in a certain sense, an even longer process of change in relations between husband and wife.

Still, women never did attain full awareness of the opportunities for bringing about changes in their position in the patriarchal family, which was already in the process of breaking up, and as far as change was concerned they remained far more its unconscious vehicle than its conscious agent. In the situation offered by the seigneurial order, women represented the embodiment of all the conservative forces of society.[21] Geographically immobile, and confined to a narrow sociocultural universe, they were undeniably more conservative than men, and in that respect represented a stable element in society. It was the sons, not the daughters, of the manor who received their education in Europe, and who were the political and social innovators, even introducing changes in feminine fashion. On the other hand, these new trends affected only the youngest men, and left the older generations untouched. In the final analysis, women remained far removed from the currents of social and political change, and their isolation was deliberately fostered by the men who remained openly hostile to woman's participation in any and every activity that went beyond the bounds of the family.

The exclusion of women from the focal points of sociocultural change is exemplified by the way that various secret societies that existed during the colonial epoch recruited their members. Around the end of the eighteenth or beginning of the nineteenth century the first Masonic lodge was founded at Bahia, soon followed by other secret societies. The political movements that grew out of these societies (especially the Masonic lodges) were those of a white, male elite, and participation was effectively barred to anyone from the lower strata and to women. To be sure, participation in these movements was not the only means to promote change in the established order, but it was one of the few deliberate expressions of conscious social action. The exclusion of women, particularly those belonging to the ruling elite, hence constituted an effective barrier to their achieving an awareness of the country's political and economic problems. Under these circumstances, even though the women of the upper stratum contributed unconsciously to undermining the existing status quo, the disintegration of the slavocratic order was not, and could not have been, matched by a parallel process of female emancipation.

Originally, ownership of land was the sole source of political rights, and indeed in this respect women were no better off than slaves.[22] Many women, however, became property owners through inheritance and proved themselves quite capable of meeting the responsibilities that that task entailed. On the other hand, those who had capable husbands were never given the opportunity to demonstrate their abilities. Indeed, the woman herself was sometimes considered an economic good.[23] The right to bequeath to a third party was contingent on the condition *si in viduitate permanserit*. Thus, if a woman married again, she lost the third party right, as well as the right to keep and raise the children from her first marriage. Society faced a woman with a dilemma: she was obliged either to renounce being a woman and live only as a mother, or to relinquish her rights as mother in order to marry again. Usually a widow would renounce the property and children of her first marriage, since she was then free to find a successor to her first husband. The sexual taboos surrounding women during the colonial period were backed not only by social sanctions but by physical constraint. In prohibiting women exercise of the right of property, Brazilian colonial society added to its caste division a social stratification based on sex. This rigid system of physical and moral constraint of the female segment of the population, created and maintained by the androcentricity of the patriarchal family, left deep marks on the life and mentality of Brazilian women.

Changes in the Family Structure:
The Nineteenth-Century Transition

With the spread of urban life in the nineteenth century, the life of women in the manorial class underwent corresponding changes. Although their social position remained essentially unchanged, women no longer had to live in manor houses. The city environment provided opportunities for more social contacts—at feasts, church, the theater. The patriarchal family lost some of its rigidity, allowing women to become freer and more at ease in their attitudes and bearing. Yet their education was still neglected, except that in addition to their instruction in domestic duties women were taught the art of conversation to grace social gatherings with their presence.

Meanwhile, poverty and prostitution continued to spread outside the homes of the wealthy landowners, and disintegration of the slavocratic order proceeded apace. The white woman, however, lacking education and devoting herself almost exclusively to her family, the Church, and the great feasts, remained oblivious to the changes taking place in the world around her, including the ferment of public opinion over the question of abolition that raged in the cities during the last ten years of the empire. Since the abolition movement thrived on the written word, Brazilian women had no chance to develop a critical stand on the conditions of their existence.

Like the later movements for independence from the metropolis, the abolition movement was the work of men. Although the end of slavery did not bring about the momentous changes it might have, it had many consequences for the life of women in the seigneurial class. The mere fact that master and slave no longer lived together in the same household reduced the tensions generated by easy access to black women. Of course, many blacks, male and female, continued to work for their old masters and hence to share the same household, but their relationship changed. Blacks too were individuals, free beings, and part of the social world. To be sure, prostitution continued, but no longer by virtue of the black woman's status as slave. The universalization of wage labor helped to lay bare its economic roots, in addition to the moral degradation suffered under slavery.

Changes effected in the caste system by abolition, however, were not accompanied by equivalent changes in the system of sexual stratification. Indeed, with the disintegration of the caste system, the black woman acquired at least a formal freedom which had previously been denied her. Her status was inferior to the black male's inasmuch as the emancipation of the "black races" did not bring her full human rights. Under the new order, the male ex-slave was considered a Brazilian citizen for electoral purposes, while women, both white and black, were marginalized from the selection of popular representatives to the government. Though abolition therefore may have meant emancipation, albeit unstable and incomplete for the black woman, for the white woman it represented a veritable step downward relative to the status of the black man. Once the caste division of Brazilian society was eliminated, the sex factor took on a new significance in the class society then emerging. Just as race had done in caste society (and still does, for that matter, in today's competitive societies, although perhaps to a lesser extent), sex now served effectively to conceal the social tensions generated by a fully formed but not yet fully developed capitalist system of production.[24]

Abolition had more immediate effects on the structure of the family group. Now that the black female slave was free, the head of the family no longer was able to give free rein to amorous impulse. The sexual decision was not unilateral any more, and extramarital sexual relations suffered corresponding restraints. With prostitutes, of course, payment in effect sustained the unilateral nature of the decision, although from another perspective it brought out the impersonal and contractual character of a commercial relation in which the wills of both parties have to be taken into account. Naturally, this does not mean that prostitution was voluntary. The pressures the social structures of capitalism exert to drive a considerable segment of the female population into prostitution are too well known to permit that conclusion. Nevertheless, whereas the freedom of the nonslave to prostitute herself remained abstract, in a system of free labor power prostitution is a purely commercial proposition, and as such essentially amounts to the exploitation of one social class by another.

One of the most salient effects of the disintegration of the slavocratic-seigneurial order and the patriarchal family's loss of its *raison d'être* was to uproot the white and mestizo populations that had lived in the shadow of the manor house and give them a certain social, and, above all, domestic autonomy. A great amorphous mass of people emerged from the state of near anomie in which it had existed under the slavocratic order and began to gradually develop perceptible contours of its own. These people were gradually absorbed into the lower strata of the new society, where they formed more or less stable monogamous families, although there was already discernible the instability inherent in the nascent urban proletariat. Yet, given the conditions under which it had to live, this social layer retained the distinct features of its former social structure. Common law marriages continued to exist alongside the legal monogamous family.[25]

The disintegration of the patriarchal family did not proceed evenly throughout the entire country. Even today, the Brazilian family presents a wide variety of structures, extending from the semipatriarchal family to the modern married couple that has lost its ties with family and tradition. As the family lost its patriarchal foundations—a process which varied in accordance with the pace of the nation's economic development—the family head saw his despotic rule weakened, as a result of the loss of some of his previous political and economic functions. Of course, he continued to wield authority over his wife and the minor children. However, the source of that authority gradually shifted from his male identity alone to his role as family wage earner.

The Uneven Spread of
Urbanization and Industrialization

Urbanization, which began in earnest during the second half of the nineteenth century, and industrialization, which received its biggest boost in the 1930s, had profound repercussions on family structure. However, since neither urbanization nor industrialization proceeded evenly throughout Brazilian society, the restructuring of the family group became a function of the modernization of economic life (although in the countryside family structure sometimes lagged behind economic development). Immigration provides an example.

The importation of foreign workers, which had been encouraged to promote the coffee economy of the South, might have been an innovative force in family structure, but this was subject to the cultural values the immigrants brought with them. The importation of European labor frequently only reinforced the patriarchal family pattern. São Paulo, for example, received southern Italians, with all their paternalistic tendencies, and Syrians, who brought with them a semipatriarchal family structure. The result has been that, despite that city's remarkable economic development, its social structures have not changed much. The pace of social change varies: in some areas of social life it is brisk and rapid, in others it plods along under the weight of history. Accordingly, while southern Brazil has achieved a high level of economic development, family structure has not been equally responsive to modern needs.

Immigrants from other parts of Europe—for example, Germans—have had little influence on the restructuring of the Brazilian family. In the majority of cases they either formed veritable self-contained enclaves which effectively blocked cultural exchange, or else isolation, scanty means for coping with their environment, and other factors produced effects that were just the opposite to those that might have been expected from their cultural heritage. It was not uncommon to see the German immigrant transformed into a backwoodsman.

Where they developed together, urbanization and industrialization gradually changed woman's roles, and gave her life new dimensions. Work in factories, shops, and offices brought many women out of the isolation in which they lived, and in the process also altered their attitudes toward the outside world. Courtship took on entirely new aspects. Parents no longer arranged marriages; now the children saw to it they had a say in the matter, and their efforts were made easier by the new customs of going to dances and movies. Once the system of sexual segregation and domestic seclusion of women was undermined, differences in the degree to which men and women participated in cultural life also diminished.

This major readjustment of the family structure to the new conditions of urban life brought about profound changes in female education. Although education in household duties remained the ideal, the need for formal schooling was becoming increasingly evident by the end of the nineteenth century. Of course, this did not mean that it was thought that women should receive the same education as men, or that the roles traditionally assigned to the two sexes should be on an equal social footing. Then as now, society put up considerable resistance to the education of women, and this resistance increased the higher one climbed the educational ladder. In any event, the broadening of women's cultural horizons, the wider possibilities for birth control, and the growing utilization of legal means to dissolve the marriage bond were open testimony to the fact that woman's status was in the midst of a process of continuous redefinition, at least in the dynamic centers of Brazilian social life.

By contrast, the extension of the legal family to more and more social groups meant *de facto* and *de jure* a reinforcement of the sexual taboos surrounding girls and married women, except among the more educated strata of the urban industrial centers. Even now, although an increasing number of nonvirgin women marry and are no longer condemned to a life of prostitution, this is true only for those groups that are furthest removed from the value system of the middle social strata. There is no sociological evidence to suggest that such behavior takes place on a broad scale. The vast majority of Brazilians belong to the Catholic Church, whose ethic provides no prospect for breaking the virginity complex, and society has put up strong resistance to social groups that have tried to introduce fresh ways of thinking in this area. Furthermore, in a society that maintains a double moral standard and legitimizes prostitution, there is no compelling reason why the virginity complex should ever disappear.

Machismo, still the essence of the male ideal, also does much to maintain sexual restrictions. A survival from the patriarchal manners of the colonial family, this "Don Juan-

ism" is a true emblem of the male supremacy that exists in
the family and the society in general. A woman's loss of
virginity before marriage is felt to permanently detract from
her husband's manliness, and the consequences of that attitude for relations between the sexes in the family are obvious. Under these circumstances a Brazilian wife is not really
a companion to her husband; indeed, this has been cited as
one of the most important factors in the breakup of numerous marriages.[26] The historical evolution of the family from a
consanguinous group to a more conjugal one seems to have
depended on the changing role of the wife and consequent
reduction of inequality in relations between the sexes. However, resistance to these changes has been intense and has by
no means come only from men. Women, too, have found it
difficult to accept changes, insofar as they have not had to
confront directly the demands of a rapidly changing world
and have allowed themselves to remain hidebound in an
antiquated tradition. It is no wonder, then, "that the Brazilian man learns to formulate his self-esteem to a large extent
in terms of sexual potency."[27]

For the Brazilian woman, marriage in no way loosens the
social restrictions to which she had been subject as a girl.
Indeed, even in the cities she is forced to give up some of her
freedoms when she marries. She not only has to avoid certain
actions that are taboo for all women regardless of their civil
status; she must also allow no behavior, no matter how
innocent, that might encourage inferences prejudicial to her
reputation as a married woman. Although this morality is
dominant in the middle strata, both the upper and the lower
classes are much more relaxed about their morals, albeit for
different reasons. The lower classes still have fewer biases and
prejudices, even none at all, about casual marital unions,
although it has been among this segment of the population
that the legal family has been making its latest inroads in
Brazil.[28] The economic instability and poverty among this

population is not conducive to stable marital ties; these are dissolved and resumed without great ceremony. This example illustrates the kind of changes in family life wrought by the fact that urbanization preceded industrialization in many parts of the country.

The family structure in the countryside stems directly from the patriarchal family of the colonial epoch. More resistant to the changing patterns of urban industrial life, it displays features that hark directly back to its historical roots. Although the father's say in the choice of mate has been considerably curtailed, and companionship between young lovers is becoming more and more common, the casual flirtation is still tolerated only with misgivings and only within limits. Flirtation often consists merely in the exchange of glances, leading directly to engagement or marriage. The boy ordinarily does not visit the house of his chosen one, but when he does he jokes and converses with the other members of the family instead of with the girl. Feasts and dances do not offer much opportunity for closer contact; many dances are exclusively for men as modern ballroom dancing for couples is generally looked on with disfavor by more conservative parents (although this too is changing in the countryside). Some girls are not permitted this type of dancing at all, and for those who are, decorum requires that the fiancé be passed over in favor of other young men. All these obstructions placed in the way of close contact between young men and women fulfill very well-defined functions in an isolated environment where intimacy on the sly would be very easy. Even engagement, which generally lasts about a year, is often abruptly cut short to prevent intimacy from progressing in a way that tradition could not condone.

Although there are cases of deflowering and flight that result in a declaration of marriage in absentia, the abduction of a betrothed is not always considered a breach of traditional patterns of morality. Many abductions, or pretended abductions, occur with the connivance of the parents, who hope in this way to escape their obligation to host the traditional feast. When money is scarce, elopment is made-to-order. Occasionally, it is not followed by legal marriage. However, free unions of this sort more often involve widows, widowers, or others whose marital situation has been dissolved; families with single daughters will usually try to secure legal sanction. Free unions entered into as second marriages, on the other hand, do not at all diminish the reputation of the parties involved. Even male bigamy is accepted, and does not cause rivalry between the two women. True, such cases are not very frequent,[29] but there are enough of them to show a lingering pattern of old colonial ways in male sexual behavior and they bring to light the conformism that continues to permeate women's upbringing.

For women, matrimony is regarded as the soundest social fate, even in urban areas; while the countryside has no place for the bachelor. The social position of a young girl bereft of her parents is totally indeterminate and her economic situation extremely insecure. So powerful are these forces that in the countryside a girl who has passed the ideal marriage age will sometimes break the traditional reserve and embark upon amorous conquest, though she may be aware that the life awaiting her after marriage is a grim one. If young bachelors are scarce, she will attach herself to a married man, since even a free union of this sort is considered preferable to the life of a spinster.

The married woman occupies a singular position in the rural, backwoods family of southern Brazil. She may do as much subsistence labor as the man, although she will be spared the heavier tasks, and in addition she does all the household chores, including caring for the children. Yet once outside the intimacy of the home, a woman is not her husband's equal. In the presence of strangers she withdraws into the background, not daring to enter into conversations or even to remain nearby. At feasts her role is to prepare the food, and she enters the dining room or hall only to serve the guests. One more observation will round out the picture of the conjugal inequality of rural life: "On journeys or trips into town, the husband may be seen riding on the family's only horse, with the wife trotting along behind bearing the youngest child."[30]

This describes accurately enough the situation in the state of São Paulo, a region which has seen most of the disadvantages as well as advantages of modernization. In areas that have been economically stagnant, vestiges of old patriarchal family patterns linger on in even greater abundance. There, broken by the strenuous farmwork and household chores, crushed by an endless succession of maternities, and reaping only marginally the benefits of increasing opportunities for social contact, it is only by humble submission that a woman may secure the social position and economic security made necessary by rural isolation. Since women still perform a basic economic function in the rural family, there is no need to mystify her by concealing her social heteronomy under an outward show of equal treatment at the personal level.

The persistence of the patriarchal family structure may no longer be evident inasmuch as the extended family is being pushed increasingly into the background by the conjugal family, but old patterns remain very much present in the institution of the godparent. Family solidarity has come more and more to reside in the godparents, who have effectively become part of the kinship structure in that they fill the place of natural parents. While their obligations with regard to socialization and religious training have become superfluous, their closeness and companionship continues to be very much coveted and still performs its traditional functions.[31] In urban areas these ties are becoming looser, and traditional obligations are undergoing a process of redefinition, as the younger generations gradually effect change in the structure of kinship by marriage, through the religious sacrament of baptism. In rural Brazil, where kinship by marriage serves an important function, godparent relations do not show any notable signs of disintegration.

Thus, relations between husband and wife have undergone substantial changes only in the more urbanized areas of the country, where the conjugal family has taken root. Although at its core it has clung to the old moral traditions, the urban family has adjusted to the new roles that economic change has brought for women. Education is being extended to growing numbers of women, and in so doing has induced members of both sexes to initiate a process of redefinition of women's social roles.[32] But formal schooling is only one aspect of education, and hence while some aspects of the female personality are being brought into line with modern life as a result of exposure to new conceptions of the world, others have remained immersed in tradition. The male personality also shows the effects of uneven development, but it is among women that the process has been most conspicuous. The most recent social and economic changes have had deeper repercussions on women; specifically, their roles have undergone transformations that have sometimes clashed with religious and moral conceptions. History, of course, does not proceed by a series of synchronized ruptures in all of society's structures at once, so that this uneven development is to be expected. But what is important is that a process of redefining the world, and, within it, the social roles of men and women and their relations with each other, has begun. In this process education occupies a place of fundamental importance, and it is to this that we now turn.

CHAPTER 7

Education for Women in Brazil from the Colonial Period to the Present

The Eternal View of Women

Education never did become a social value in the rough society that was colonial Brazil, with its predatory, exploitative, profit-seeking economy. Its first meaningful role was as a tool of religious instruction for the children of the white colonizers and Indians, the adults of the emerging society whom the Jesuits hoped to win over to the Christian faith.[1] The Jesuits pursued their educative mission, founding primary and grammar schools during the first century of colonization, and by the time they were expelled in the eighteenth century they could boast of a vast educational network. Expulsion occurred when the Order of Saint Ignatius ran up against the authority of the manorial landlords, who reigned supreme within the patriarchal family, but the Jesuits in fact continued the spiritual conquest of lesser members of the colonial seigneurial family. As the sole force capable of setting itself up against the excesses of patriarchal authority, the Jesuits implicitly endorsed the existing order and subtly and ably indoctrinated the boys in the schools and the girls in the chapels and churches. In the short term, the Jesuits undoubtedly played a constructive social role by bringing elements of literacy to the male children of the free population. For women, the Jesuit fathers symbolized the possibility of refuge that religion offers to those under the yoke of arbitrary power. In this respect, their influence on women was only negative; they offered women no means of liberation, but taught them submission to the Church and to their husbands in accordance with the precepts of the Apostle Paul. That, indeed, was hardly a difficult task, perfectly in keeping with the traditions of the Iberian peninsula which condemned women to a life of social inferiority and ignorance. European cultural traditions, together with the scarcity of white women and the licentiousness of manners, explain the life of reclusion to which men bound their daughters and wives during the colonial period. The Iberian practice of sexual segregation, approved and encouraged by the Church, was a weighty factor in shaping the female personality, creating a sedentary, submissive, and religious creature who took only a limited part in cultural life. Shyness and ignorance remained the essence of the female personality throughout the entire colonial period, as many a foreign traveler noted:

> The traditional situation of inferiority in which women were placed by custom and the laws, the nonexistence of a social and worldly life for women, and their almost complete lack of education (at that time women rarely learned even to read and write) engrained in them a timidity and reserve that made them blush on being caught up by strangers or left them disconcerted before guests and outsiders.[2]

The religious orders, Jesuits included, sanctioned the role the social order had cut out for women. Their reclusion and ignorance were the obverse of the loose mores that united master and female slave. As two different aspects of the same system, neither could be altered without changing the other. If the priesthood acquiesced to, and even benefited from, the amorality that reigned in the slave quarters,[3] it obviously could not seriously conceive of altering the conditions under

which the women of the seigneurial stratum were forced to
live. The Catholic Church instructed woman in the philosophy of renunciation of worldly pleasures to her greater glory
in life after death. Between the authority of the head of the
family and the moral authority represented by the holy
fathers, a woman did not have much room to grow. The
metropolitan government contributed heavily to sustaining
this climate, as may be seen in the ordinance concerning the
duties of tutors:

> Look after the persons of orphans in a good and true manner,
> instructing them in the precepts of the Church and teaching them
> their prayers, instilling in them a fear of God, shielding them
> from evil and guiding them toward the good, teaching the boys to
> read, write, and do sums, and the girls to sew, wash, and make
> lace, and all the other usages that women undertake with their
> hands, and all good habits and manners."[4]

These instructions did not constitute discrimination against
the women of the colony. In Portuguese culture, there was
simply no place for female education, which was regarded as
a veritable social heresy. The ideal of pedagogy for women
did not extend beyond the domestic arts.

In the sixteenth and seventeenth centuries, in some regions
of Brazil, women did not even know how to speak Portuguese. Living as they did amidst the Indians, and lacking
contact with Europeans, many women and children could
express themselves only in the language of the natives.[5] As a
result, according to Alcântara Machado's gleanings from
sixteenth- and seventeenth-century testaments in the state of
São Paulo, in over four hundred wills, one phrase occurs time
and time again to explain the absence of the testator's signa-
ture: "For she is a woman and does not know how to
write."[6] In seventeenth-century São Paulo, only two women
knew how to write their names: one was a Dutch woman, the
only "enlightened" woman in the first half of the century,

and the other was a Brazilian educated in Bahia, the first to sign a document in the Piratininga territories in 1699. Women's ignorance of even the rudimentary aspects of Portuguese culture not only extremely limited their participation in cultural life, but also placed their economic security in jeopardy. There were, for example, cases in which women were bilked of their fortunes because they did not know how to read.[7]

Religious Education:
The Role of the Convents

Convents were the only places where a woman could receive an education. The Conceiçao retreat, a lay institution founded at Olinda in 1595, was intended solely for preparing orphan girls from good families for marriage. Even in Bahia, the cultural hub of colonial Brazil, there were no schools for girls. Some young girls of the seigneurial layer sought in the monasteries of Portugal the education they could not obtain in Brazil. The first convent in Brazil, the Order of Santa Clara, was founded in 1678 at Bahia. Apart from one established at São Paulo in 1685, no others were founded until the eighteenth century: two in Rio de Janeiro in 1750 and 1780, and two in São Paulo, one in 1774, and the other not until 1811. Although reading and writing were offered along with music, singing, organ, and domestic skills, the Brazilian retreats were convents providing only primary-level education. To take their vows, the sisters had to go to Portugal, where they could also broaden their education. However, only a very small number of Brazilian women entered convents. A total of twelve girls were at the Santa Theresa retreat, the first of the São Paulo convents, in 1728.

In the early nineteenth century, the government began to

place difficulties in the way of establishing convents, claiming the colony was threatened with depopulation, and suggesting that the retreats undertake to educate women as pupils rather than as future nuns. But the Santa Clara retreat in Sorocaba, after obtaining a license to become a teaching establishment, in the end became a cloister. To maintain appearances, it kept six pupils during the first year, but because of the type of education they received four of these ended up in nun's habits after all. Because the Brazilian convents were not under canon law, the nuns could discard their habits any time they wished and some of them did so, but the majority settled down permanently to a life of contemplation.

With the arrival of the Portuguese court a few modest opportunities were created for women to receive lay instruction. Jean Baptiste Debret mentions two private *colégios* in operation in the viceroy's capital in 1816.[8] Of course, these schools bore no resemblance to what a *colégio* is understood to mean today. At that time, they were places where Portuguese and French women taught sewing and embroidery, religion, the rudiments of arithmetic, and the national language to girls whom they took into their homes as boarders. The arrival of these women—followed a little later by Germans—helped a bit to broaden the cramped intellectual horizons of the Brazilian women, and brought the first rays of enlightenment. Still, these girls' boarding schools do not appear to have been widespread, even in the capital, and often the foreign tutors performed their functions as domestic governesses and lived in the homes of their charges. Ina von Binzer mentions two such boarding schools in Rio de Janeiro in the 1890s. She herself had worked at one, but later worked only as a domestic tutor.[9] Although the didactic efforts of these women from abroad sowed the first seeds of intellectual concern in the newly liberated fledgling society, they could not serve as a basis for a national system of education for women. With the advent of independence, the initiative for building a national school system to meet the needs of the population had to come from the imperial government.

The Imperial Education System

Like the breathing spell from the expulsion of the Jesuits and the dismantling of their educational organization in 1759 to the first serious attempts to reorganize this system on lay foundations under royal auspices in 1772, there was also a relatively long interval between the end of the colony and the first measures to set up the imperial education system, based on individual courses leading to no degree. The 1823 Constitution took up the idea of providing education for women. The draft bill which provided that a commendation for distinguished service to the nation and decoration with the Imperial Order of the Cross be extended to the citizen who, before the end of 1823, presented "the best treatise on the physical, moral, and intellectual cultivation and education of Brazilian youth" was amended, on the proposal of delegate Maciel da Costa, to read "of both sexes." [10]

But the liberal tendencies in the 1823 Constitution were snuffed out when the assembly was dissolved, and the 1924 Constitution states only that "primary education is free to all citizens," and mentions "colleges and universities where the sciences and arts shall be taught." [11] To the deputies elected to the legislature of 1826 fell the task of drawing up, discussing, and approving bills on national education. The draft bill signed by deputies Januário da Cunha Barbosa, José Cardoso Pereira de Mello, and Antônio Ferreira França, which dealt with the organization of public primary education under the Empire provided:

> There shall be primary schools teaching the elements of literacy, in all the most populous cities, towns, and villages of the empire. . . . Teachers for girls shall be appointed and certified by

examination in the manner indicated above, for the most populous cities, towns, and villages where the president of the province on proper counsel deems such an establishment necessary, and these mistresses shall be women who, by their purity of spirit, wise judgment, and knowledge have shown themselves worthy of such instruction, which shall also include sewing and embroidery.[12]

Although the paragraph referring to women's education is justified in the name of woman's maternal functions,[13] the need for it is at least acknowledged.

The law that emerged from the draft bill on education on October 15, 1827, exempted the schoolmistress from the obligation to teach geometry and limited the teaching of arithmetic in girls' schools to the four basic operations. Finally, it introduced different curricula for boys' and girls' primary schools; that provision stemmed primarily from the prevailing views on woman's social roles, for which a knowledge of geometry would be useless, but also from a realistic awareness of the level of ignorance of the women who applied for teaching posts. The law provided for equal pay for male and female teachers. Still, since whether or not geometry was taught provided the criterion for salary differentials, female teachers were in fact the more poorly paid.

The greatest difficulty in applying the 1827 law was finding enough teachers to staff the girls' schools. Despite the fact that women predominated in the teaching of domestic arts, the few who showed up to direct the classrooms had such poor command over the subjects that in the end they failed to transmit what scanty knowledge they did possess.[14] The 1827 law defaulted in practice "for want of suitably qualified teachers, who could not be attracted by this scanty pay, despite the guarantee of a lifelong position. The girls' schools were even worse off: in 1832, Lino Coutinho counted less than twenty in operation throughout the entire empire."[15] Thus, the realities of Brazilian life frustrated the implementation of the first plan which would have given women at least the rudiments of schooling. The 1827 law was in fact an instrument of discrimination. To be sure, it was the first piece of legislation giving women the right to education and on that account it represented a historical milestone, but it admitted girls only to primary schools, the so-called pedagogical schools, and reserved the higher levels (*liceu, ginásio, colégio*) to the boys.

Since coeducation, always a difficult goal in predominantly Catholic countries, was not allowed, the curriculum of girls' schools continued to stress needlework rather than schooling. The social expectations attached to woman's role made schooling in the formal sense almost totally superfluous: many fathers took their daughters out of school as soon as they learned their needlework, to prevent them from acquiring a solid knowledge of the three Rs. The persistence with which the district inspectors, the chamber supervisors, the inspector general, and provincial presidents alike urged teachers to show diligence and application in the teaching of needlework revealed the same orientation. One schoolmistress, Benedita da Trinidade, was harshly criticized for having dispensed with instruction in manual arts on account of the little time it left her to teach her pupils reading, writing, and arithmetic. The same move had more serious consequences for Professor Maria da Glória do Sacramento, who was "not qualified to receive her salary by reason of not having fulfilled one of her duties, which was to teach the domestic arts."[16]

In 1830, when the parliament was debating the government proposal for the creation of primary schools, Ferreira França suggested that instruction in the manual arts be given separately from instruction in literacy. In such a system, children would spend the entire day at school, learning the arts in one period and letters in another. Thus arose the first idea of creating vocational schools for practical training in a trade to prepare the less advantaged for an occupation. The idea, however, did not bear fruit and elementary education remained precarious and divorced from Brazilian realities. Another of Ferreira França's proposals became a practical reality at a later date, namely, that "teaching posts in public primary schools should be given preferentially to women."[17]

The 1827 law, which was almost wholly frustrated in its application, presupposed one fundamental principle if it was to be effective: that legislation on education be centralized. This would have been the only guarantee to uniform and universal education. The constitutional amendment of 1834 cut off this effort to unify education by conferring on the provincial assemblies the power to legislate public primary education and to regulate establishments set up for that purpose, while leaving legislation on secondary and higher education in the hands of the central government. Greater importance was thereby ascribed, in a country of illiterates, to more advanced education than to subjects on which the social and economic development of the nation depended. From that time on, the shaping of the nation's intellectual climate and mental outlook was in the hands of the provinces, while the central government was left with the task of caring for those areas of education where regional diversity would have been more effective.[18]

This amendment dealt a mortal blow to equal pay for elementary school teachers as specified by the 1827 law. The first law on primary school education in São Paulo enacted after the amendment authorized the president of the province to "provisionally appoint the teachers for girls' schools without competitive examination."[19] The shortage of competent women and the maintenance of sexual segregation obliged the authorities to keep many women teachers who were basically unqualified. Thus, rather than endeavor to promote professional training for women, the provincial governments sought to uphold the principles of traditional morality, which were against both coeducation and male teachers for little girls. The law set the pay of women teachers not appointed by competitive examination at two-thirds of the regular salary and retained them at their posts only until they could be replaced by other teachers with better credentials. This served as a real incentive both to open additional primary schools and to improve the training of women teachers; it also signified legal acceptance of incompetent female teachers, and to a certain extent even discouraged them from advancing their own education. Within a social environment which, for the most part, saw a woman's teaching functions as a continuation of her functions as a mother, rather than as a profession requiring special training, and which constrained women, in conformity with social expectations, to accept lower wages than men, this law gave formal sanction to the continued existence of woman's cultural inferiority.

Girls continued to be excluded from public secondary education at the Pedro II Colégio, to which they gained admission only in this century. Whereas boys' secondary schools aimed principally at preparing youth for higher learning quite remote from the realities of Brazilian life and its practical needs, female education pursued the ideal of preparing women for marriage. This ideal gave a distinctly domestic cast to post-primary education for woman, and prevented her from intellectually going beyond the objective of social "conversation," for which special emphasis was placed on foreign languages, especially French.

Under the empire, not only was the quality of female education persistently inferior, but there were also fewer schools, and hence fewer girl pupils. In 1855, in the municipality of Côrte, there were seventeen primary schools for boys and only nine for girls, with enrollments of 909 boys and 533 girls, respectively. That same year, the private school system had ninety-seven establishments, incuding primary and secondary schools: fifty-one for boys and forty-six for girls, with enrollments of 4,490 and 2,864 respectively. Two years later, the public primary shcool system had grown by one boys' school and two girls' schools, with enrollment rising to 1,473 boys and 743 girls, and in 1861 enrollment had increased to 1,892 boys and 1,091 girls. Four years later, this difference had diminished (1,860 boys to 1,530 girls), but it was only in the private schools that a rough equality was reached (2,111 boys and 2,056 girls).

However, this process of gradually equalizing the number of boys and girls receiving formal schooling was uneven. In 1866, for example, a regression occurred, with 2,863 boys and only 2,080 girls in private schools.[20] While general public neglect of female education continued, as the initiation of women to the elementary acquisitions of culture became more and more a part of the aspirations of the upper strata of the urban population, private enterprise took liberal advantage of these heightened ambitions, and the number of girls enrolled in private schools grew.

The Growth of Normal Schools

A need for normal schools to train primary and secondary school teachers was duly reflected in various ministerial reports and draft bills providing for the creation of such institutions. The first efforts, however, got nowhere, and it was only in the last years of the empire that normal schools began to be established in earnest. Created to put an end to the improvised teacher, they became institutions on which improvisation was merely raised to a higher level. As a result, the first normal schools, founded at Niterói in 1835, at Bahia in 1836, and at Ceará in 1845, did not get off the ground. The schools at São Paulo and Rio de Janeiro also were failures. For example, the São Paulo school had only one teacher. Founded in 1846, it was abandoned in 1867, and reopened in 1874. After failing again in 1877, it finally opened for good in 1880.

The failure of the first attempts to establish normal schools in Brazil was not due solely to the absence of staff capable of providing a better quality of instruction to persons seeking careers in teaching. The normal schools were intended chiefly to train primary school teachers, and they tended to draw their enrollment from the less privileged strata. In a country with a high illiteracy rate, these strata did not see education as a means for social advancement; that view had to wait for the effects of intense industrialization and urbanization to set in. In this sense, the normal school was not actually a social need for Brazil at that time. Rather, it was just one of the many liberal ideas engendered in countries with more developed economies, and imported to Brazil by the national intelligentsia. On the other hand, the failure of these schools was just one more symptom of the general disorder in the nation's education system, or rather, of its *lack* of one.

Secondary education, consisting of two different types of institutions—under two separate political jurisdictions, state and federal—was indicative of the diversity of views on the nation's educational needs. In reality, the Pedro II Colégio was the only institution for secondary education. The provincial *liceus* were inferior in status to Pedro II and did not give direct access to higher education. The consequence of this was the preservation of a system of preparatory studies as the logical outcome of a series of disconnected preparatory courses incapable of providing genuinely formative intellectual training. As it was essentially a preparatory system, secondary education was meant for students who intended to continue their studies, and that, in effect, excluded all but a very few women.

First, there were no incentives for students who intended

to go on to higher studies, and second, the way that Brazilian secondary education was organized made it difficult for women to get into higher institutions. Since the Pedro II Colégio was an all-male establishment, with a status that no other provincial *liceu* or *colégio* had, any woman who wanted to enroll in a higher institution (or for that matter any boy who did not have a diploma from the Imperial Colégio) had to take an examination to qualify for entry into higher courses of study. This examination, initially given only at the Pedro II Colégio, proved to be a real obstacle to higher education for women.

In any case, the structure of higher education in imperial Brazil had no relevance to women for adapting to a way of life which saw them more and more gainfully employed outside the home.[21] Social conditions themselves stood in the way of a woman's acquiring a profession in all sectors that had traditionally been considered the domain of men. What is more, the influx of women into primary school teaching was not the result of liberal currents; rather, it was a natural result of the lack of teachers in primary girls' schools where the moral precepts of the Catholic Church and the moral attitudes prevailing in the society at large required the observance of sexual segregation. The appearance of the first normal schools sparked off a negative social reaction to the recruitment of women, and the first women students at the normal schools were even considered immoral.

The rare public efforts to provide education to impecunious girls tended to channel them into careers as primary school teachers. In 1825, the Seminário de Nossa Senhora da Glória was founded at São Paulo as a girls' school, subsidized by the emperor, to instruct orphan girls in the three Rs. Although it gave preference to indigent girls, it also accepted paying boarding students from other social strata to supplement its budget. Despite the precarious material and intellectual situations of the girls at the Seminário, they were given preference, in the law of March 16, 1846, for teaching posts in girls' schools. In 1847 the government created a normal school at the seminary in response to needs for reorganization that were beginning to be felt; however, it never opened its doors. It was not until a women's section was created at the normal school of São Paulo (today the Caetano de Campos Institute of Education) in 1874, that the students at the Seminário da Glória were given a real opportunity to receive the training they needed for a proper career. In 1882 the number of those preparing for elementary school teaching increased perceptibly when twenty girl graduates were appointed to posts as primary school teachers in public schools. When the normal school was reopened in 1880 (after being closed since 1877) the seminary girls henceforth were able to train for careers as primary school teachers. Yet the school, which continued to offer both elementary instruction and professional training for primary school teaching, never really became a normal school in the strict sense of the word.[22]

These girls' schools represented only a timid first attempt to make young girls without means into useful members of society and did not solve the problem of women's education, which remained precarious in all schools, public and private, throughout the imperial period. The normal school did not originally have the characteristics of secondary *liceus* or *colégios;* it was an extension and sometimes a complement to primary school, and was subject to different regulations according to the province. Initially intended for professional training, it provided one of the few opportunities for women to continue their studies, and thus came to function in ways for which it had not been intended: it was frequented increasingly by those seeking only to acquire more formal schooling. While secondary education was distinctly aristocratic in character, the normal school served women who aspired to professional training for women, and even to their mere formal schooling, the normal school attracted women insofar as it also prepared good housewives and mothers. Thus, most girls enrolling in normal schools did so with a view toward obtaining competent training for the performance of traditionally feminine roles, while professional training was money in the bank, as it were, to be used in the future if needed.

From its very beginnings, then, the normal school was predominantly a female institution. In 1880—the first year of its functioning—the normal school of the municipality of Côrte had 105 male and 177 female students. True, 31 of the girls were enrolled in needlework classes, but others studied calligraphy and drawing, and still others the sciences. In practical respects the normal schools were highly deficient, but they did broaden women's range of knowledge, and gave them experience in social contact with the other sex.[23] Coeducation, which had been instituted in the primary school not long before, encountered intense and broad resistance,[24] to be expected in essentially Catholic countries. In such countries, coeducation is adopted more as a measure to save resources than out of a real understanding of its social significance. From this point of view, the normal school represented quite an innovation, since sexual segregation continued for a long time in secondary schools, and there were extremely few of these for girls throughout the entire imperial period. Aside from the rare provincial *liceus,* there were only the private schools, generally religious, which did not confer the baccalaureate.[25] "The first two girls who ventured to pursue secondary studies leading to the baccalaureate received their diploma in Letters" only in 1907.[26]

By this time, however, girls had already qualified for higher studies through preparatory examinations taken after completing a secondary course. In the March 22, 1879, session of the legislative assembly of Pernambuco, Tobias Barreto spoke in defense of a draft bill providing a stipend to the daughter of Romualdo Alves Oliveira, graduate of the

provincial secondary school, for medical studies. Though he
did not feel that the time was ripe for woman's political
emancipation, Tobias Barreto fought for civil and social
emancipation. Not only did he vote for the petitioner's
grant-in-aid, he also proposed that a similar subsidy be
provided at the same time to one of his former pupils.[27] Yet
two years were to pass before the first woman student
enrolled in a higher course of study.[28] The lack of a public
system of secondary education for girls made it extremely
difficult for them to get into higher institutions. As of 1930,
Brazilian women had not yet gained a foothold in higher
education or the university.[29]

The concentration of women in the denominational,
mainly Catholic, schools was a major obstacle to the educational changes that were pressing for attention. During the
last decades of the Brazilian empire, however, new ideas
began to confront Catholic conservatism.

Catholicism Defends Its Role
in Education

In the two decades preceding the proclamation of the
Republic, there was intense discussion of ideas directly inspired by foreign liberalism and "scientism," which from
various perspectives dealt with the changes needed in the
Brazilian social structure. Each current of thought inter-
preted woman's social roles and educational needs in the light
of the particular social and political reforms they proposed.
Within this historical context, the Catholic Church represented conservative thought, redoubling its efforts to preserve
the order in which it had staked its interests. In an attempt to
preserve the patriarchal family structure, Catholics, arguing
that fundamental differences existed between men and
women, advocated a corresponding inequality in civil and

political rights. Adopting the age-old position that the proper role for women was in the family and there alone, Sá e Benevides denied them the right to any political or administrative activity—for moral and social reasons.[30] Consistent with their policy of administering imminent social change in controllable doses, the Catholics hoped that women would continue to serve as a brake on attempts to put through any bold changes.

The low level of education among women was also defended in the name of the moral and social need to preserve the family. Tito Lívio de Castro countered this ahistorical argument in defense of the family with a "scientific" line of reasoning that drew on both history and the natural sciences. "If the education and intellectual progress of women causes the breakup of the family, the first concern of a people embarked upon the path of civilization must be to abolish the family in its present form—which means educating women."[31] Though he believed that women were in fact intellectually inferior to men, he did not attribute this to anatomical or physiological factors but to the permanent state of neglect to which they were condemned by society's refusal to educate them. If intellectual inequality between the sexes was due to historical factors, therefore, there was no reason why women had to remain in a state of ignorance and intellectual and social inferiority. The solution lay in education: only with female education would the family really become a "sexual and social contract," instead of being seen as a "hallowed institution." Rejecting the Catholic argument which saw the education of women as a threat to the stability of the family, Tito Lívio de Castro argued that the family as a social institution is subject to constant mutations as history unfolds. He saw in women a motive force for superseding an "immoral form of family organization which owed its existence to the ignorance and enslavement of women."[32] Female education was, on the one hand, necessary for the establishment of a just social order, and, on the other, the cornerstone of social reform policy.

Enemies of Catholic conservatism found themselves increasingly opposed to the existing state of affairs. Catholicism remained the state religion. However, whereas it formerly had been unchallenged, now it had to defend itself against the arguments, positivist and otherwise, of liberalism and scientism, and had to compete with Protestantism in the saving of souls. The Catholics could not proceed on the assumption that Catholicism would continue to be the state religion, in which case a state monopoly in education would have served their purposes admirably. The situation instead foreshadowed a complete separation of Church and state. Through recourse to dogma, the preaching of asceticism, and the condemnation of human vanity, the Catholics tried to hold back the course of history in an effort to retain at least part of the power Brazilian society had originally conferred upon them. Placing faith before science, and morality before education, the representatives of Catholic conservatism believed that a full education necessarily meant a religious education; thus they regarded compulsory education and schooling as lying outside the state's rightful domain, and an infringement of the rights of the individual and the family. Catholics tried to obstruct every legislative effort to reform the sickly and decrepit Brazilian education system.

Perceiving that the separation of Church and state would mean their interests would be better served if they focused their attention on their ties with particular areas of education, they concentrated on higher education. In fact, the Church was already deeply involved in higher education, both in theory and practice. Higher education was one of the strongest bastions of conservatism in Brazil, completely abdicating its function as a center for dissemination of the new ideas that were of such importance for the country's development in the last two decades of the empire. "Newspapers, books, and parliament do far more to spread new ideas than the schools. . . . It is the self-taught students, far more than their teachers, who are fighting for the new view of things, and are even endeavoring to see that it takes root in the schools." [33]

At the same time, they recognized the need for allies. Thus Catholics came to defend liberal arguments, even though they were opposed to liberalism in its defense of freedom of opinion and its support of the establishment of liberal education. In defending freedom in education the Catholics knew that competition between religious and public schools would take place only in theory. In practice, as long as the interests of the Church coincided with those of the state in maintaining the established order, it was up to the latter to defend those interests. In other words, the Church's apparent liberalism, as reflected in its advocacy of educational freedom, was rooted in its self-identity as the state religion, either *de facto* or *de jure*.

The Liberal Challenge

The classical liberals were the most moderate; their aim was not so much the emancipation of woman as the improvement of her preparation for carrying out her functions as wife and mother. For example, Antônio de Almeida Oliveira, following Fourier, took the condition of women as an indicator of the degree of civilization attained by a people. [34] Yet his concern with woman's role in the home is reflected in his 1882 Draft Plan for the Organization of Education, in which he attempted to strike a proper balance between general formal schooling and the domestic arts, and to blend co-education with certain devices to maintain sexual segregation. [35] Although they were timid in their approach to the problem of women's education, the classical liberals were the first to bring it up for discussion, and it was due to them that people began to be aware of the need for equivalent schooling for both sexes.

Despite the life of a domestic recluse to which it condemned women, positivism was bolder in its approach to the subject of female education than was classical liberalism. The positivists' policy stemmed from their own view of the differences between the sexes and their respective social roles. Men and women were conceived as complementary beings—mentally and socially, as well as biologically. Thus woman's superiority in the emotional sphere is matched by man's greater strength of character, and man's analytic intelligence is counterbalanced by woman's capacity to synthesize.[36] The logic of this position, however, meant that if women grasp ideas by a different process than men, it is not possible to teach them together; although the teachers should be the same, women should be educated separately and by different means.[37] Thus, positivism did not advocate equal education for men and women, and only sounded the call for women's education at all because boys were brought up by their mothers. Woman's vaunted moral and social preeminence proved to be no more than a cloak to hide her economic and political heteronomy.[38] Positivism did not strive for the emancipation of woman; on the contrary it wished to emphasize her dependent and subservient condition in the family and in society at large:

> In the family, only he who works outside the home is its head, and everything he needs to live and perform his duties should belong to him: the home, his raiments, the tools of his trade, the books, etc. The aged shall be given shelter and sustenance, and should not go out to work or be placed in homes, nor should women or children.[39]

The most forward-looking ideas of the time were put forward by scientistic liberals, some of whom showed a breadth of vision that enabled them to pose in realistic terms the problems attached to any social reform that entailed a major redefinition of female roles. The most representative on the question of women were Tobias Barreto and Tito Lívio de Castro. Although they did not approach all aspects of their society with the same realism as they did the problem of education,[40] they did have an unshakable belief in the power of education as a factor in social change and in achieving social justice; indeed, they saw education as the key question upon which the progress of Brazilian society depended. In this broader sense, education was seen as central to any program of social reform, and woman's education was viewed as more than merely a necessary step forward in the just cause of achieving social equality with men. It would permit the family to become a sexual and economic contract between intellectual equals. Beyond that, the idea of educating women went directly counter to some of the established beliefs of the time concerning teaching and instruction at the primary level, beliefs which in a certain measure anachronistically persist even to this day. For example, Tito Lívio argued firmly against the employment of women as elementary teachers, on the grounds that occupational qualifications are more important for doing a job well than any affinities that may exist between the agent and object of labor, in this case teacher and pupil.[41]

Obviously, one cannot share Tito Lívio's belief that education can develop intellectual capacities that could then be transmitted by heredity; one may, however, agree that education is a constructive social force, whether as it relates to women's role in the family, or from the perspective of providing women with training in a skill. In this sense, as a socializing process, education shapes the personality traits the social system requires of its members, thereby facilitating individual adjustment to various spheres of activity. Education, which in the case of the primary school teacher was initially just technical training for that post, gradually be-

Table 1
Post-Primary Education (1880s)[42]

Type of school	Number of schools			Number of pupils		
	Men	Women	Total	Men	Women	Total
State secondary schools	1	—	1	154	—	154
Provincial schools	16	1	17	1,933	180	2,113
Public courses apart from official secondary or classical schools	46	—	46	690	—	690
Boarding schools or private secondary schools	67	40	107	2,804	1,289	4,093
Private secondary courses or classical studies	16	—	16	125	—	125
Church seminaries at pre-secondary and secondary level	10	—	10	797	—	797
Vocational schools	9	—	9	658	—	658
Total	165	41	206	7,161	1,469	8,630

came integrated into the totality of responses mustered to meet the social requirements of the capitalist system of production.

Tito Lívio's realism was the product of an objective view of the situation in a country with a mortality rate of 37.6 percent before the age of fifteen, in which 42.1 percent of the population was without an occupation or profession, in which only 0.7 percent was employed in nonmanual occupations, in which 78.1 percent of the free population over the age of five was illiterate, and in which only 12.7 percent of the boys and 6 percent of the girls received any schooling at all.[43] And the situation beyond primary school level was even more dismal.

Although the effort was not immediately successful, the protests of "scientism" and liberalism initiated a slow but steadily growing awareness of woman's situation. The most immediate thrust of this protest was to begin the arduous but necessary process of preparing public opinion to understand and accept as legitimate these strivings for a better education for women. Agitation around this issue in the 1880s paved the way for numerous legislative bills on the organization of education at all levels, including education for women.[44] But the common fate of these bills was to gather dust waiting for an overall reform of public education that was always just around the corner.

Thus attempts to set up an integrated national system of basic education all failed during the pre-republican period, along with efforts to restructure higher education and to establish links between the two levels. The question now was whether, with the end of the monarchy, a victorious liberalism would be able to organize national education along the lines that social and economic changes would require.

The Education of Women
Under the Republic

The 1891 Constitution of the Republic established the principle of secular education, and thereby expressly freed formal education from its ties to the Catholic Church. But it also gave formal sanction to the decentralization of education legislation,[45] the result of which was the creation of a system of basic education that not only was not uniform but also relegated the state to an ancillary role. The consequences of decentralization are well described by Fernando de Azevedo:

> From the educational and cultural point of view, the Republic was an abortive revolution. It contented itself with a change in regime without having the thought or decisiveness necessary to

bring about the radical transformation of the educational system that alone could have effected an intellectual rejuvenation of the cultural and political elite so necessary to the new democratic institutions.[46]

Not only was higher education left with its traditional elitist trappings, removed from the problems of the nation, but it was a throwback to the empire. The system of secondary education was maintained as before, with emphasis more on the accumulative than the formative aspects of learning, and designed to prepare pupils for higher education and the privileges of the well-off layers of the population.

The gulf between primary and higher education, already apparent in the period of the empire, continued under the new regime, in both the state-administered and the federal school systems. The system of primary, normal, and technical and vocational schools existed side by side with the systems of secondary and higher education, with no links between them. Since the former was the educational system for the masses, while the latter was for the elite, the Republic was without issue as far as the democratization of learning was concerned. Since there were no central guidelines for a national educational policy, the school system that did emerge could only be the offspring of the most sundry local rulings. The liberal spirit that pervaded the laws on education passed under the first Republic allowed a wide margin of action to the Catholic Church, which by tradition and because it possessed a practiced cadre was far better equipped than any lay organization to perform the tasks of education. In other words, the Church had become, as it had foreseen, the major beneficiary of the establishment of the principle of freedom of education. Since the elite of the republican government had no educational philosophy to back up the new political ideal, and since they lacked the means to create a body of teachers who could cope competently with the educational tasks of the secular state, they were unable to "replace the catechism of the period when Church and state were one with an order to match the new regime of full and total individual responsibility which they had just proclaimed."[47]

Because of this, the religious secondary schools drew large numbers of their pupils from the ranks of the economically, socially, and culturally heteronomic group—women. However, because these schools were not free, large segments of the population were effectively barred from them, and this, of course, had serious repercussions on the education of the female population.[48] Since there were not enough normal schools, many girls attended secondary school courses at Church schools instead, but as the Church schools were not on an equal footing with the public schools, they neither gave direct access to higher education, nor enabled their students to later prepare for a career.[49]

Protestant Schools

The Protestant schools, in contrast, did a lot to widen Brazilian women's cultural horizons. In 1871 the American School was founded in São Paulo; it later became Mackenzie College, to which a secondary course of study and the College of Commerce were added in 1886 and 1902, respectively. This and other initiatives undertaken by the Protestant denominations, principally Methodist and Presbyterian, were an invaluable contribution to the education of Brazilians, especially women. In the first place, as Protestantism had close affinities with the scientific spirit (in its austerity of mind and analytical bent), it coexisted comfortably with republican ideas and even flourished under the new regime. In the second place, as coeducation existed from the beginning, these schools did much to reshape relations between the sexes along modern lines, offsetting sexual segregation and tempering its deleterious effects on the education of women.[50]

Protestant schools, however, were in no position to compete with the educational empire of the Catholics, for three reasons: first, they were few in number; second, the Catholics had dominated the teaching profession for centuries; and third, it was for the most part unthinkable for Catholic families to send their children to Protestant schools. As a result, the Protestant schools which appeared in the last days of the empire and the beginning of the Republic caused only a tiny ripple of change and were unable to seriously challenge the traditional dominance of the Catholic Church in education.[51]

In failing to establish a unified system of secular education, the Republic perpetuated two serious defects of the old system. We have already examined the first of these, namely the dominant position of the Catholic Church. The second was the existence of two distinct school systems—one offering education and occupational training for the masses, and the other designed to prepare the elite for their rulership role. The situation of women in Brazil being what it was, before 1930 few entered or graduated from the latter system. The accompanying tables show the numbers of women receiving higher education for the country as a whole, and for the state of São Paulo, long the hub of the nation's economic life.

These statistics indicate that the tendency for women to gravitate to certain socially less valued areas of education, which began during the imperial period, became more marked under the Republic. They also show that:

1. Of the few women receiving higher education before 1930, most were concentrated in pharmacy and, to a lesser extent, medicine and dentistry. The greater number of women in pharmacy can be accounted for by the profession's loss of social prestige: pharmacists have retained their tradi-

Table 2
Higher Education in Brazil, 1929

Course	Number enrolled		Number completing course	
	Men	Women	Men	Women
Medicine	5,787	72	609	4
Dentistry	680	71	156	13
Pharmacy	816	178	167	62
Philosophy and letters	62	3	6	1
Law and social sciences	3,180	20	401	2
Civil engineering	2,007	24	212	1
Geology and surveying	—	—	—	—
Industrial engineering	16	—	—	—
Agronomy	Advanced specialized courses			
Mechanical engineering	Advanced specialized courses			
Architecture	23	1	—	1
Electrical engineering	282	2	42	1
Industrial chemistry	—	—	—	—

SOURCE: *Estatística Intelectual do Brasil, 1931.*

Table 3
Advanced Specialized Training in Brazil in 1929

Subjects	Number enrolled		Number completing course	
	Men	Women	Men	Women
Agronomy and veterinary science	970	10	145	2
Commerce	18,892	4,260	2,458	627
Dramatic arts	47	53	—	1
Fine arts	1,146	133	29	—
Music	616	4,910	31	588

SOURCE: *Estatística Intelectual do Brasil, 1931.*

Table 4
Total Enrollment, State of São Paulo, 1930

Courses of study	Total enrollment		
	Male	Female	Total
Pre-primary and primary courses*	244,483	210,780	455,263
Preparatory courses	559	1,938	2,497
Secondary courses†	21,530	6,309	27,839
Vocational courses:			
(a) seminary	535	—	535
(b) teaching	691	7,010	7,701
(c) liberal arts	178	1,584	1,762
(d) technical††	11,827	6,912	18,739
(e) agricultural	138	—	138
(f) nautical	83	—	83
(g) commercial†	—	—	—
(h) obstetrics	—	43	43
Advanced courses:			
(a) law	822	4	826
(b) medicine and surgery	284	11	295
(c) veterinary medicine	25	—	25
(d) engineering	447	7	454
(e) pharmacy and dentistry	1,516	536	2,052
(f) arts and sciences	45	—	45
Total	283,163	235,134	518,297

SOURCE: *Estatística Escolar de 1930, p. xvii.*

*This item includes 597 pupils under official state guardianship and 113 from the primary course of the church schools for girls.

†Figures include pupils in the common courses of the commercial schools.

††Includes students in special typing and shorthand courses, and also those at the "José Bonifacio" school, run by the Patronato Angrícola, in Jabuticabal.

Table 5
Higher Education, State of São Paulo, 1929

Subjects	Number enrolled		Number completing course	
	Men	Women	Men	Women
Law	711	4	84	1
Medicine, surgery, pharmacy	684	121	153	34
Arts	41	—	—	—
Engineering	473	3	54	1

SOURCE: Estatística Intelectual do Brasil, 1931.

Table 6
Advanced Specialized Courses, State of São Paulo, 1929

Subjects	Number enrolled		Number completing course	
	Men	Women	Men	Women
Veterinary and Agronomy	230	—	26	—
Commerce	10,356	2,168	1,467	362
Theology	173	—	20	—
Dramatic arts	22	47	—	—
Fine arts	756	67	4	—
Music	269	1,694	6	166

SOURCE: Estatística Intelectual do Brasil, 1931.

tional functions only in small communities, where there are no doctors, where wages are sufficiently low to prevent patients' seeking professional help, or where traditions are still alive in which the apothecary plays a part. This loss of prestige—the pharmacist is now no more than a vendor of manufactured remedies—is probably the major factor in the entry of women into the field. This is reinforced by the fact that the number of men choosing this course of study has been very low, not even 14 percent of the number going into medicine. Over the past thirty-five years the number of female graduates in pharmacy has grown at practically the same rate as the number of male graduates in that field.[52]

Since the last days of the empire, there has been a high proportion of women in the conservatories, since music was and still is considered a woman's vocation. While the Imperial Academy of Music and Opera was in existence there were slightly more men than women enrolled: in 1857, there were forty women and fifty-two men. A balance was almost struck two years later, forty-six women and forty-eight men, and when the Imperial Academy closed its doors in 1860, women students became a majority at the Conservatory of Music. In 1861, forty-two of the seventy-seven students enrolled at the Conservatory were women, and by 1882 this preponderance had grown: one hundred women and thirty-seven men.[53]

The number of woman students enrolled in higher level commercial studies in 1929 in São Paulo was high compared with other areas of education, but there were still far fewer women than men. Women's tendency to move into this field can be explained on two levels. First, the growth in the number of jobs in the tertiary sector in São Paulo, and in Brazil generally, was abnormally fast. Second, the commercial courses were designed to train people for jobs in subordinate positions, so that students did not need to show special qualities of initiative and leadership.

2. The statistics for education in the white-collar professions (which are available only for São Paulo and hence are incomplete) do not give a true picture, since they include students in specialized typing and shorthand courses, and many of the women receiving training in this area were very likely enrolled in quick-training courses for tertiary jobs which are highly valued by the lower social strata and the lower middle classes. The high concentration of women in

this area indicates that many people were beginning to see in occupational training for the female members of the family a means for the social advancement of the family as a whole.

3. The fact that only a tiny proportion of secondary school students were girls is obscured by the inclusion of commercial students, among whom, as we have seen, there was a substantial proportion of women. To further complicate matters, these figures are for first-level commercial courses, which correspond to the *ginásio,* but are much more geared than the latter to training people for jobs in the tertiary sector. Nonetheless, compared with the number of male students in secondary education, the number of female students is quite low.

4. Women traditionally dominated the few normal schools.[54] Male enrollment was less than 10 percent of female enrollment and this tendency later became even more marked. In 1964, for example, 95.2 percent of the total number of students in normal schools were women, while in 1965 the figure was 94.6 percent.[55] At times, primary school teachers were almost exclusively women, as in Rio de Janeiro in 1935, when 99 percent of the teachers in elementary education were women.[56]

Because normal schools, both public and private, played an important part in the occupational training of women and in raising their level of culture in general, an examination, if only a cursory one, of the functions of the private normal schools for the state of São Paulo may be of some value.

Normal Schools Under the Republic: The State of São Paulo

Law 2,269 of December 31, 1927, established independent normal schools in the state of São Paulo to train primary school teachers. In 1928, twenty-six private normal schools (two in the capital and twenty-four in the rest of the state) applied for and obtained certification with the same standing as the public institutions.[57] In their first year of operation, these independent schools already had an enrollment of 1,503 students, and turned out their first batch of teachers in 1930, by which time the enrollment had doubled.[58] Although private normal schools had far fewer students per course unit, almost as many teachers graduated from them in 1930 as from the public teacher training schools.[59]

Despite the positive role these schools performed, they had some serious defects. The course of study they offered was shorter than that of the public schools, and up to 70 percent of their places were filled without entry examinations, when there were fewer applicants than places. Many of them gave religious instruction, notwithstanding the principle of secular education. Furthermore, as we have seen, neither public nor private normal schools qualified their students for entrance directly into higher education, which meant that their studies were effectively over. Fernando de Azevedo was correct when he stated that the schools in São Paulo prior to the 1933 reform "were upper-level primary, or secondary schools which were no more than incomplete *ginásio* courses, with a slight professional flavoring given them by material in psychology, educational theory, and teaching technique."[60]

However, de Azevedo is mistaken in claiming that the normal schools were units unto themselves with no possibility of linking up with the *ginásio,* that is, with a secondary school that did prepare students for institutions of higher learning. In the second decade of this century, legislation was amended in São Paulo to allow a degree of liaison between the two lines of education. *Ginásio* graduates and persons who had had college preparatory courses were allowed to take supplementary courses to qualify for primary school teaching, and normal school graduates could obtain *ginásio* or preparatory course certificates and go on to higher education.[61] By taking examinations in subjects that were not a standard part of their main course of study, secondary level normal school graduates[62] qualified for the same degree as conferred by secondary schools.[63] This right, granted by law to secondary school teacher trainees, was later extended to everyone studying in normal schools.[64] Under Law 374, dated September 3, 1875,[65] and Law 1,341 of December 16, 1912,[66] which were still in force, *ginásio* students could qualify for primary school teaching alone, or for both primary and secondary school teaching.

Although giving secondary school graduates the opportunity to obtain normal school certificates, and normal school graduates the opportunity to obtain *ginásio* or preparatory school diplomas by means of examination did not substantially alter the original distribution of students, especially women, among the different areas of instruction, a number of people did take advantage of the rights granted them by law.[67]

Education After the 1930 Revolution

In 1930, the revolution that had been simmering for a decade broke out, and to the new government fell the task of reorganizing Brazilian education. It was able to pose in new ways the most pressing problems of a social order in the midst of conscious self-transformation. The enthusiasm for education, so evident in the decade just ended, was reflected in the restructuring of the system of higher education proposed in Decree 19,851, dated April 11, 1931, and in Decree 19,890, issued a few days later. These provided for a total revamping of the system of secondary education, changing it from a preparatory course of study for access to higher education, to a system of broad general education to extend over a seven-year period, divided into two parts. The first part, five years in length, was designed as a broad and basic course of study to be followed by a second, two-year period, the purpose of which was to begin preparing the students for their future specialized professions.

This reform of secondary school education had several extremely important consequences; for our present purposes, however, let us concentrate on the effects it had with regard to women's increased chances to obtain a formal education. Decree 19,890 permitted the implementation of certain ill-defined desires for educational reform that had taken shape by the end of the 1920s. In the early 1930s the normal schools in several states underwent certain reforms before their ultimate integration into the school system, from which they had hitherto remained more or less apart. In São Paulo, during Fernando de Azevedo's term as superintendent of public education, teacher training underwent a radical reform, with courses of a general educational nature being separated from specialized courses related specifically to teacher training. Thereafter, the teacher training school offered a two-year course of training for primary school teaching; the admission requirement was the five-year *ginásio* course graduation certificate.

This reform was a distinct boon for women, who made up the greater part of those enrolled in the normal schools. Besides extending the term of schooling for women, the reform meant that women would henceforth have access to at least some secondary school education and it put off the choice of professional specialization in the *ginásio* from age twelve to seventeen. This, in turn, gave women greater leeway in determining the direction their education would take.

However, the reorganization of education was instituted more at the regional level, by the states, than on a nationwide scale by the central government; it affected directly the primary, normal, and vocational schools while leaving secondary and higher education essentially untouched. The old dual school system continued to serve as an obstacle to the creation of an integrated and unified educational system for the entire nation. When the central government was given the exclusive right (established in the 1934 Constitution and ratified by the 1937 Constitution) to set the general guidelines of educational policy and to draw up a national plan for education, the last legal obstacle to a bridge between the two systems was removed.[68] Although ideas about the democratization of culture did not succeed in transforming secondary education from an elitist system to a popular one, they did make education available to broader numbers by increasing the number of schools. There was a notable increase in the number of secondary school students in Brazil in the 1930s.[69]

Despite the achievements of the Brazilian educational system, including some significant victories for the female population, the Comprehensive Law on Secondary Education (Decree 4,244, April 9, 1942—the Gustavo Capanema Reform) in a sense represented a backward step. Without going into its qualitative aspects, by the mere fact that it expressly provided for "secondary schooling for girls," it set up women as a separate group and struck a blow at the acceptance of coeducation. Although it did not go so far as to make sexual segregation compulsory, it did suggest that women should be educated in exclusively female classes.[70] Although there was not much difference between the secondary school curricula for men and women, segregation is present in the phrasing of the reform—in such expressions, for example, as "woman's calling in the home," or the "femininity of her personality." The contradiction lies in the fact that secondary school education was the only way to gain direct access to higher education.

Normal school graduates were first allowed into courses in the colleges of arts and sciences by way of Decree 1,190, dated April 4, 1939, which set up the National College and allowed normal school graduates to take educational theory, romance languages and literatures, Anglo-Germanic languages and literatures, classics, geography, and history.[71] Even teachers without a normal school diploma were extended this right, although on a different basis. The Comprehensive Law on Teacher Training[72] in 1946 formally confirmed this right by splitting the program into two parts, a short course for primary school assistants and another full-length one for primary school teachers.

As for enrollment in the higher level courses, it was not until 1953 that a broader equivalence among secondary level courses was achieved.[73] But by that time there was already a clear tendency for women, a majority in the normal schools, to enroll in higher level courses in preparation for teaching posts at the secondary level. Because of the kind of training the normal school graduates received, they showed a pronounced preference for courses in educational theory. The Caetano de Campos Institute of Education actually came to function as an advanced-level institute, although even then it was attached to the college of arts and sciences. Even after Law 1,821 established broader links between normal school education and higher education by means of supplementary courses,[74] there was no great change in the situation, and normal school graduates continued in large numbers to choose courses in educational theory and other advanced subjects.

Teaching was generally regarded as a typical, or at least appropriate, occupation for a woman, and this attitude was by then reinforced by the fact that the enrollment of normal school graduates into other advanced courses was either governed by legal restrictions or was contingent on passing examinations. Such enrollment was a decisive factor, therefore, in determining a woman's choice of career. Society thus decided which economic activities the female worker would engage in, independently of what she felt her calling to be. Even today women gravitate to courses in education and humanities, although in actual number they are still not as numerous as the male students.[75] It was only at the end of 1961 that the intermediate level courses were given equal status, and this did not produce any radical changes in the distribution of normal school graduates among the advanced-level courses. Such changes may be facilitated by legislation, yet they depend in the final analysis on economic and social factors. In recent years the number of women enrolled in universities, although still less than a third of the number of men, has increased by leaps and bounds, above all in the college of arts and sciences.[76] Such colleges were oriented from the beginning toward the education of women, and the first to be set up, in 1933, was for female students.[77]

On January 5, 1934, the second state-supported college of arts and sciences was established at the University of São Paulo, and five years later, the National College of Arts and Sciences was set up as part of the University of Brazil. Rapid growth followed over the next twenty years: the number of universities grew from four to fifteen between 1937 and 1953. More and more colleges were set up, some as independent institutions and some attached to universities. In the state of São Paulo, there was a great drive to create independent colleges, so that now no less than eight of the eighteen independent institutions are colleges of arts and sciences. The proliferation of such establishments, and of education courses within them, was a great boon to female education, and set off a process of eliminating men from secondary school teaching, just as they had been eliminated from primary school teaching.

However, the number of women remained substantially below the number of men at both the university and at other levels. In 1955, 51.7 percent of the Brazilian population was illiterate, and of these 23.4 percent were men and 28.2 percent were women—in other words, there were 8,570,524 illiterate men and 10,311,962 illiterate women. In the same year, the total enrollment in secondary schools (including the *ginásios* and *colégios*) was 311,996 men and 261,768 women, and 39,540 men and 35,832 women had completed their studies the previous year. The overall difference seems small, but most of the female students only attended the *ginásio*. Of the 35,832 girls who completed secondary courses in 1954, only 1,103 took the arts and humanities program as compared to 1,197 boys, and only 2,790 girls completed the science and math program as compared to 10,303 boys. Of the total of 35,832 girls no less than 1,939 did only the *ginásio* course.

That same year, 5,058 female students completed courses in commercial studies, and of these 3,114 went on to do the second level; the corresponding figures for men were 12,134 and 7,867. A total of 16,808 women and 2,559 men completed studies in normal schools. Of 802 women who completed vocational training, 12 took the technical course and 115 received master's certificates; for men the figures were 1,699, 344, and 117, respectively. A total of 12 women did vocational courses, of which 11 received master's certificates; the figures for men were 324 and 236, respectively. In 1963, a total of 498,418 women were enrolled in the first level of secondary courses out of a total enrollment of 1,212,691, while the enrollment at the second level was 171,000 out of a total of 351,165.[78] Overall, then, by the time women achieved numerical parity in secondary education, they had not done so in higher education, where they still made up less than a third the number of men. The actual figures for those completing university studies in 1964 were 20,282 men and 6,890 women.[79]

Contrary to what is often supposed, the proportion of women among university students does not rise with the increasing economic development of a region. To take just a few examples, the number of women enrolled in higher education in 1965 relative to the number of men was 28.5

percent in São Paulo, 29 percent in Guanabara, 33.3 percent in Rio Grande do Sul, 34.5 percent in Goiás, 38.8 percent in Espírito Santo, 45.2 percent in Sergipe, 45 percent in Amazonas, and 62.5 percent in Maranhão.[80]

As a result of the intense urbanization of the South, there was a rapid expansion of the job structure in the tertiary sector, which normally requires a moderate degree of schooling. This, allied to the fact that women traditionally are not brought up with a career in mind, has meant that women have sometimes acquired professional training prematurely. Urbanization has at the same time been one of the driving forces for women acquiring an intermediate-level education, by opening the ranks of the middle classes to larger numbers of people, increasing aspirations among the people at large, and providing the opportunity to combine work with study. But while higher education has been internalized by the middle classes as a prerequisite for a man's social advancement, it is not necessary for a woman's intellectual development vis-à-vis a career. The prospect of early engagement and marriage still limits the education and training of the female workforce. The desire for social advancement, which is to a large measure responsible for the greater attention paid today to woman's education and to her occupations outside the home, has still not, however, overcome the fact that class society, in order to maintain its own equilibrium and stability, must order men's and women's occupations hierarchically. While professional training certainly affects woman's occupational position, stratification by sex often determines the training she receives, and thus ultimately the place she will occupy in the job structure.

CHAPTER 8

The Female Workforce

General Considerations

The employment of male and female labor power assumes different patterns in different socioeconomic formations. Not only do the types of work performed differ according to structural type, but also, in societies based on private ownership of the means of production, whether capitalist or pre-capitalist, the work performed by women differs from that done by men. Each mode of production has laws specific to it which govern the development of the material and non-material forces of production, including labor power. The way the essential characteristics of a socioeconomic system work to determine how it is put to use is further complicated in the interplay with the natural traits of individuals. For example, racial and sexual features may be used socially to mystify essentially economic phenomena, such as the relative positions of individuals in the system of production. This serves to block perception of the system's true nature.

The sex factor is an example which operates in all social systems to disguise the essential characteristics of a historical socioeconomic formation and so conceal the true manner in which the particular mode of production functions. Although less useful than race as a means for enabling the privileged strata to maintain its position of domination, sex is always at least potentially a discriminatory, and hence a stratificatory, factor. It has accordingly had a major hand in providing the various types of free-enterprise societies the camouflage they need to keep social tensions at a low ebb, and in that way to protect the social structure from changes which would be fatal to the existing mode of production, or which would accelerate structural transformation.

It has been a mistaken belief that the development of productive forces puts an end to the use of factors such as race and sex to justify the marginalization of large groups of people from the productive system and power structure of a society. Yet, as social techniques become more and more refined, we can see human behavior being steered along lines which, while giving the semblance of voluntary conduct, maintain the dominance of the privileged classes, in effect if not by intention. Far from discovering a negative correlation between the development of productive forces and the employment of irrational criteria to legitimize the existing social order, we find that the correlation between these two phenomena is highly positive, although subtle. Under capitalism, the economic foundations of society are laid bare for all to see; for that reason, capitalism needs the broadest and most elaborate camouflage to conceal its social injustices. Capitalism thus makes the most thorough and rational use of the most irrational criteria,[1] such as the physical weakness, emotional instability, and low intellectuality of women, to defend purportedly higher values such as stable family relations, smooth functioning of domestic services, preservation of traditional ways of upbringing, and respect for the moral principle of separation between the sexes—all to keep female labor in a subsidiary status, and to make women the key element in that vast group of human beings directly marginalized from productive functions.

On the surface, the developed capitalist societies are the ones which have the most elaborate social plans for woman and her work. But the changes wrought by the advent of industrial capitalism brought into relief the economic functions of women who exercised occupational activities outside the home, and concealed their role in the domestic industries which had preceded the mammoth factories, and at the same time marginalized a large number of women from the dominant system of production. The employment of some women outside the home was to serve as sufficient evidence of the broad acceptance female labor supposedly enjoyed and the freedom class society gave women to choose a professional career or marriage, or both. The ideological window-dressing of capitalist societies encourages the belief that the number of economically active women increases in proportion to economic and social progress.

Actually, the real movement of capitalist societies is away from employed female labor. Capitalism has been able to absorb growing numbers of women into the dominant system of production, but only up to a certain point. The transition to a capitalist system of production has required partial utilization of female productive labor from precapitalism. If we view society as a totality, the advent of capitalism brought about a diminution in the directly productive functions performed by women. This, of course, does not mean that once a society has embarked upon the road to capitalism the majority of women will become economically inactive. Their performance of domestic functions represents a certain saving that must be added to the household budget. Still, domestic functions prevent women from becoming the economically independent individuals valued by urban industrial capitalist society. With the family continuing to function as the basic productive unit of the economy, household functions and directly economic functions are divided between the sexes, the man receiving a relatively large share and the woman a relatively small share of economic independence.

Of course, this marginalization of women from the dominant system of production of goods and services serves a valid purpose if it accompanies the development of capitalism in general. Moreover, it does not preclude the large-scale use of female labor power during certain periods. Whenever there is an urgent need to hold down production costs—whether because the society is passing through the stage of primitive accumulation, or because it must increase its rate of economic growth—capitalist entrepreneurs have found it very much to their advantage to employ female labor in abundant measure. Were it not for the way society in general reacted to the substitution of female for male labor, employers could have used female labor on a large scale to their obvious advantage throughout capitalism's development.

Subject to a high degree of exploitation, and in many ways still tied to nondominant and even outdated modes of production, female labor represents the forces of society's historical past which, defined and exploited anew, operate to aid the evolution of a new economic structure. In societies based on free enterprise, women do not take part in the building and development of the economy merely as labor power in general; they constitute a special group within the labor force which is especially vulnerable to the ups and downs of the economy. They are paid the low wages that go along with subsidiary jobs, not only because their technical qualifications are lower but also because, to a great extent, the female personality has not absorbed the traits a worker needs to function in the capitalist system of production. The relative lack of skills among the female labor force serves a needed function in maintaining the stability of a society in which human labor is becoming less and less important relative to the other factors of production. Even where a woman does have the requisite technical training, however, that in itself is not sufficient incentive for her to try to participate in the occupational structure. Even though the drive to "get ahead" is a major item in the personality inventory of an individual raised by the canons of class society, a woman does not normally seek social advancement for herself. If she decides to take on gainful employment for reasons of upward social mobility, it is more often to promote the chances of the family's male members than to advance her own.

Thus, personality traits adapted to the workings of a market economy appear in a special light when they occur in women, and their ultimate roots in the climate created by class society are obscured. From this vantage point, woman, generally speaking, represents a negation of capitalism for a number of reasons: (1) she is more a part of economic structures associated with nondominant modes of production; (2) her socialization is at variance with the attainment of the cultural goals set by class society; and (3) her ties with the individualism of competitive societies are at best remote. Nevertheless, it is just this negation that is among the most convenient for the development of free-enterprise economies, facilitating as it does the development of an economy with periodic ups and downs at the partial expense of subsidiary modes of production. The ejection of large numbers of women from the dominant system of production of goods and services creates a reserve labor force for that system as well as a means of regulating the wages of workers employed in it. The actively employed female workforce of a country thus functions not simply according to its degree of development (decreasing with increasing development), but also as a means of revitalizing those sectors which are considered most appropriate for women, as the example of Brazil makes clear.

Employment of Women in Brazil

Although it is difficult to compare the distribution of the population of Brazil in the various branches of the economy at different periods in the country's history,[2] the available data show that the distribution of women in certain areas of the economy varied according to the economic structure. The data also show that there was an expulsion of female labor as a result of the establishment of a full-fledged capitalist system in Brazil. According to the first Brazilian census, in 1872, if we ignore the figures for those who were unemployed, 45.5 percent of the workforce of the nation were women, of whom 33 percent were in the domestic service sector (no less than 81.2 percent of the total employed in this sector were women). It should be borne in mind that the structure of the Brazilian economy at the time was only marginally differentiated, and that the majority of the workforce was employed in agriculture, with domestic services in second place for women. Of the total number of men employed, 68 percent were in agriculture, with general farm laborers and herdsmen (including day laborers) making up 81.2 percent of the working male population (in that sector). Of women employed apart from 35 percent in agriculture and 33 percent in domestic services, 20 percent were in dressmaking, 5.3 percent in the textile industries, and 6.7 percent in other activities. It is interesting to note that as textiles was practically the only manufacturing industry that existed in the country (the number of those employed in the hat and shoe industries was negligible), women constituted a majority of workers employed in the secondary sector. The percentage of women gainfully employed was fairly high in 1872; even excluding those in domestic jobs, women represented 37.4 percent of the nation's total number of employed.

The 1900 census showed little change in the proportion of

women in the employed population.[3] Again, the fact that the textile industry accounted for almost all manufacturing was responsible for the predominance of women in secondary occupations, with the domestic services, arts, and public employment diverting a significant number of women away from agriculture. However, this near numerical equality was not to last.

By 1920, the proportion of women in the working population had fallen from 45.3 percent to 15.3 percent, excluding persons who lived on unearned income, gave no profession, or were without one. Women constituted only 9.4 percent of those in primary occupations, no more than 27.9 percent of those in the secondary sector, and 22.2 percent of those in the tertiary sector. The growth of industry, which received a boost from World War I (the working population expanding by 83.3 percent in a space of thirteen years),[4] was accomplished through the broad use of male labor, while the percentage of women employed in secondary occupations decreased. The rapid growth in industrial production during the 1930s further accelerated this trend.

Thus, contrary to general belief, industrial development did not bring about a substantial increase in the employment of female labor. Although there was an increase in the absolute number of women employed in the three major sectors, the increase in the number of men employed was substantially greater, so that the proportion of working men to working women was almost the same in 1940 as it had been two decades earlier.[5]

The proportion of women in domestic work increased even further over the next ten years. In 1950, only 10 percent of the total female population over the age of ten worked outside the home, while 84.1 percent were engaged in domestic activities or attended school and 5.9 percent were unemployed. Women constituted no more than 11.3 percent of all persons working in jobs outside the home.[6] Since the economy was unable to absorb the whole of the nation's available labor power, women were to a large extent marginalized from the productive process, such marginalization justified in terms of traditional conceptions of female roles.

The industrial upsurge which took place between 1955 and 1960 (during the presidency of Juscelino Kubitschek) substantially raised employment levels in the urban areas, with consequences for female employment. In 1960, women constituted 17.9 percent of the total employed labor force of the country, yet this increase of 3.2 percent over the 1950 figure was not due to an increase in the number employed in essentially urban sectors. Industrial expansion diverted the male labor force away from agriculture and into urban jobs, and in so doing altered the previous proportions of men and women employed in the three sectors of the economy and raised the percentage of women working in the primary sector to 10 percent. Although the proportion of women workers in the secondary sector increased to 17.9 percent, women's share of jobs in the tertiary sector fell to 30.7 percent. In the southern region, the region most affected by the upsurge, the proportion of women gainfully employed was less than that in the eastern region.[7] If we compare the southern region with the northeastern region, where industrialization was minimal in 1960, we find that the proportion of women among the urban employed was considerably greater in the Northeast. There, women made up 9 percent, 36.5 percent, and 35 percent of the total number of workers in the primary, secondary, and tertiary sectors respectively, or 17.3 percent of the total employed population in that region, which was almost identical to the percentage for the southern region.

Although the proportion of women in the employed population rose slightly between 1960 and 1970, it remained fairly low, at 21 percent. Women made up 27 percent of wage earners, 10 percent of self-employed, 4.1 percent of employers, and 24 percent of unremunerated workers. The proportion of women in the primary sector was 9.7 percent; this figure rises to 24.7 percent in the category of unpaid workers, and falls to 6.5 percent for the other three categories taken together. Women constituted 12.2 percent of industrial workers, which is almost the same as the percentage (12.1 percent) receiving income (wage earners, self-employed, and employers); 24.7 percent of persons working without pay were women. In the tertiary sector 37.8 percent of the employed were women, this percentage falling to 23.5 percent of those working without pay and rising to 38.3 percent of the total in the other three categories combined. Although 50.5 percent of the population ten years of age and older are women, only 13 percent of these are gainfully employed, compared with 36 percent of men in the same age range. Thus there are three times as many men working as women.

Although a rigorous comparison of the data presented is impossible, they indicate convincingly that the participation of women in directly economic labor in Brazil underwent a considerable reduction between 1872 and 1960, or to focus on this century only, between 1900 and 1960. The development of industry in Brazil did not occasion a greater participation of women in the national labor force, just as it did not in other countries. On the contrary, the number of women who devote themselves exclusively to domestic activities that are not directly remunerated has grown. The special situation of the peripheral economies in the world capitalist system has hindered a greater utilization of the labor force in general by virtue of labor-saving technology. The limited dissemination of birth control techniques or the incorporation of medical and paramedical techniques for health care, at least in urban centers, accentuates even more the problem of unemployment. This obviously does not mean that a country that develops along the path of capitalism is able to absorb the whole of its available labor force. In such countries, the labor power factor is gradually replaced by technology, that is, it diminishes as the use of machinery increases the productivity of labor. Even this phase of increased employment, however, which permits a more rapid accumulation of capital and enables income to be distributed to segments of the population that will later be marginalized from the system of production, does not occur in countries with dependent economies. International purchase of machinery considered obsolete in the country of origin makes it very difficult to maintain employment levels in countries on the periphery. Quite apart from the effects of such commercial transactions on the balance of payments and the repercussions this has on the domestic economy, the importation of machinery drives labor from the secondary sector, not only because it increases productivity, but because domestic production of such machinery is almost out of the question. For this reason, the problem of unemployment, both apparent and concealed, is much more serious in countries with dependent economies than in the center of the international capitalist system. The marginalization of female labor, which is often explained almost exclusively in terms of prejudice, the vestiges of a "traditional society," and the low level of economic development, turns out to be a consequence of the full development of capitalist relations of production.

In Brazil, the establishment of a full-fledged capitalist system of production accelerated the expulsion of women from directly economic roles, as the above figures have demonstrated. The practice, inherent in capitalism, of eliminating labor to increase surplus value is compounded in dependent economies by two other factors which also hinder the full use of female labor. First, the transfer of the surplus value to the highly developed capital-exporting countries holds back the pace of capital accumulation in the developing countries by inducing domestic entrepreneurs to alter the organic composition of capital in their enterprises in favor of constant capital, while reducing variable capital to the absolute minimum. Also, the showcase effect of the high standard of living enjoyed by workers in countries at the center of the international capitalist system has led Brazilian workers to demand higher wages, which has limited the appropriation of the absolute surplus value.

It is certainly true that in some remote regions of Brazil, especially where vestiges of the slave economy remained, capital accumulation took place almost exclusively through the appropriation of absolute surplus value. In the large urban centers, however, where almost the whole of industry was located, labor legislation placed broad curbs on capital accumulation through the appropriation of absolute surplus value quite early in the industrialization process. All these factors (and others which would need an economic treatise to analyze) have combined to marginalize female labor, and demonstrate that the vestiges of "traditional society" have *facilitated* the establishment of capitalism in Brazil, in a way that could only be possible at the periphery of the international capitalist system. Seen in this light, the arguments furnished by a traditional outlook to justify woman's domestic role have not contributed to the backwardness of the Brazilian economy or held back its development. On the contrary, even at the stage where the level of employment and hence the use of female labor could have been at its highest, Brazil's state of economic dependence made for the underutilization of labor power.[8] Although there has been no massive exploitation of female labor to accelerate capital accumulation in Brazil in the recent period, the employment of women has always allowed appropriation of a greater portion of surplus value because of the discrepancy between men's and women's wages. The statistics for industrial wages in 1920 show a high concentration of women over fourteen in the lower wage brackets.

Table 7
Industrial Earnings in 1920, According to Sex

Monthly earnings (thousands of réis)	(Percent)	
	Female	*Male*
Below 2,900	40.7	10.9
3,000 to 3,900	21.3	12.0
4,000 to 5,900	25.4	33.4
6,000 to 7,900	9.6	24.2
8,000 and over	3.0	19.5
Total	100.0	100.0

Among the industrial workers under fourteen, although the male-female wage differential was smaller, it still existed. The greatest discrepancies, however, in industrial earnings were among the adult population. Even in the textile industry, where the majority of workers were women, men's wages were higher.

Table 8
Monthly Earnings Among Textile Workers
in 1920, According to Sex

Earnings (thousands of réis)	Percentage of women in the same bracket	Percentage of men in the same bracket	Total
Below 2,900	73.8	26.2	100
3,000 to 3,900	63.2	36.8	100
4,000 to 5,900	49.9	50.1	100
6,000 to 7,900	42.1	47.9	100
8,000 and over	21.8	78.2	100

Statistics on the average earnings of day laborers show that in the textile industry the average wage of adult women was 70.6 percent that of men; in the food industry it was 57.9;

and in the clothing and cosmetics industry, 54.5 percent. In rural areas, the average wage of a woman field laborer, including food and lodging, was 92.3 percent, or 66.9 percent excluding food and lodging, of the average wage for a man doing the same work.

The view of women's work as subsidiary labor encourages the offering and acceptance of lower wages. It is true that women have the worst paid jobs, but this is in large measure due to the fact that they are less qualified, whether this is seen merely in terms of technical skill or whether it is regarded as embracing the entire range of characteristics and personality traits of the individual attuned to the achievement of economic success. These factors, together with the fact that women tend to be seen as temporary labor, are still very much operative in Brazil, and are at least partially responsible for the fact that the male-female wage differential underwent little change between 1920 and 1960. Women have not abounded in the more highly paid positions in any type of occupation, as Table 9 shows.

Table 9
Average Monthly Income in 1960, According to Sex
and Type of Work, for Population over Ten Years of Age

Average monthly income	*Primary sector*		*Secondary sector*		*Other work*	
	Men	*Women*	*Men*	*Women*	*Men*	*Women*
Below 2,100	24.8	24.0	6.3	29.1	7.8	46.5
2,101 to 3,300	19.8	9.8	9.0	12.7	7.2	11.6
3,301 to 4,500	13.9	4.0	11.2	8.9	8.5	7.0
4,501 to 6,000	9.1	2.2	4.7	21.1	17.7	10.2
6,001 to 10,000	6.1	1.1	29.4	17.8	27.0	12.2
10,001 to 20,000	2.3	0.5	13.1	2.6	19.1	7.1
20,001 and over	0.7	0.1	4.4	0.1	8.4	1.2
No income	22.2	57.8	0.5	5.6	1.2	2.0
No statement	1.1	0.5	1.4	2.1	3.1	2.2
Total (percent)	100.0	100.0	100.0	100.0	100.0	100.0

Moreover, comparing wage statistics for different regions shows that economic growth does not bring about any fundamental change in women's situation.

In both developed and underdeveloped regions of Brazil, the female representation in well-paid occupations is low, as the following tables show. These tables give the average monthly income (in cruzeiros) and correlate it with the percentage of women out of the total number of workers for each type of work. They are broken down by region, and consider only the population over the age of ten.

Economic development brings about great changes in the distribution of both male and female labor, shifting workers from the primary sector to the secondary and tertiary sectors. In the later stages of development, labor is channeled from the secondary into the tertiary sector. In Brazil, however, as a result of an excessive pace of urbanization unmatched by a corresponding degree of industrialization, the tertiary sector grew prematurely. Although the number of

Table 10
Southern Region (Percentage of Women)

Income	Primary sector	Secondary sector	Other work
Below 2,100	12.7	31.9	78.8
2,101 to 3,300	6.4	36.8	56.3
3,301 to 4,500	2.9	11.4	37.9
4,501 to 6,000	2.4	18.2	22.7
6,001 to 10,000	1.6	13.6	15.7
10,001 to 20,000	1.5	4.2	14.4
20,001 and over	1.3	1.9	5.0
No income	26.5	15.3	46.5
No statement	5.4	23.2	25.3
Total	10.7	15.7	27.6

Table 11
Northeast Region (Percentage of Women)

Income	Primary sector	Secondary sector	Other work
Below 2,100	8.7	63.4	64.8
2,101 to 3,300	4.8	13.8	26.6
3,301 to 4,500	2.5	13.4	17.0
4,501 to 6,000	3.9	6.4	15.0
6,001 to 10,000	3.1	6.7	25.0
10,001 to 20,000	4.4	3.9	13.4
20,001 and over	2.3	1.3	3.7
No income	16.8	87.3	55.0
No statement	21.8	0.0	20.2
Total	9.3	35.9	35.2

Table 12
Eastern Region (Percentage of Women)

Income	Primary sector	Secondary sector	Other work
Below 2,100	10.2	38.5	73.0
2,101 to 3,300	5.1	19.4	42.5
3,301 to 4,500	4.3	12.0	24.0
4,501 to 6,000	2.8	12.5	19.6
6,201 to 10,000	2.8	8.8	21.0
10,001 to 20,000	3.2	2.8	14.6
20,001 and over	2.0	3.3	7.5
No income	25.0	60.0	44.2
No statement	8.4	24.4	24.7
Total	10.9	14.4	32.7

Table 13
Monthly Income in 1971, Guanabara, Rio de Janeiro,
São Paulo, Parana, Santa Catarina, and Rio Grande do Sul

Average monthly income as a proportion of the minimum salary	*(Percentage of Women)*		
	Primary sector	*Secondary sector*	*Other work*
Below ¼	31	37	78
¼ to ½	27	32	79
½ to 1	8	26	46
1 to 2	2	10	19
2 to 3	0	2	7
3 to 5	0	0	10
5 to 7	0	0	5
7 to 10	0	0	0
More than 10	0	0	0

SOURCE: *População, Mão-de-obra, Salário, Pesquisa Nacional por Amostra de Domicílios, Fundacão IBGE, 4° trimestre de 1971.*

women employed in the tertiary sector increased, this did not lead to any radical redistribution of women among the various income brackets. Women still continued to hold the lowest paid jobs in all sectors of the economy and in the South, where development was at its most intense, the proportion of women in the unskilled occupations even increased at times. There is a higher proportion of women in the lower income brackets in the South than in the Northeast or the East, both in the primary sector and in the category of "other types of jobs." In 1963, approximately 80 percent of the 275,000 women workers of all ages in the state of São Paulo were in the lower layers of the working class.[9]

At the root of this unequal distribution of female labor within the occupational structure are, even more than the precarious technical qualifications, the attitudes of women and society in general toward the role of women at work. An important factor in more highly paid jobs, quite apart from the better technical qualifications that they require, is that they demand also a degree of permanence, normally determined by the role a worker's occupation plays in his or her life. But it is only in special cases that a woman works with a view toward career advancement. In general, the pursuit of a career is contingent, both upon its financial return and on the extent to which it is compatible with the tasks which a woman may also have to perform for a family.

At the beginning of this century, when the fledgling Brazilian proletariat was struggling for labor legislation, large numbers of women participated in strikes.[10] Unfortunately, both the anarchist and socialist wings of the trade union movement adopted the short-term objectives of winning improvements in workers' living and working conditions, and totally ignored broader national issues. The trade unionists did not even try to adapt socialist ideas to the Brazilian situation. As a result, there was a complete lack of contact between the industrial proletariat and other layers of the urban masses and the rural workers.[11] The trade union movement concerned itself with developing the class consciousness in terms of an ideology which totally negated the capitalist status quo and on that account wholly neglected any analysis of Brazilian society. To that extent, there, it was utopian and hence unmindful of the possibilities for improving woman's social situation, by demanding, for example, that the state help to provide training for women workers, many of whom were in the textile industry, or provide public facilities to enable married women to work.

Although the socialist trade union movement posed the question of women's emancipation—the periodical *Anima e Vita,* which dealt specifically with the problem, was started in 1910 in São Paulo by Ernestina Lesina—the labor unions of the time never went so far as to take up the struggle for equal pay, and limited themselves to merely seeking general salary increases and protection for working women.[12]

If the labor unions did little in the first three decades of this century to defend the interests of the working woman, in the years following the revolution of 1930 there was not even the possibility of such action. The industrialization which took place in the 1930s absorbed huge numbers of workers who, though without technical skill, could be quickly trained for factory work. The high rate of population growth in Brazil and the relative stagnation of agriculture were instrumental in drawing large numbers of people to the large urban centers where they formed an industrial reserve army regulating the price of labor. Structural unemployment, a problem Brazil had never been able to solve, took on a new form after 1930. On the one hand were the plans for industrialization, never really fulfilled, in response to popular pressures for increased consumption; on the other was the inability of the secondary sector to absorb the increase in the urban population, which had swelled as a result of internal migration. Thus, the aspirations of ever growing numbers of people to enjoy the standard of living in an urban industrial society were frustrated by the deficient capacity of Brazilian industry to absorb available labor power, and this discrepancy persisted even in periods of intense industrial growth.[13] Under these circumstances, it was not possible to try to keep up the level of employment of women of working age, and even less possible to boost the percentage of women in the nation's total employed labor force. There was, however, no general consciousness at the national level that the country's social and economic development was taking place in part at the expense of keeping a vast number of women in the home. Quite the reverse: feminine organizations, upholding an ideology which stopped short of total negation of the capitalist status quo, saw the structural expansion of Brazilian society along the path of capitalism as an opportunity for extending professional status to women on a large scale and thus for investing them with a social role that was more in keeping with the times.

CHAPTER 9

Manifestations of Feminism

Sources and Perspectives

The ideas, ideals, and aspirations which characterize the developed nations have also influenced the development of countries with dependent economies. Many of the "solutions" adopted by Brazilian governments for the nation's problems have been directly inspired by foreign social situations, and have been only marginally, if at all, applicable to Brazilian realities. It has not been rare to see positions adopted on social questions as the result of social pressure exerted by segments of the population more influenced by ideals originating in countries with different lifestyles. The showcase effect of the industrially advanced countries has left its mark on broad areas of social life, and affected many layers of the population, especially the lower middle classes. Even the proletariat has not escaped as the demands of foreign workers came to dominate Brazilian unions in the first decades of the century.[1]

The results that liberal ideals had on legislation in education under the Republic provide another example of just how effective imported measures can be, and since Brazil had no infrastructure capable of response, the establishment of free competition in education was ineffective, and even harmful. Some discrepancy between the problems of a backward or underdeveloped society and proposed solutions is probably inevitable. However, because political behavior and intellectual attitudes are easily imitated, they may arise apart from material conditions and indifferent to economic development. Because ideas are so easily imported, ideologies play an important role in both reformist and revolutionary movements in developing countries. Truly revolutionary movements have the potential to rebuild society on new foundations, whereas reform movements are seldom able to go beyond the surface. This is why movements calling for innovation, and the ideas that inspire them, often go no further than superficial agitation, and the gap between thought and concrete action only widens. Many conceptions, without a totalizing perspective, also lack the terms necessary to situate[2] the object of their thought and the actions they propose. The classic order of things then becomes reversed: instead of a nation's juridical structure lagging behind the social structure, for example, the opposite occurs.

In the case of Brazil, although the laws have as a rule changed more slowly than social relations, the importation of ideas and ideals has often meant that the juridical element has proven more dynamic than certain infrastructural factors. Judging from legislation such as the Afonso Arinos law of 1951, empowering the government to penalize abuses of the equal rights provisions of the constitution, Brazil might seem quite advanced as regards the elimination of prejudices and the receptiveness to new ideas.[3] However, conservatism has continued to be the underlying determining force, sustaining and even strengthening a number of racial and sexual prejudices.[4] The result has been real discrepancies in various areas of Brazilian social life between existing social relations and the juridical framework provided for them, with the former proving incapable of absorbing the rationality of the latter. In this respect, the legislation the Brazilian feminist movement proposed was also irrelevant to the needs of broad layers of the female population.

The Code for Women: Early Struggles

The first manifestations of feminism date from the period following Dr. Bertha Lutz's visit to London just prior to World War I, at a time when English feminism was in one of its more violent phases. After receiving her degree from the department of science of the University of Paris, Bertha Lutz returned to Brazil in 1918, where she became the first spokeswoman, in the press and on the podium, for women's emancipation.[5] By 1919 she had assumed the leadership of the Brazilian feminist movement and in the same year she and Olga de Paiva Meira represented Brazil on the International Women's Council of the International Organization of Labor. At the first conference of this council two general principles were approved and adopted: (1) equal pay for equal labor, without regard to sex; and (2) the duty of every government to set up a supervisory body partly staffed by women to ensure the observance of laws and regulations protecting workers.

Following the Pan-American Conference at Baltimore, to which she was the Brazilian delegate, Lutz returned to Brazil and founded the first Brazilian feminist association, the League for the Intellectual Emancipation of Women. In Baltimore she had met with the American feminist Carrie Chapman Catt, a contact which not only provided her with a direct incentive to organize women to defend their own interests, but also provided support for the formal creation of the Brazilian Federation for Women's Progress (BFWP), a short time later in 1922. The BFWP defined its struggle in terms of the following seven objectives, spelled out in Article 3: (1) to promote the education of women and raise the level of their formal schooling; (2) to protect mothers and children; (3) to obtain legislative and practical guarantees for female labor; (4) to encourage female initiative and enterprise, and guide women in their choice of occupation; (5) to foster a sense of solidarity and cooperation among women and to stimulate their interest in questions of general and public concern; (6) to ensure the political rights granted women by the constitution, and instruct them in the intelligent exercise of those rights; and (7) to strengthen the bonds of friendship with other American countries with a view toward maintaining perpetual peace and justice in the Western hemisphere.[6]

One of the BFWP's first achievements was realized through Lutz's efforts at the Congress on Education in 1922 (at which she represented the National Museum). This was to open the day school of the Pedro II Colégio to girls. An equally important concern was the question of equality of labor opportunities, although Brazilian women already had begun their attack on this issue both in their directly practical activities and through their participation in the International Labor Conference.[7] The spirit of the times, however, required that organized struggle begin around the question of woman's suffrage. The sixth item in the BFWP's list of stated objectives, therefore, took on cardinal importance, inasmuch as political rights were seen as fundamental to any guarantees based in law, and the federation took up the struggle in various areas to achieve this end. Because of the divergent legal interpretations of the franchise provisions of the 1891 Constitution, feminists were able to argue that women's political rights were already guaranteed by the first Republic

Constitution.[8] In 1917, the opinion of Ruy Barbosa on a case concerning a woman's eligibility to compete for a post in the Ministry of Foreign Affairs referred to Barbalho's statement that "the right to assume public posts ranks among the list of political rights."[9]

Nevertheless, when the first Republican Constitution was drafted, amendments explicitly granting women the right to vote were rejected, either on the grounds that women were already included under the term *Brazilian citizen,* or because the drafters were unwilling to grant them their political rights. Consequently, during the 1920s, the opinion prevailed that woman's suffrage was unconstitutional.[10] The BFWP fomented public indignation and, gaining sympathy of several members of parliament, including Deputy Juvenal Lamartine, managed to have clauses expressly granting women the right to vote detached from the electoral reform bill and treated as independent bills. Senator Justo Chermont introduced a bill to the same effect in the Senate, but this body resisted pressures to grant women political rights, and ten years were to pass before the bill was again brought up for debate.[11]

The candidacy and subsequent election of Juvenal Lamartine to the presidency of the state of Rio Grande do Norte marked a partial victory for feminist demands. In his political platform of April 1927, Lamartine not only proclaimed his sympathy for feminism and its goals, but also stated that during his term of office, he was looking forward to women taking an active part in the choice of popular representatives and in the drafting of laws. As the Rio Grande legislative chamber was at that time trying to bring the state electoral laws into line with the reforms introduced by the 1926 Constitution, Juvenal Lamartine, then a senator, had the following proviso included in Article 77 of the General Conditions: "In the state of Rio Grande do Norte, all citizens who meet the conditions specified in this law shall have the right to vote and to run for office, without any discrimination as to sex."[12] This was approved by the outgoing state president, José Augusto Bezerra de Medeiros, and in 1927 the first woman voters registered.

There were twenty registered women voters by February of the following year, fifteen of whom voted in the April 1928 senate elections held to fill Juvenal Lamartine's seat. The Committee on Senatorial Powers, however, did not recognize woman's suffrage, given the federal laws in force at the time, and judged null and void the fifteen votes given to the sole candidate for the senate post, Dr. José Augusto Bezerra de Medeiros (although it declared him elected nonetheless).[13] The demonstrated constitutionality of the Rio Grande legislation on women's political rights had encouraged many women from several other states to solicit and secure voters' registration,[14] and the BFWP responded to the senate's refusal to accept this legislation with a Feminist Manifesto on the rights of women. (See Appendix I.)

During Juvenal Lamartine's administration, although still without political rights at the federal level, the Rio Grande do Norte women could both vote and run for office in state elections. A number of women were elected to municipal legislatures, and in the city of Lajes, Alzira Soriano roundly defeated her opponent in the race for mayor.

These events in Rio Grande do Norte, however, were not enough to guarantee women the exercise of their political rights, and the feminists redoubled their efforts to achieve their electoral aspirations. Bertha Lutz was active on many fronts. In 1922, the same year she founded the BFWP, she also founded the Professional Union, the Union of Public Employees, and the Independent Electoral League. Finally, in 1929, she founded the Female University Union.[15]

The 1930 revolution took up and continued the campaign for electoral reforms to abolish sexual discrimination. The provisional government was importuned to take seriously women's demands for suffrage which had been reaffirmed by the Second International Feminist Conference organized by the BFWP at Rio de Janeiro in 1931. While the head of the provisional government, Getúlio Vargas, was not particularly sympathetic to feminist aims,[16] he nonetheless saw to it that feminist political objectives were reflected in the electoral code set out in decree 21,076 of February 24, 1932. Nevertheless, as long as the principle of genuinely universal suffrage was not incorporated into the nation's constitution, the question would not be fully resolved. Article 108 of the 1934 Constitution, which two women helped to draft,[17] established women's suffrage once and for all.

The Code for Women, 1937

Once the suffragists' struggle was victorious, the Brazilian feminist organizations shifted focus, redoubling their efforts (in particular through their representatives on legislative bodies) to obtain female labor legislation and protection for mothers and children. Bertha Lutz proposed various legislative bills during the period 1936–1937, when she represented the Federal District in the lower chamber of the National Congress.[18] But long before that, in 1922, she had worked with the Union of Commercial Employees to obtain a reduction of the working day from thirteen to eight hours. Although by 1936–1937 the Women's Labor Code was in force (see Appendix II), female labor legislation still left much to be desired. [19] Lutz, stressing woman's economic functions, drew up a Code for Women, dealing with political, economic-social, civil-commercial, and penal issues. The Code for Women incorporated many of the precepts already enshrined in the 1934 Constitution and effectively superseded the Women's Labor Code in that it improved its terms in women's favor. Special maternity leave was increased to three months, with the woman receiving either full wages if she worked in the public sector, or two-thirds of her wages if she worked for private enterprise. These benefits also applied to cases of preventive or accidental abortion. The new code retained the provision giving a working woman the right to two half-hour periods per working day for nursing her child during the first six months after birth, and reduced from thirty to twenty the number of women employees obliging an enterprise to provide nursery facilities on the premises.

The innovations showed that, while Lutz felt that the public authorities, that is, the society as a whole, should shoulder the burden of maternity, she did not apply the same reasoning to capitalist entrepreneurs. The net effect, therefore, was that the defense of women's interests was subordinated entirely to the interests of the entrepreneurial bourgeoisie, who, by paying only one-third of the wages of women on special leaves-of-absence, were able to make up for this expense through the greater profits accruing from female labor, which was absurdly low-paid.

In addition to its provisions for the protection of maternity, always a source of discrimination against the working woman, the Code for Women also set out some uncalled-for and discriminatory protective measures for certain types of female workers. Paragraph 8, Article 34, establishes the "right of women manual laborers and counter girls to be absent from work two days per month without loss of wages," thereby making female labor even more of a special case than it already was, and damaging the cause of female labor in general by offering it excessive protection. Any protective legislation for female labor which goes beyond what is strictly necessary for maternity weakens their bargaining power by creating conditions which perpetuate and even reinforce their organized and systematic exploitation. Indeed, protection became a sore point which the unions, using even the most drastic pressure techniques at their disposal, would never succeed in eliminating.

From the feminist viewpoint, the Code for Women was a contradictory document. Notwithstanding the sincere belief that sexual equality was possible in capitalist society, the spirit that pervaded its drafting revealed a broad lack of understanding of the principles and mechanisms whereby class societies functioned, and at another level, showed an ambivalent attitude with regard to measures designed to regulate female labor. This was true right down to the question of a common working day; the Code for Women gave favored treatment to women workers, for whom it introduced the "English week" (i.e., a five-day work week) and "a rest period of ten minutes for each work period, without increase in the hours of the working day." Employers, however, purchase workers' labor power for a certain amount of time each day (then, eight hours) and their profits depend in part on their being able to actually utilize the labor power purchased. Any reduction in the working day for any social group will be a weighty factor in expelling individuals belonging to that group from the class structure. The special provisions for women manual laborers and counter girls amounted to a reduction of five hours and forty minutes per week for the first category and of nine hours and fifty-seven minutes for the latter two. Obviously, businesses operating on an individual profit basis cannot afford the excessive expenses incurred by the observance of these special conditions, and are therefore forced to make up for any reduction in women's working day through lower wages, or by hiring only men, which deprives women of jobs.

Thus, the attitudes of employers toward female labor, in themselves quite consonant with the purposes of capitalist exploitation, were given additional backing from protectionist and petty-bourgeois feminism. By making woman's status as a worker extremely vulnerable, the Code for Women, had it been put into effect, would have helped expedite women's elimination from the class structure. In this respect, the legislation supported by Brazilian feminism represented a stand in favor of the capitalist status quo, yet one that did not perceive any of the implications the class structure had for female labor, nor the contradictions between competitive society and sexual equality.

Indeed, Paragraph 1 of Article 46 of the Code for Women reads as follows: "They (i.e., married women without chattels, income or lucrative occupation, who look after the home and children) shall be assured 10 percent of the combined family income for their own expenses in recognition of the services they perform for the home." Thus, it was expected that the same wages (the husband's) should pay for the labor of two persons (husband and wife), although the man's wages do not represent all the items he produces, and the work the woman performs in the home is responsible for releasing at least some of a man's free time to engage directly in gainful employment. If 10 percent of the husband's income were allocated to his wife both would be doubly exploited: the head of the family because not only are his wages incommensurate with the total value he has created, his income corresponds only to a working day, whereas actually to that time would have to be added the time spent by his wife working in the home so that he can work as a wage laborer. And the woman is doubly exploited because the 10 percent of the husband's earnings are not adequate remuneration for the services she performs in the home, nor is it full compensation for her alienation from the dominant system of production. This approach to the problem of woman's economic dependence was clearly inferior to that of family subsidies, which at least do not use part of the husband's wages to pay for his wife's nonproductivity.

Brazilian feminists do not seem to have bothered with

either an analysis of the realities of the nation's socio-economic life or with any deeper examination of the capitalist social order. Initially taking their cues from the European feminists, and more recently from the North Americans, they continued to broaden their contacts as feminism forged onward in other countries, and then attempted to transplant to Brazilian soil the legal measures they saw adopted elsewhere. The proposal that the employee, the employer, and the government shoulder equal shares of the costs of maternity, a benefit which was to be available to all working women between the ages of eighteen and forty-five, was directly inspired by Argentine legislation. In like manner, the Lutz proposal for a National Women's Bureau that same year was modeled directly after the U.S. Department of Labor's Women's Bureau, an agency created at the end of World War I to promote legislation for equal job opportunity and equal pay in industry. After observing how the American bureau was unable to act in certain areas of social life because its functions had been limited to that of an information and counseling service, however, Lutz endowed the Brazilian bureau with executive functions as well.

The proposal for a National Women's Bureau illustrates a common tendency: as women develop an awareness of their own problems, a measure of animosity arises between those who have already succeeded in securing a niche for themselves in respected positions in society, and the vast majority of women who do not enjoy such social prestige. A tone of marked hostility was present in the discussions between Bertha Lutz and Carlota Pereira de Queiroz in the Committee for the Code of Women on the subject of creating a National Women's Bureau. Although the animosity stemmed from their divergent views, it was abundantly clear from the general course of the discussions that this was not the only factor generating heat. The two women, proceeding from equal positions of power, were in fact both vying for social approval of their practical actions. In this they saw each other, rather than men, as essential rivals.[20]

While the draft bill was still in the discussion phase, Carlota Pereira de Queiroz presented her objections. She first opposed the proposed autonomy, which would have allowed the bureau to function effectively as a ministry. Since the National Women's Bureau should be in charge "of services bearing on female labor, the household, public assistance to women, children and maternity, and social security throughout the whole of the territories of the Republic,"[21] she concluded that it already impinged upon at least three of the already existing ministries—those of education, justice, and labor—and thus not only confused its functions with those of the other three, but also betokened a real segregation of the sexes. Since education and health ranked above labor on her list of priorities, she proposed that the bureau be attached to the Ministry of Education and Health, and that it be called the Department for the Support of Women and Children. Not only would this be in consonance with the 1934 Constitution,[22] but it would represent the first step toward the ultimate creation of a Social Aid Bureau.

Carlota Pereira de Queiroz also criticized the fact that Lutz had specified that the posts in the new bureau be staffed entirely by women. Pointing out that a number of men had contributed to the feminist cause, she objected to barring men from the responsibilities Bertha Lutz had defined for the National Women's Bureau and called for strict observance of Proviso 3 of Article 121 of the 1934 Constitution, which limited the preferential job categories for women to those concerned with children, mothers, and the home.

Counterattacking, Lutz assailed minds incapable of "grasping the idea of creating *something for women alone,*" and accused them of being fainthearted and shackled to tradition. A specifically feminine institution would, in her opinion, serve as a symbol for the position women had achieved once they gained respect for their rights as human beings. She did not agree that the creation of a separate institution to deal with all aspects of a woman's life signified a segregation of the sexes; on the contrary, it was a sign of growing equality between the sexes. As for creating a Department for the Support of Women and Children, she rejected it emphatically.

> I can accept the name Department of the Home, Female Labor, Social Welfare, and Motherhood just as I accept, advocate, and demand for women the natural right to care for her child. Yet, the term *Protection for women* is totally unacceptable. . . . The need for protection is not inherent to woman's condition. The objective the feminist movement had in mind when it solicited and obtained constitutional guarantees for the home, female labor, and motherhood was not that women should become the passive beneficiaries of the state, but active collaborators in the progress of the nation. For us, woman's maternal function covers more than just its physical and clinical aspects; it has its exalted social and spiritual sides as well. In public life, woman does not merely represent a quantitative increase in the number of society's individual members; she also symbolizes the aspiration toward a transformation of values. Whereas men are interested primarily in party questions and technical and economic problems, women prefer to devote themselves to establishing and maintaining harmonious human relations and to human welfare.[23]

De Queiroz saw this position as segregationist and individualist, the expression of a feminism that was heading toward a struggle between the sexes in Brazilian society:

> It is she [Lutz] who says "I demand for women." As long as I am a member of the constitutional assembly I shall combat this individualist feminism, which would lead inexorably to a battle of the sexes. If elected by popular vote to the legislative chambers, a woman can participate in them in a cooperative spirit. To what end, then, should she insist incessantly on holding herself apart, proposing to defend only the manifest interests of her sex and no more, as if it constituted a class? I am becoming more and more convinced that in Brazil, where women have already been granted political rights, there is no place for this struggle between the sexes. What is needed is elementary cooperation, and only that, faithful to our traditions, between the representatives of the two halves of mankind.[24]

In fact, both positions were contradictory, and could not stand any test of their internal consistency. The nonfeminist, even anti-feminist, São Paulo delegate opposed the defense of feminine interests once women had gained their political rights, but only then. So long as these rights had not been won, she, too, seemed to agree that women had to struggle for sexual equality. Women's political rights were considered prerequisite to their achieving sexual equality in all other areas of social life. If, however, once women had gained the right to vote and to run for public office they would achieve social equality with men simply by working together with them, they would obviously not need the type of protection, aptly reflected in the phrase "support for women," that de Queiroz wanted to provide.

Moreover, the place assigned to female labor on de Queiroz' priority list is a clear indication that woman's path toward economic independence was not one of her concerns. In its main lines, her thinking reflects the position of persons belonging to the "traditional families": social advancement and equality with men is admitted for women of the ruling strata, but women of the underprivileged sectors are seen as creatures who require state protection because they are unable to move forward on their own. Once woman's suffrage was resolved—apparently to her genuine gratification—de Queiroz steered her thoughts and actions in a direction that was totally consistent with the class division of society and with the preservation of ruling class privilege. Her criticism of the sexual segregation implicit in the government agency of which Lutz made so much may indeed have been valid; on the other hand, even though she knew that political rights remained abstractions for women who had no access to jobs or education, she saw no reason, in the light of the protection she proposed, to provide them with the means for their emancipation. On the contrary, support offered to economically dependent women only deepened their dependency both materially and psychologically.

Finally, in her proposal to deal with the problems of women through the creation of a Social Aid Bureau (intended to supersede the Department for the Support for Women and Children), she was actually groping for some palliative to ease the misery of the underprivileged and hence to provide an outlet for the tensions generated by poverty and promiscuity. The welfare role de Queiroz cut out for the agency created to deal with women's problems thus reflected the markedly conservative cast of mind so typical of native "Paulistas."

Bertha Lutz's activities, on the other hand, reflected her identification with the ideals of the middle layers of society as regards social advancement. The whole of her efforts was directed toward promoting expansion of capitalist structures in Brazil so as to open up new paths for women toward economic emancipation, including the state's assumption of functions that could earn it the title of a social welfare state. The inconsistencies in her thinking derived from her failure to adopt a critical stand toward the structure of competitive society. She was hence unable to establish "a nuclear structure that could give rise to an administrative body within which women could go on to perfect the human and social factors concentrated in the cornerstone of society—the home," without furthering sexual segregation at the same time. Although she did not speak out against the class division of society, Lutz had no particular interest in maintaining Brazil's social structure as it was. Her reformist position, tied as it was to middle-class aspirations for social advancement, required legislation that would ensure social equality for the sexes and at the same time show women the way to emancipation. Despite the limits imposed by a line of reasoning that set a figure of 10 percent of the husband's wages as adequate recompense for a housewife, she was nevertheless able to link woman's economic emancipation with emancipation in other areas of social activity. Although she offered nothing new in women's liberation with regard to their reproductive functions, she did seek the means for women to educate themselves and to provide for their health, and strove to obtain their full civil rights, the only real means whereby women could be ensured of economic independence from men.

Lutz also brought the full force of the feminist movement to bear in opposing divestment of the civil rights of married women prescribed by the Civil Code of 1917. The preliminary draft for the creation of the Women's Code contains ideas which were not to bear fruit until the Civil Code Reform Law (4,121) of 1962, as well as some which were not realized even then. For example, Article 41 of the proposed code stated that women's legal powers should not be changed because of a change in their civil status. "Marital preemption shall persist only when mutually authorized by both parties to the marriage or by virtue of an obligation assumed by the economically dependent spouse to attach the goods of the other." Although the 1962 law incorporated this provision, a further section, stating that a married woman is not obligated to take the name of her husband, was not included.[25]

Further, Paragraph 3 of Article 45 of the Lutz proposal made it illegal for a husband to prohibit his wife from having a gainful occupation; Paragraph 2 obligated the wife, in the case where she is gainfully employed, to contribute in a measure proportional to her income to the upkeep of the home and any minor children begotten of that marriage. These two principles were incorporated into Law 4,121, thereby assigning equitable obligations to both husband and wife and abolishing the need for a wife to obtain her husband's permission to take on gainful employment as had been provided by Article 246 of the Civil Code. However, the law of August 1962 seems to leave the way open for the husband to seek a judicial decision to determine if his wife's employment was prejudicial to the family order.

Other provisions of the proposed Code for Women have not yet been enacted. Article 43, for example, bound both spouses to "fidelity, mutual aid, upkeep of the home, and the care, support, and education of the children of that union."

Although the provisions do not refer explicitly to the head of the family or to the person who is to exercise that function, the idea is implicit that both the wife and husband are to strive zealously to maintain the harmony of the family group. That is not true under the 1962 law, which, although it stipulates that the wife is to collaborate in the management of the family, recognizes the man as its head. Article 233 of that law states: "The husband is the head of the conjugal union, and exercises this function with his wife's collaboration, in the common interests of the household and the children." So although the wife is admitted to the exercise of the functions of the head of the family, she has a secondary, merely collaborative status.

Society's negative reaction to the innovations that have been proposed for the family was—and still is—of such a magnitude that in 1966 the government of Castelo Branco was forced to withdraw another Civil Code reform bill from the National Congress.[26]

Left-Wing Movements and Brazilian Feminism

There is no doubt that the Brazilian feminist movement historically has played a constructive social role. Although it was not fully successful, and even at its peak did not enjoy the active support of broad masses of women, it did perform an important service in broadening female awareness not only of women's problems, but of all the problems of the modern world whose influences, whether direct or indirect, they, too, ultimately experienced. The impetus for Brazil's feminist movement came from imported ideas which did not get much of a hearing in Brazilian society (whereas had it been fully successful, from its inception it would have created a wide gap between women's legislation and the actual social relations that kept women in an inferior status). Still, for many persons it did kindle the first spark of ambition to liberate and emancipate themselves through work, and that process was nurtured further as women began to enter areas hitherto reserved exclusively for men. In this sense, though feminism may have been "imported prematurely," its net effects were positive inasmuch as it enabled the maturation of feminist ideas to keep broadly in step with the progress made with regard to particular issues, such as work outside the home, education, and participation in social life in general. The right to vote, obtained more than a decade later than in France, did not broaden significantly women's participation in political life. This, however, is hardly surprising, considering that a low level of political engagement is generally typical of class societies.

Brazil has also been an arena for the development of women's movements organized on more political foundations.[27] Although they too struggled for women's rights, and in that sense were feminist, their range of action and their outlook set them off from the feminist movement proper, which purported to be autonomous with regard to political ideologies. The struggle of left-wing women's movements focused on political issues and the high cost of living, and was only secondarily waged in behalf of women's rights. Many groups were therefore short-lived. For example, the Woman's Union, founded in 1934, had hardly enough time to recruit a membership of any serious proportions among intellectual and working women. Part of the National Alliance for Liberation, it was declared illegal in 1935 and all its leaders arrested, some remaining in prison for over a year.

The next efforts occurred while the Brazilian government was deliberating whether to enter World War II. Working- and middle-class women organized committees throughout the country, but mainly in São Paulo and Rio de Janeiro, to collect woolens for the Brazilian soldiers at the front, to struggle against the rising cost of living and the black market, and to combat fascism and Nazism. One of the organizations which led the way in these activities was the Woman's Division of the League for National Defense. The number of organizations grew, yet lacked coordination. There was a generally felt need for an association organized on a nationwide basis to carry out these activities more efficiently, and as the war went on, the idea of a Federation of Brazilian Women took shape and matured.

When hostilities ceased, leaders of various women's and feminist organizations and a number of nonaffiliated women held a round table discussion that lasted three days. In attendance were women from the middle classes, as well as from the hills and the shanty towns, whose life experiences instilled the discussions with an air of realism and immediacy. The need for social equality between the sexes and for breaking down old prejudices about women was only one of the problems considered. The need for a nationwide organization to unify the women's movement was stressed over and over again. Some women, dismayed by the vehemence of the discussions and by the form this idea of a nationwide organization was taking, tried to put it off.[28] Some time later, however, a meeting attended by delegates from the various states was held in the Federal District and out of it emerged the Brazilian Federation of Women (BFW), in 1949. It was unable, however, to send its president as representative to the Council for the International Democratic Federation of Women convened in Moscow in that same year; her passport had been held up by the Brazilian authorities and delivered only after legal measures had been taken, by which time it was too late.[29]

The BFW struggled actively for its objectives and organized national meetings, congresses, and a Latin American Conference, which was attended by women's delegations from almost all the countries of Latin America. Branches were set up in all the states of Brazil, active ties were maintained with like-minded organizations in Brazil and abroad, and new ties established with the Trade Union's Women's Division, with which it organized a number of campaigns.

During the same period that the BFW was founded, other organizations also grew out of the women's movement. With the war ended, it picked up new momentum, especially in the large cities, to combat the hoarding of daily necessities and extortionist prices. Organizing themselves into neighborhood committees, women denounced the hoarders, and pressured the authorities to put a stop to the rampant economic abuses.

The Federal District Women's Convention, which brought together a large number of women—both members of existing organizations and free agents—gave birth to the Federal District Women's Association, which ultimately numbered about a thousand sympathizers from the various neighborhood organizations of Rio de Janeiro. The association was committed to tackling the particular problems of the neighborhoods, to the struggle for peace, and to the defense and protection of children, and it launched intensive campaigns on these issues. The neighborhood branches held weekly meetings at which they appointed representatives to the central committee meetings, where the various problems were taken up for joint discussion, and campaigns planned. The association often participated in campaigns started by other organizations, joining ranks with them, for example, in defense of the state monopoly on petroleum, of national sovereignty and freedom. The high cost of living was attacked by the Federal District Women's Association in numerous demonstrations and round table discussions and, in general, by their unremitting vigilance.

At the same time as these neighborhood committees were

immersed in their activities, a strong movement for amnesty for political prisoners was gathering force throughout the rest of the country. In Rio de Janeiro women joined forces with the National Students Union to found the Women's Committee for Amnesty, in which they played a militant role. Amnesty was won and the committee was transformed into a Women's Committee for Democracy, which over a five-year period devoted itself to the struggle for women's rights and to broadening women's cultural and political horizons—later it obtained the support of the Woman's Institute of Constructive Services, which was committed to the same program.

In the early days of Juscelino Kubitschek's government, in 1956, the Brazilian authorities suspended the activities of a number of women's organizations, among them the Federal District Women's Association and the Brazilian Federation of Women, of which it was an affiliate. Although some of these organizations undertook their own legal defense (the BFW, for example), their activities were prohibited by law six months after they were first suspended.[30]

On April 21, 1960, on the occasion of a huge public demonstration at the Brazilian Press Association in honor of the first president of the BFW, on the tenth anniversary of her death, the Women's League of the State of Guanabara was founded with the same goals as those organizations that had gone before it. During its brief existence, the league was extremely active: it founded a children's library, organized courses in tailoring and sewing and manual skills in general, in gymnastics, in reading and writing, in housekeeping, and in amateur and puppet theaters. It arranged a number of discussions on various topics, including many of a political nature, and presented puppet plays for children in working-class neighborhoods. It was the motive force behind a vigorous campaign against the high cost of living, ranging from street demonstrations to radio and television appearances to round table discussions with economists, union leaders, and students in outlying areas. Members of the Women's League showed up on a number of occasions at the plenary meetings of the national price regulatory commission (COFAP) to protest against the high price of food. Together with economists and technical workers of the Ministry of Agriculture, the league carried out studies to determine the causes of the exorbitant prices demanded for items such as milk, meat, grains, and vegetable products, and made its findings public through broad press coverage. The results of its research in hand, it presided over the organization of a movement against the rising cost of living in other states, and arranged a caravan, joined by more than 200 women, to Brasilia where it sent a petition with 100,000 signatures to President João Goulart proposing ways to combat the high cost of living.

The Women's League took active part in the campaign for amnesty for the participants in the barracks rebellion at Brasilia, and together with unions and student organizations, it demonstrated on numerous occasions against the government of Carlos Lacerda. It was forced to cease its activities when its leaders suffered persecution in the aftermath of the 1964 April revolution.

Conclusions: Feminism and the Feminist Mystique

Despite its limitations, there is no denying that petty-bourgeois feminism played an important role in competitive societies; it destroyed many prejudices, broke down longstanding taboos, and created a new perspective on women's social roles. Yet seen in terms of actual direct participation in the dominant system of production, women's situation in class society represents a step backwards compared with their participation in the economic life of other social formations, the productive forces of which were not so developed. In this respect, some of the rights won by women in competitive society betokened merely a refinement of the techniques whereby large numbers of women are marginalized from the class structure. Hence, even though the goals of feminist movements generally may have been to institute real social equality between the sexes, the actual attainment of the goals feminist organizations set for themselves has been dependent on the structural possibilities offered by the major types of social formations, in which different degrees of equality obtain and in which the field of what has been historically possible is structured differently.

In most Western countries women now enjoy the same legal rights as men, with the exception of a few concerning marriage. Feminism was not brought to a standstill by the attainment of political rights. Tactics, of course, changed considerably when women began to gain seats in parliaments. Because of the aggressive features often assumed by the movement for women's suffrage, petty-bourgeois feminism historically has been identified with that movement and nothing else. It is true that a large number of women, even organized feminist militants, considered their job done when their political rights were won, but these were by no means all the women who had fought for the vote. Local and national organizations in many countries continued to struggle for the extension of all civil rights to women and for woman's social advancement. They fought, for example, to obtain civil rights for married women, to establish equal educational opportunities for men and women, to broaden women's chances of employment, and to protect mothers and children. These national organizations formed themselves into a confederation, which took up the struggle for peace and for the destruction of Nazism and fascism, and strove to raise the level of women's personal aspirations across the world.

As formal rights became more and more universal in many industrial societies, and even in some countries less socially and economically developed, however, middle-class women found more and more ways to accommodate themselves to a situation of partial equality with men, while feminism itself, although still alive and active, was unable by word of mouth alone to maintain the spirit of struggle that had hallmarked the suffragist movement—and that spirit was essential if women were to advance further toward their goal of total liberation. Actually, these two developments were two sides of the same phenomenon. The acceptance by middle-class women in class society of a partial equality with men and petty bourgeois feminist efforts to broaden women's rights and chances of employment without overstepping the structural limitations of capitalism represented differences of degree only in a social consciousness which basically accepted the class structure. The petty-bourgeois feminist movement may have been more progressive in the sense that it was not content merely with obtaining formal rights for women, but it was never able to see the question of sexual equality in terms of a social structure that negated this equality. It strove and is today still striving to destroy the prejudices that have kept women subservient to men, and has always endeavored to get men to adopt a positive attitude toward female wage labor, altering women's own image in the process. But in so doing the petty-bourgeois feminists have neglected to promote those things which could really improve women's chances for integration into class society—in particular, they have failed to effect a change in the view taken of female labor. Work in capitalist society may be alienating and alienated, but a large number of jobs still give satisfaction. Nevertheless, the occasional chances that work offers for self-fulfillment are not so adequate to produce a balanced human personality and achieve a harmonious union between the individual and society. The need to work must derive from more than a mere shortage of money; it must become an integral component of the female personality.

If this were to happen, women would surely find incentives with men for the most diverse positions and the struggle against their discrimination on biological grounds.

This solution would certainly be a blow to the feminine mystique—for one thing it would increase the female employment rate—but it would not mean complete sexual equality, nor would it increase the irrationality of the capitalist system of production. In fact, it might even aggravate the social contradictions that are continually threatening the stability of competitive societies. Any reduction in the social differences between the sexes that would result from allowing more women into the class structure would accentuate the lines dividing the social classes; at least it would expose the class roots of a good number of personal successes and failures in the economic world. To abolish the various factors, such as the social discrimination of women, that camouflage the class structure of society would expose its basic contradictions to the view of groups that heretofore had been partially or wholly mystified by it; this also would help to sharpen the conflict between the social classes. Indeed, any reduction in the social differences between the sexes is a threat to the continued existence of capitalist society, just as a sharpening of the class struggle in general should ultimately bring about its destruction.

On the other hand, while making work into a genuinely felt need for women goes far beyond any other solution to the problem of female labor that has been proposed or applied so far, woman's unique position requires that she think about other aspects of her life as well. In competitive society a man's occupation is the focal point of his existence (as it would be for a woman if her labor were seen in a different light), but in woman's existence there are other factors which make her a worker of a fundamentally different kind (worker being defined here merely as a person doing work). A society based on the private appro-

priation of the economic surplus and subject to recurrent
crises of overproduction based on the private appropriation of the economic surplus is not able to achieve full employment, nor can it afford to absorb the entire cost of
maternity as a social expenditure; this being so, woman's
special position must perforce detract from her ability to
function as a worker in capitalist societies.

Of course, the social tensions generated by the market
under capitalism are handled in different ways in different
countries, and these therefore will tend to approach the
woman problem in different ways, depending on their position within the overall international capitalist system. In the
leading capitalist countries, which have become warfare or
welfare states, it is easier to allay the social tensions caused
by male and female employment. War places a temporary
moratorium on crises of overproduction by employing more
of the reserve workforce; capital investment at the system's
periphery siphons "international surplus value" to the system's center, where it is used to create a more just distribution of income, at the international level, and over the long
term to build a social welfare state. This is perhaps the chief
reason why women in the advanced countries enjoy more
freedoms, although these freedoms also help to increase the
alienation of all, both men and women, who receive the
benefits of the social welfare state.

Yet, it is also true that while war and underdevelopment
indirectly may bring a certain order and stability to the
economics of the leading capitalist countries, they provide
neither a total nor a sound and lasting solution to the woman
problem. It is therefore only partially correct to say that
economic growth and social development bring women more
freedoms. The capitalist nations employed female labor
rather flexibly as their economies grew, but its use may be
restricted drastically as class society enters its maturity,
since that flexibility was made possible by the social and

economic underdevelopment of vast regions at the periphery of the international capitalist system.

Whatever revolutionary content there is in petty-bourgeois feminist *praxis,* it has been put there by the efforts of the middle strata, especially the less well off, to move up socially. To do this, however, they sought merely to expand the existing social structures, and never went so far as to challenge the status quo. Thus, while petty-bourgeois feminism may always have aimed at establishing social equality between the sexes, the consciousness it represented has remained utopian in its desire for and struggle to bring about a partial transformation of society; this it believed could be done without disturbing the foundations on which it rested. As the productive forces of capitalist society developed, opportunities for women's employment grew, and large numbers of women workers entered the class structure. In this sense, petty-bourgeois feminism is not feminism at all; indeed it has helped to consolidate class society, by giving camouflage to its internal contradictions. There can be only one conclusion from this; namely, that the feminist position is wrong when conceived as autonomous.

In reality, there is no such thing as an autonomous feminism, independent of a class perspective. Petty-bourgeois feminism has always been, fundamentally and unconsciously, a feminism of the ruling class, since the "middle classes" could always be found tailing along behind one or the other of the classes opposing one another in the system of production. It thus played a broad role in sustaining the myth that competitive societies can exist without classes and without sexual biases. When analyzed carefully, petty-bourgeois feminism is found to be not a product of sharpened social tensions, but a means for allaying these tensions, both within particular nations and internationally.

As the tensions between the opposing classes abate in the countries at the center of the international capitalist system, the contradiction between underdevelopment and development becomes more acute. Here, classical feminism has had an additional role to play, in that it has helped ease the tensions between these two poles of the international capitalist system by making the woman problem contingent on an economic development that was supposed to be hindered by archaic structures rather than the interests of the highly developed countries in destroying precapitalist structures, in shaping new attitudes toward women taking work outside the home, or in restructuring patriarchal family patterns. The upshot of this has been of course that classical feminism believed that the key to the triumph of feminism lay in the recruitment of all women, independent of class. Hence, paradoxical as it may seem, feminism will only really find itself when it has become an integral part of a consciousness "capable of considering society from its central aspect, as a coherent whole, and hence capable of acting in a central way in changing reality."

Socialist feminism may not have been completely successful in its efforts to liberate women, but that petty-bourgeois feminism was even less so should be plain from the foregoing. The comparison, however, is not completely valid since socialism has yet to reach its maturity. The maturing process undergone by these two types of society must be viewed in the light of the premises on which the two systems are based: While capitalism moved toward its maturity (represented by its monopoly phase) along a path of privatization and concentration of property, the path of socialism was toward collectivized property. Complete sexual equality, therefore, may very well become a reality in socialist society as the socio-economic relations in that society mature. On the other hand, in the case of capitalist society, as its productive forces mature, female employment stagnates at the same level or even declines. The degree of actual utilization of female labor during the periods of growth and the mature phase of economies based on private enterprise; the ebbs and flows in female employment and the arguments advanced in justification of these phenomena; and the level of consciousness which women and men attain of this process and the forms which it takes in each particular society will vary, however, within the limits we have set down, as a function of specific historical conditions in which the capitalist system of production evolves in each case. Expressed in other terms, the analysis of each particular social formation will show how the general properties of that system are expressed in each set of concrete historical circumstances.

In its general contours, the analysis of feminism given in the first part of this work is equally valid for Brazilian feminism. A feminism which is concerned exclusively or primarily with the immediate problems of women, and outwardly independent of political ideologies, is essentially a product of a mode of thought with the following features:

1. It is *utopian,* if it really believes that a deep-going transformation of the roles and social standing of women in competitive societies is possible without at the same time altering the foundations on which social life is built. In this case, feminist consciousness is unconsciously compromised with the capitalist status quo.

2. It is *in conscious league with the competitive social order* if, in its struggle for total social equality between the sexes, it nevertheless accepts a partial equality which is fully compatible with the competitive order, even in countries where differences between men and women have been abolished in the formal legal sense, yet *de facto* inequalities still exist.

However forward-looking the progressive side of petty-bourgeois feminism may be, it is unable to exceed the bounds of its fealty, conscious or unconscious, to the social order of a capitalist economy. In this respect it is just as little a "pure" feminism—despite the claims of its apologists—as are "socialist feminist" movements or women's movements. Whatever the level of consciousness feminism is able to achieve with regard to women's problems, the problems themselves are always defined in the terms of a particular social order, and any possible solutions to these problems, short-term or long-term, must be gotten from within this order.

Socialist feminism, even in its most practical, nontheoretical forms, such as exist in Brazil, represents a much fuller consciousness than its petty-bourgeois counterpart. Since it proceeds from a vantage point that is highly critical of the capitalist status quo, it has been able to see the problems of women as merely one aspect of a social totality in which a number of other determining factors are also operative, and to discern among the latter those which call for immediate attention. In Brazil, however, left-wing feminism has almost always been clandestine, camouflaged under labels that would be palatable to the society at large. While this enabled it to penetrate into areas inaccessible by any other means, it made organizing extremely slow, even atomized, because it lacked continuity. The broader national political movement with which it linked up always lacked a solidly based organization deriving its intellectual sustenance from a dynamic analysis of Brazilian realities, for which it substituted ready-made, and hence ineffective, formulae. Indeed, this was typical of all women's organizations, even those which, like the BFW, avoided decision-making from the top down at all costs.[31] The negative reaction of capitalist societies to socialist movements, whether or not they were engaged in the struggle for women's rights, set their main thrust against just that lack of a broad popular base, which had been so much a fact of life in Brazil. However, even if left-wing feminist organizations in Brazil had taken care to avoid this separation between leadership and base, they would still have suffered from the organizational vices of the broader political movement of which they were a part. This certainly does not explain all the flaws and failures in their efforts to politicize women, but it unquestionably has been a weighty factor in holding back women's awareness.

Another quite serious criticism of these women's organizations as both left-wing and feminist groupings is that they elected to give the defense of women's civil rights priority over the need for women to receive training for remunerative employment. This shows a negligence, if not ignorance, of the potential embodied in female labor outside the home for shaping an independent and critical awareness in women. Even more than this, it indicates an indifference to the possibilities offered women by a position in the class structure and by the social contacts and economic independence ensuing from that position.

Although feminism in general has never penetrated very deeply into Brazilian society, it has left an indelible mark on the personal histories of many urban women over two generations, and gained many civil rights. True, these rights have never, even today, had more than an abstract existence for a vast segment of the nation's female population; but they will always represent possibilities, to be used at any moment to facilitate women's entry into certain areas of social life by removing the legal obstacles in their way. The conquest of political and civil rights for women, however, also entailed certain reactions on the part of society, among which it is necessary to distinguish those which indicated a genuine acceptance of the new female roles, and those we might call "prejudicial refinements," that is, the intelligent use of social techniques to conceal prejudices against women.

The denial of civil and political rights to women belongs to a specific phase in the development of competitive society. In some countries, the concession of such rights may not fit the realities of everyday life, although they may be compatible with the general framework of ideas sustained by capitalist society as a whole. Thus, the hegemonic center determines the "level of reality" in the subsystems,[32] and sometimes actually widens the gap between ideas and the actual state of things, or between the juridical structure of a nation and the social relations that have evolved within it. Aside from the serious discrepancies it creates between the various levels of social phenomena,[33] this determination of the "level of reality" from without in the dependent subsystems also gives rise to incongruities between different domains of human behavior. For example, it heightens the ambiguity of female roles, and thereby increases women's ambivalence toward them. This ambivalence, in turn, sustains and refuels mystificatory processes, and makes it difficult for women to distinguish functions they have the qualifications to fulfill, and the limits beyond which their conduct would be considered deviant. Throughout their lives, then, women assume an attitude lacking the aggressiveness required by competitive society, which has come to see them as passive creatures. This characterization becomes a self-fulfilling prophecy that makes it difficult for women to develop a critical awareness.

As it is consciously or unconsciously compromised with the established order of class society, petty bourgeois feminism is not capable of effecting a total mystification of feminine consciousness. It can find no other way to proceed than to attribute to the female gender a degree of autonomy it does not possess. Socialist feminism does provide a richer perspective from which to analyze the problems of women in competitive societies, but its simplifications leave much to be desired. Theoretically—and practically, perhaps for the same reason—it has failed to come up with any completely satisfactory solution to the feminine question. That is why the "feminine mystique" can still operate even in societies in which many women have become aware of their problems. Although this consciousness is precarious and simplistic in its petty-bourgeois form, in its socialist form it obliges class society to refine the processes by which it mystifies women. Once again, the workings of the hegemonic center of world capitalism are in evidence. The export of science, technology, and the techniques of social engineering to the periphery makes available ways and means to reelaborate and refine the prejudices and preconceptions that discriminate socially against the female population. Although science and technology did not originate at the periphery of world capitalism, they are used there with the object of establishing a level of reality compatible with the goals of the system at large. Thus although some of its features may vary from country to country depending on tradition, the feminine mystique has universal features, so that it may be ascribed to *class society* as a structural type. It is valid, therefore, to say that mystificatory processes, whatever their origin, have no nationality insofar as they are used rationally, with the end of maintaining and justifying a social order whose particular features may vary from one nation to another, yet have the same foundations in all cases—namely, class division. Considering the showcase effect exercised by the dominant capitalist nations, social engineering techniques evolved in the economically and socially more advanced countries have all the basic requirements needed to make them universally applicable. In its universal aspect, the feminine mystique represents a refined social technique which in underdeveloped countries assumes exaggerated features as a result of the impressively effective ability of tradition to control the pace of change of women's social roles. On the other hand, however, the mystique serves as a foundation, and a substantively rational one, for traditional techniques of controlling the evolution of feminist consciousness.

Appendix I:
Feminist Manifesto.
Brazilian Federation for
Women's Progress, 1928

The following document is contained in *Educação* 3, no. 2 (May 1928), published in São Paulo.

1. Women like men are born free and independent members of the human race, endowed with equal faculties and called on equally to exercise without impediments their individual rights and duties.

2. The sexes are mutually dependent, and owe each other their respective cooperation. The denial of the rights of one must necessarily be detrimental to the other, and hence to the nation.

3. In all countries and epochs, laws, prejudices, and customs aimed at restricting women, limiting their education, impeding the development of their natural aptitudes, and subordinating their individuality to the judgment of another person, were based on false theories, which in modern life cause broad social instability.

4. Autonomy is a fundamental right of every adult individual; the denial of this right to women is a social, legal, and economic injustice which has negative repercussions on the life of the community and holds back general progress.

5. Nations which oblige their female citizens to pay taxes and to obey the law without granting to them, as to their male

citizens, the right to participate in the making of those laws, or in the voting for those taxes, are exercising a tyranny which is incompatible with governments founded on justice.

6. Whereas the vote is the only legitimate means for defending these rights of life and liberty, proclaimed inalienable by the Declaration of Independence of the American Democracies, and today recognized by all the civilized nations of the earth, women shall have the right of suffrage.

Appendix II.
The Women's Labor Code, May 17, 1932

Following are excerpts from the Women's Labor Code, taken from *Consolidação das Leis de Assistência e Proteção a Menores e Mulheres,* Brasil Editôra, n.d.

Article 7. In all industrial and commercial establishments, public and private, it is prohibited for a pregnant woman to work during the four-week period prior to childbirth and for four weeks afterward.

§4 The four-week periods prior to and following childbirth may each be extended by up to two weeks in exceptional cases if certified by a physician.

Article 9. Any woman excused from her job pursuant to the provisions of Article 7 and attendant paragraphs shall have the right to one-half her normal wages, defined as the average for the six foregoing months, as well as the right to return to her original job.

Article 10. In the case of miscarriage, subject to corroboration, a woman shall be allowed a rest of two weeks and shall have the right to receive during this period financial support as provided in the preceding article, as well as the right to return to her original job.

Article 13. Employers shall be forbidden to dismiss a

pregnant woman on grounds of her pregnancy alone and without giving good reason for such dismissal.

Article 14. The financial assistance provided for in Articles 7, 9, and 10 shall be disbursed from funds created by the Institute of Social Security or, where these are wanting, by the employer.

PART III

The Feminine Mystique and the Scientific Era

INTRODUCTION

Rationality
and Irrationality

The increasing rationalization of the modern world is often viewed as if it signified no more than the replacement of old, traditional modes of conduct, basically irrational, by others that are in substance rational—that is, arrived at through the use of reason. Such an interpretation, however, breaks down under even the most superficial examination. Rationalization, which molds so much of life in modern society, has much more to do with functional rationality, which refers to behavior directed toward achieving a predefined goal, independently of whether that goal itself is rational. In this sense, even acts that bear the stamp of tradition may be functionally rational if they are situated within, and discharge functions as part of, a larger context of actions organized to attain a specific, preselected goal. Social techniques may be rational or irrational in substance, but functionally they are always rational inasmuch as their purpose is to shape human behavior to achieve some specific end. If the rationalization of modern life has such a general and abstract quality about it, it is in its functional, not its substantive, aspect that this is true. It is this which gives the appearance of rationality to the manipulation of large masses of humanity and to the re-elaboration of tradition in pursuit of some specified end.

The scientific method is usually rational in substance, as well as functionally, in both its pure and applied forms. The scientist makes use of reason to arrive at some objective, which may be determined by the needs of technology at the time, or by the international power structure; or it may merely be the desire for knowledge. Science is still suscep-tible to error; its degree of functional rationality will, when it comes to practical application, depend on the use made of its discoveries and inventions. Since this use, or social fate, is normally not determined by scientists, in its practical appli-cation science may find itself divested of the constructive role it has played as an instrument of human control—again in a substantive sense—over nature. Science makes mistakes, and has had its share of fallacies; indeed, these are an integral part of its growth and perfection. Aside from that, scientific knowledge can also be made to serve ends that are totally alien, and even contradictory to, any goal scientists them-selves set or even think possible. Thus, science is a tool, rational in substance, that may be used rationally, in the functional sense, to attain substantively irrational ends. Science can be used to achieve such ends at essentially three junctures: (1) when scientific knowledge is held valid because it is not impugned by empirical facts or other findings; (2) when its conclusions are still unconfirmed, in broad need of testing, and constitute no more than working hypotheses; and (3) when its discoveries and inventions are reinterpreted and distorted by society.

Although the natural sciences, too, are susceptible to being used to attain irrational ends, at any rate in the first two ways mentioned above, the social sciences are by their very nature much more vulnerable to such use, as history, particu-larly World War II, has amply borne out. The physical world yields to human control only under conditions in which the techniques used to this end are grounded in principles that adequately reflect its structure and movement. Social life, on the other hand, is so malleable that human behavior may be shaped in many different ways even when the consequences constitute a mutilation of the human body or person. This being the case, it is evident that the social sciences are much more susceptible to being used to attain substantively irrational ends. Moreover, their discoveries are difficult to test, and this widens the range of their possible uses, even where social reinterpretations have subjected them to profound distortion. The human sciences constitute a highly effective instrument for enhancing the functional rationality of social processes, independently of their ends, by giving this rationality a scientific foundation, so dear to modern societies. They have contributed immeasurably to processes of mystification, and to the feminine mystique in particular. Indeed, the feminine mystique has very often drawn nourishment from the hypotheses and fallacies of science, and from discoveries transfigured by social reinterpretation.

Perhaps no other scientific theory has so much influenced the ideas of the past quarter century as psychoanalysis: contemporary literature, art, philosophy, psychiatry, psychology, sociology, and anthropology all bear its indelible imprint. The educational sciences, and even the judgments of common sense, are steeped in psychoanalytic concepts. The term *rationalization,* for example, has become so thoroughly a part of everyday speech that many of our judgments about others now make allowance for the possibility that a person may, consciously or unconsciously, substitute reasons which are socially acceptable for the real motives for his or her actions. Because the value of a knowledge of origins is basic to human existence, not only in archaic societies but in socialized civilized societies as well, it is worth an examination—historical as well as conceptual—of psychoanalytic theory and the role it has played in capitalist society.

CHAPTER 10

Psychoanalytic Theory and the Feminine Mystique

Freudian Theory

A desire to know the origin of things has been a hallmark of Western society. Indeed, the eighteenth and nineteenth centuries abounded with attempts to explain the origin of the universe, life, the human species, society, religion, language, and other human institutions. In the twentieth century, the continuing inquiry into origins experienced a major breakthrough in one of the human sciences. Psychoanalysis shifted the focus of this inquiry from the history of society to the life histories of individuals. It sought the source of maladjustment and pathology in the primary constituents of an individual's life. Early childhood acquired key importance because it was found that during this period occur the events which explain the structure of personality. This meant, moreover, that an individual's subjective childhood experiences could be manipulated, revived, or at least recalled as part of a therapeutic process aimed at reshaping the individual's personality.

But psychoanalytic theory and psychoanalysis radically altered our way of looking at human life in another respect as well. Its focus on, and attempts to explain, problems that were directly or indirectly sexual, and its insistence on the importance of sexual factors in the shaping of the human personality, broke new ground for science; for the first time, matters which society had traditionally considered taboo became subject to scientific scrutiny. The resistance psychoanalysis encountered in both academic quarters and society at large attests to its profoundly innovative, even revolutionary, quality.

Yet paradoxically, although Freud's theory did so much to revolutionize our approach to sexual questions, even to the point of working deep changes in social mores, it also did its part to keep woman enshrouded in myths, whose continued existence broadly circumscribed the transformation of women's social roles. Freud's explanation of woman's psychological traits made the same mistake as the myths constructed on biological foundations—namely, that anatomy is destiny. Perhaps the anatomical explanation put forward by Freudian psychoanalytic theory should be viewed simply as an attempt to construct a "culture-free" theory; but because it made constitutional factors responsible for the qualities assumed by the female personality at a particular period of history, it in effect took a system of values which had meaning only within a specific historical context and made them into absolutes by rooting them in the concrete facts of biology. That is why orthodox psychoanalysis has had such a poor record with regard to woman's social adjustment in a society which needs her collaboration.

According to Freudian theory, although masculine and feminine dispositions are discernible in childhood, "with the arrival of puberty, changes set in which are destined to give infantile sexual life its final, normal shape."[1] The essential lack of sexual difference in childhood derives from the coincidence of libidinal development in the two sexes and the fact that, for both girl and boy, the mother is the first love object. With the advent of puberty, while the boy's leading erotogenic zone and his love object remain the same, the girl must change both: her erotogenic zone shifts from the clitoris to the vagina, and her father replaces her mother.

The transformations of puberty, which Freud saw as the key to certain feminine neuroses, are compounded by the castration complex. For a boy it takes a quite positive form, that is, he fears being deprived of something he already possesses. For the girl, however, castration anxiety is a negative experience; it signifies an absence. She feels seriously wronged, and falls victim to penis envy "which will leave ineradicable traces on [her] development and the formation of [her] character and which will not be surmounted in even the most favorable cases without a severe expenditure of psychic energy."[2]

The lack of a penis, the cause of the castration complex and woman's envy, is basic to Freud's theory, the germ out of which he developed all his later ideas about woman's nature. The absence of a penis is seen as a basic defect, and as such determined, according to Freud, woman's emotions, attitudes, interests, and desires. Anatomy, then, is the basic determinant of woman's behavior; therein also lies the reason for her incapacity to form a superego able "to attain the strength and independence which give it its cultural significance."[3] It is responsible, too, for her denial of her sex, her defiantly rebellious exaggeration of her infantile masculinity, her clinging to her clitoral activity, her vanity, her need to be loved more than to love, her lesser capacity for intellectual achievement, her desire for independence, etc.—in short, for all the so-called feminine personality traits which function as a compensation for her original anatomical defect.[4]

Freud also invoked penis envy to explain female inventions whose origins were more obviously social. Thus, the techniques of plaiting and weaving were supposed to have been invented by woman, who made clothes to cover her defect, just as nature concealed her genitals with pubic hair.[5]

Three possible lines of development start from this anatomical defect:

> One leads to sexual inhibition or to neurosis, the second to
> change of character in the sense of a masculinity complex, the
> third, finally, to normal femininity. . . . This means, therefore,
> that as a result of the discovery of women's lack of a penis
> [women] are debased in value for girls just as they are for boys
> and later perhaps for men.[6]

In the boy the castration complex and Oedipus complex
are in opposition; but the former destroys the latter, and the
boy can free himself from his erotic identification with his
mother, which results in the formation of a severe superego,
aimed at perfection. "What happens with a girl is almost the
opposite. The castration complex prepares for the Oedipus
complex instead of destroying it."[7] The absence of a penis,
for which she blames her mother, drives her from her attach-
ment to the latter into taking her father as a love object.
Since her castration is a consummate fact, she has no motive
leading her to surmount the Oedipus complex. "Girls remain
in it for an indeterminate length of time; they demolish it
late and, even so, incompletely."[8] This is why women have
less capacity for sublimation, and hence are unable to aspire
to perfection.

It follows, then, that puberty is a phase of libidinal intensi-
fication for the boy, whereas for the girl it involves growing
repressions. Instead of the libido expanding, libidinal energy
becomes compressed, as it were, in the girl, predisposing her
to neuroses, and hysteria becomes for her a natural illness.
Because female development consumes so much energy,
women are deprived of the amount needed for their full
psychological development.

> A man about thirty strikes us as a youthful, somewhat unformed
> individual, whom we expect to make powerful use of the possi-
> bilities for development opened up to him by analysis. A woman
> of the same age, however, often frightens us by her psychical

rigidity and unchangeability. Her libido has taken up final positions and seems incapable of exchanging them for others. There are no paths open to further development; it is as though the whole process had already run its course and remains thenceforward insusceptible to influence—as though, indeed, the difficult development to femininity had exhausted the possibilities of the person concerned.[9]

Because of his failure to consider the extent of cultural influence on the working of the individual personality, assuming what he took to be general in his own culture to be universal, Freud did not see that given the social conditions under which woman lived in his time, she had no choice but to assume "final positions" before the age of thirty or never to assume them at all. Marriage, the most highly valued "career" for women was situated before the age of thirty. When a range of choice is reduced to one, it is not surprising that the person who must submit to this choice should display the rigidity and unchangeability Freud observed in his patients. His mistake lay in his not seeing the relationship between female character traits and the social conditions under which women then had to live, rather regarding them as fixed in woman's biology. Many years were yet to pass before some societies were to celebrate the mature woman as a triumph of modern life over nature.[10] With this triumph and the sociocultural changes it brought with it, the distance between the psychological characteristics of today's woman and those of the women Freud observed grows greater with each passing day.

Freud compounded the myth of female servitude (which thrives even today, fed especially by popular love-story literature) with the myth of passivity. In associating active with masculine and passive with feminine, Freudian theory gave scientific currency to an age-old myth, and in this way facilitated its acceptance. The myth of feminine passivity became truly a self-fulfilling prophecy. Women came to believe that passivity was a trait inherent in the female personality, and were supported in this belief by the scientific literature of the day, popularized and reelaborated by popular romance. A woman thus began to define herself as a passive creature and reinforce this self-image through her overt behavior. An assertion that at most had been no more than a scientific hypothesis became for her a supreme truth, although psychoanalysis was later to reject the hypothesis. As R. K. Merton says: "Creative prediction begins by a false definition of the situation, which provokes a new behavior which makes the conception, false to begin with, true." [11]

Freud carried his equation of active with masculine and passive with feminine to its ultimate conclusion: if libido is force, energy, and hence activity, how could it exist in women? Through his theory of bisexuality he showed how woman, because she possesses libido, does, after all, have a little bit of man in her, but that to speak about a "feminine libido" is without any justification.[12] While conceding woman a certain amount of activity (masculinity) with the one hand, Freud takes it back again with the other:

> If . . . we are inclined to describe it [the libido] as masculine we must not forget that it also covers trends with a passive aim . . . [It] is our impression that more constraint has been applied to the libido when it is pressed into the service of the feminine function and that—to speak teleologically—nature takes less careful account of its demands than in the case of masculinity.[13]

For Freud, the aim of biology, accomplished in the sexual act, was entrusted to the aggressiveness of men—independent of women. In theory, therefore, it follows that woman gains the opportunity to be a positive creature through her libidinal capacity for activity. In practical terms, however this opportunity is never realized, since feminine goals are passive goals, and energy at the service of passivity is transformed into its opposite: inaction.

"Universal woman," like "universal man," is a mental

construct with no counterpart in the real world. What exists are human beings, determined by the concrete sociohistorical situation in which they live, and it is in this and only this context that they are to be observed and explained. "A person's very features," observed Simmel, "depend on the milieu within which he is accustomed to move."[14]

Freud and Social Theory

Although to distinguish the normal from the neurotic personality[15] on the basis of sociological criteria alone is no simple task, there is no other way to make this distinction without ascribing an absolute status to factors that are essentially cultural and therefore relative, that is, relative to a structurally specific type of society. In his disregard of the sociological perspective, Freud introduced into the discipline he founded the bias which the social sciences could not accept. The Freudian method was diametrically opposed to the methods of the social sciences, and even contradicted their findings and conclusions. Instead of attributing mental phenomena to the social factors that determined them, as is done, at least, in one tradition of sociology, Freud proceeded in the opposite direction and derived social phenomena from psychological factors, and the latter, in turn, from biological factors, completely reversing the causal sequence. As Florestan Fernandes has shown so well, when a people's pattern of social stability is destroyed, the process has disintegrating effects, both physiologically and psychologically, on individuals.[16] Of course, one must not make the opposite mistake and adopt sociological criteria as the only true ones, totally dismissing approaches which give priority to biological and psychological factors. These are valuable in that they help us to keep sight of the biopsychological underpinnings of social relations. Yet by themselves they are inadequate, because by failing to consider the opposite route of enquiry, beginning with the social, they lose sight of the true breadth of human malleability. The disastrous effects of contact between peoples who are culturally too different from one another to permit the more backward to adapt quickly to the requirements of the situation created by that contact are irrefutable testimony to the fact that "among human beings, the purely social sphere is an autonomous source of dynamic needs which have a deep and far-ranging formative influence on almost all the basic biological and psychological processes."[17]

The autonomy which Freudian theory ascribes to biological factors has negative consequences in another respect. Not only did Freud's biological bias deprive his generalizations of universal validity, but it reduced their applicability even for the society in which his patients lived. Freud failed to see that participation in the dominant culture varied from individual to individual. Not only did he not see that social norms varied according to the culture and the times, he also did not perceive the relation between behavioral patterns and the different social positions or roles defined by the specific way a social system is structured. Cultural relativism does not just apply to whole societies; it is equally relevant to the process of differentiation that takes place within social systems. The social norms of one class need not govern the behavior of another. Thus even if we accept the Durkheimian definition of normal,[18] and say that the neuroses observed by Freud in the European woman at the end of the nineteenth century and beginning of the twentieth were typical of societies similar to that of Austria of that time and in analogous stages of development, the conclusions may still not be generalized. Freud's neurotic patients were members of the bourgeoisie and hence not representative of the society as a whole. What Freud observed in them could not be found in the behavior of the women of the European proletariat of that epoch.

In other words, social classes participate in different cultural spheres, and in the same spheres at different levels. The same can be said for the sexes. Even in societies where differentiation is minimal, and sex does not function as a factor of social stratification, the sexual division of labor alone imposes different behavioral standards on men and women. Insofar as the mental life of human beings is directly linked to the conditions of their social existence, it is implausible that the insights of any school of psychology, and Freudian theory in particular, should have discovered any innate universal dispositions of human nature.

Nevertheless, we must bear in mind the cultural context in which Freud lived when he laid the foundations of his psychoanalytic theory. The academic tradition both tacitly and explicitly sanctioned the prevailing sexual taboos, yet at the same time viewed the manifestations of human mental and social life as stemming from biological characteristics proper to human beings in general. In this respect Freudian theory merely consolidated a viewpoint that had already ample support in European social life of the epoch. The therapeutic techniques Freud developed offered a wide range of possibilities for remolding the male personality; for women, however, their therapeutic value was limited by the "inherent defects" of the female anatomy.

Thus the advent of Freudian psychoanalysis did little to alter woman's condition. On the contrary, it fueled the concept of woman as unformed, passive, and rigid in countries where Freud's ideas found widest acceptance. North American women, who avidly and uncritically swallowed the hypotheses of psychoanalytic theory, were among the victims.[19] Adorned with all the refinements the techniques of mass communication and advertising would permit, these visions of woman, conceptualized by Friedan as the "feminine mystique," became for modern women a more redoubtable foe than all the prejudices of past generations. Above all, the mystique derived particular force from the fact that it was disseminated by psychologists, educators, and others in the human sciences, thought to be uncompromising enemies of prejudice and superstition. Indeed, the social sciences propagated the myth of biological determination of the female and gave it the status of scientific truth. Initially no more than a rough hypothesis advanced to shed some light on psychological phenomena, and subject to subsequent verification, it was transformed by the social process into eternal truth. Thus, the myth of feminine passivity, bearing the halo of scientific authenticity, ended up nullifying or at least drastically diminishing the potential therapeutic value of psychoanalytic techniques for modern women.

In the United States, many women who rejected or left gainful employment to become housewives, deprived henceforth of the opportunity to develop their capacities as human beings and, on that account, excellent prey to nervous disorders, found themselves suffering from what Friedan called an "undefinable malaise," of which they tried to cure themselves through the use of techniques elaborated by the same psychological school that helped to keep them in the home.

Yet this was by no means a universal development. The feminine mystique did not touch all strata of society to the same degree nor in the same way, and some it did not reach at all. While many more educated and more cultured women escaped its effects, large numbers of working women were forced by economic necessity to disregard its dictates. A job meant more than just a wage: it also placed one in a market where goods and services were relatively freely available. Modern woman challenges the feminine mystique and increasingly undermines its tenability in the very process of her daily activities (whether she does this consciously or unconsciously is not the question).

But these false notions are at the same time periodically reinforced. Myths about women and those about blacks may differ in content (above all in the arguments employed to sustain them), yet their function is essentially the same: to eliminate potential competitors, especially in activities conferring the highest social prestige. In this respect, the feminine mystique is truly a functional necessity of class society, but this is saying no more than that the stratification factor par excellence in class society is sex. There is no apparent way, either in theory or in practice, to equate social class, which is fundamentally an economic category, with the category of sex. Women are not an inferior, and men a superior, social class; both sexes experience the diverse class situations to which differentiation within a class gives rise. But men and women do not always participate in a social class in the same way. Whereas a working man participates directly in his class by selling his labor (so that, it should be added, his emotional stability and social adjustment depend on his being gainfully employed), women will most often participate in their social class by extension, and will reflect the economic status of their husbands or fathers. The capitalist system does not require paid female labor as a permanent element, and thus has not made work an essential ingredient of the ideal female personality, that of wife and mother. Although a growing number of women are acquiring vocational skills, such training is almost always acquired as personal insurance against the uncertain future that always looms in competitive societies. Work, as a means of professional self-fulfillment through an occupation, as something that contributes to the enrichment of the human personality, and even as a means of social adaptation to conditions of varying economic uncertainty, has value neither for women nor for the society at large so long as it ascribes to its female members only quite defined social roles. For women, a job is a socially acceptable means to cope with a difficult economic situation, or to increase the family income and take some of the strain off the family budget, or to achieve a higher standard of living, including even a certain degree of conspicuous consumption. Generally speaking, female labor may be viewed as a means to maintain the economic status of the family unit or to give it a boost along its way up the social ladder.

Why, then, should this be so? The exaltation of woman's role as dedicated mother and spouse, the channeling of women into jobs that men either abandoned or had never laid claim to in the first place, the exploitation of woman's purported "help-thy-neighbor" calling, and other devices are all so many ways by which society ensures its continued existence. Motivational mechanisms evolved by the social system operate to induce change in individuals (learning) or to counteract tendencies for change (processes of defense and adjustment). They enable the social actors to choose how they will fulfill the various roles they must assume from among the alternatives offered by the social system; thus demonstrating how socialization abets the assimilation of cultural values. But both personality and the social system contain incentives which produce divergent behavior. When motivating processes fail to guide the individual along pre-scribed ways, the system applies mechanisms of social control to eliminate deviant behavior. These mechanisms themselves are no more than the motivational processes of one or more actors involved in the situation.

The Feminine Mystique as a Social Control Myth

There is one form of social control of particular significance for female behavior: myths. In competitive societies feminine myths fulfill precise functions, and in this respect are a means, perhaps one of the simplest, for keeping women's behavior within certain bounds and for encouraging them to adhere to the behavioral patterns required by the system which these myths serve to legitimate. The following functions are served by feminine myths in class society: (1) to minimize the intermeshing of the kinship system with the occupational system, that is, to ensure that the two systems come together only in the head of the family; (2) to mystify woman about her roles as spouse and mother, so that she derives a sense of fulfillment from these roles; (3) to place obstacles in the way of professional ambitions, so as to keep women at a disadvantage in competition with men; (4) to glorify occupations that are not contested by men, either because they are not paid well or because they do not confer sufficient prestige; (5) to keep women's aspirations at a low level so as not to generate tensions strong enough to force a change in existing structures; and (6) to prevent the mechanisms of competition from finding their way into the family unit, not just because this would bring about radical changes in the family structure, but also because competition cannot be expanded beyond certain limits without seriously endangering the psychological stability of individuals.

Paradoxical as it may seem, the feminine mystique serves highly integrating functions in competitive societies which rely on science and technology. The mere fact that it has its strongest impact on married women, especially those with children, illuminates the way in which it works to protect the family from changes that would render it incompatible with the class structure. It is not just on this broad scale, however, that the integrative effects of the feminine mystique operate; they also operate at the level of personal adjustment. Thus the woman whose personality most nearly approximates the ideal evolved by Western culture—the woman who assumes, with the socially requisite degree of dedication, her role of spouse and mother—combines in her person all the conditions that make for a thorough adjustment to the family structure and to society in general. Obviously, this integration is achieved only if women are not compelled to enter the occupational structure.

In class society, a woman's social integration is directly dependent on how well she is able to balance off her several roles, at work and in the family. It is no exaggeration to say that a woman's participation in other structures is broadly and profoundly determined by her civil status, that the road to her integration into society at large depends on it. If this is so, it is certainly not valid to say that there is only one path to successful female social adjustment, that dictated by biology. Sex and social class together set the bounds for socially approved female behavior for each period of a woman's life. Although the feminine mystique affects most strongly married women (especially those with small children), it does not draw its legitimation solely from the specifically female condition of mother. When Freudian psychoanalysis reinforced the feminine mystique by means of biology, it deprived that concept of the fine distinctions needed to promote an integrated female personality, and to effect the coordination of the various particular structures of the social system into a harmonious whole. In reality, therefore, the feminine mystique, suckled by orthodox psychoanalysis, was unable to cope adequately with problems whose consequences extended to various levels. The foundations on which the feminine mystique is built offer no advantages over the mechanisms of social control that modern societies are capable of developing. Because orthodox psychoanalysis was unmindful of the relativity of cultures and of the internal differentiation of female roles within societies it was in many respects out of tune with the real needs of a competitive social system and, as a social technique, its lean content and inflexibility of practical application rendered it ill-suited for coping with the problem in any adequate way.

Perhaps the wide acceptance of the feminine mystique can

be explained by the relative inability of the social system to develop and perfect rational techniques of social control capable of reducing deviant behavior and thereby facilitate integration among the different structures. Yet it should be borne in mind that a perceptible amount of such behavior and the degree of tension it produces may well be a necessary component of the equilibrium class society has evolved. In fact, the effectiveness as means of social control may be the only satisfactory explanation for the degree of social acceptance and persistence in urban industrial societies of theories which, based on Freudian premises, dismiss the discoveries of the social sciences. At any rate, this seems to be the most fruitful assumption on which to begin an analysis of the persistence of theories about women created in a period that provided no substantiating evidence either in women's behavior or in the knowledge already acquired concerning the social conditioning of the "feminine personality." How else could one explain the appearance and social acceptance of Helene Deutsch's book on feminine psychology, published in 1944? Twice in this century, vast numbers of women have stepped into jobs during wartime that had been considered essentially for men, and this was just the situation that existed at the time Deutsch's book appeared. Neither then nor now have they run the risk of becoming masculine as a consequence. Femininity, like masculinity, is a meaningful concept only within the context of a social structure, the particular way it is organized, and the particular phase of development it represents. War may oblige societies to define its equilibrium in new terms, but this does not warrant Deutsch's assertion that the price women pay for achievements in domains traditionally reserved for men is their femininity. Women simply perform the roles the system demands at a particular moment.

The lack of sociological perspective led Helene Deutsch to make statements such as the following:

We often see an intellectual girl who is ambitious, pedantically conscientious, and neurotically dutiful, strengthening these qualities in adolescence and making of them an armor to protect herself from the development of feminine qualities. Such a girl seems to me the most miserable feminine type in existence, for, exactly like her rustic twin sister Dulcinea, she is often an excellent but usually an incomplete man. She too is disturbed by motherhood, not by emotional but by real maturity. In her effort to make life perfect she achieves motherhood, and her particularly dutiful devotion to her children often comes into real conflict with her aspirations. Such women are all intellect or all strength, and then subjective experience, emotional development, and intuition are completely lost. They will always do their work thoroughly but will never practice anything original stemming from the treasure of intuition, the source of woman's genius.

Only exceptionally talented girls can carry a surplus of intellect without injuring their affective lives, for woman's intellect, her capacity for objectively understanding life, thrives at the expense of her subjective, emotional qualities. Modern education unfortunately neglects this truth, and girls are very often intellectually overburdened. Sports are not an adequate substitute for deep affective experiences, nor do amusements and artistic enjoyment answer the need for real relaxation and communion with oneself.[20]

Deutsch's argument is based on premises that the social sciences had already demonstrated to be false. To take just one example, Margaret Mead's anthropological studies prior to 1944[21] illustrated the malleability of human nature in detailed investigations into the empirically observable variations in the "female character," and also the diverse significance different cultures ascribe to different periods in the individual's life. This being the case, the argument that the ethnocentrism in Freud's work was characteristic of his time, at a point when it was still unchallenged, does not work for Deutsch. Although she may have been ignorant of research in the social sciences, her own research cannot have failed to have been influenced by these discoveries; in general, science has evolved along certain specific lines, and for the most part research takes this into account. From that standpoint, Deutsch's book is incomprehensible. Yet, seen from another angle, it has proven to be socially useful: it continued firing the feminine mystique with the same sort of conceptual fuel that Freud's had done, and provided an added element.

Although Deutsch describes the psychological characteristics of women in an extremely general manner,[22] which led her to oppose modern education, she agreed with Freud that most women are not able to combine an intellectual life with an emotional life without detriment to the latter (i.e., without their becoming masculine), since subjectivity is an inherently feminine quality. Unlike Freud, however, she makes one exception—girls with talent. Once it is asserted that women are by nature incapable of exercising activities that have always been reserved for men, the social system is obliged to work out new techniques of social control to obtain female compliance when their cooperation is needed for the system's survival. In Deutsch's theory, talented women can find a justification for defining their lives on a new basis and society can take advantage of the achievements of intelligent women. Indeed, it is for just this reason that Deutsch is even more effective in mystifying women since, according to her theory, if a woman fails it is because she lacked talent, while female success becomes a natural consequence of exceptional abilities. Since its focus is exclusively on women's personal qualities, the theory provides no means to analyze the limitations the social structure imposes on women, and the success of a few serves as proof of the lack of abilities in those who fail. Ample use is made in class societies of the ideology of personal success to divert attention from the social structure and from the severe limitations it imposes on some social classes. But within these classes, women are affected by such limitations even more than men, because they are at one and the same time members of their class and members of the female sex. Herein, indeed, lies the function of the feminine mystique: it sets the terms in which women's problems are formulated and directs the search for solutions to these problems into channels that do not threaten, or even very deeply affect the established order.

After having served the mystificatory ends of some social groups, psychoanalytic theory underwent extensive reformulations. This was the result both of progress in the social sciences and the acquisition of the sound foundations that are necessary to any science. In the 1920s, Karen Horney undertook a revision of Freudian theory, proceeding from Freud's own premises and using the same methods of investigation.[23] She took up the notion of women's constitutional inferiority, but linked men's greater objectivity and greater interest in external things to the satisfaction they get from exploring their own bodies. In Horney's analysis, little girls will incline toward exhibitionism and masturbation because they are not as successful as boys in satisfying their curiosity with regard to their own bodies. However, the child's inferiority is transformed into superiority in the mature woman when, as a mother, she is able to create children. Penis envy, so detrimental to female development, now finds itself with a counterpart in a man's envy of maternity. However, the inferiority men feel as a consequence of their diminished role in procreation does not produce in them the same effects as the sense of constitutional inferiority felt by women. On the contrary, men will endeavor to compensate for their disadvantage through their objective achievements, in the positing of cultural values. It is noteworthy that in Freud's theory the lack of a penis, and in Horney's theory the inability to bear children, both betoken an absence, although the results are opposite in the two cases. Horney to some extent drew support from sociology for her explanations of the psychological characteristics of women. For her, penis envy has not led women to great achievements either because it is not as strong as a man's envy of maternity, or because it is transformed into the desire to have a husband or beget children. If, all the same, some "flight from womanhood" may be observed in women, it is woman's subjective experience of physical and social disadvantages, not a primary instinct, that is responsible.

Horney also used the advances of social science to reject Freud's explanation of feminine masochism, i.e., in terms of woman's sexual characteristics. Although she granted that masochism has a sexual aspect, she considered that less important than the fact that it results from conflicts in interpersonal relations. In shifting the explanation of masochism from the biological to the social sphere, Horney made evident the fact that masochism is not an exclusively feminine phenomenon. The error of psychoanalysts in having considered it such derives from the fact that once masochist tendencies are established they may also prevail in the sexual sphere, where they may become the condition for sexual satisfaction; and, secondly, from the fact that sociocultural pressures are brought to bear on women more than on men. Defining masochism as "the attempt to gain safety and satisfaction in life through inconspicuousness and dependency,"[24] Horney explained how the social constraints on women can lead them to try to gain "control over others through weakness and suffering, and to seek in illness an alibi for failure."[25] To the extent that women ever seek suffering, it is the result of loss of self-esteem.

When the family ceased being a unit of production, woman lost her economically active role, and without responsibility she lost her self-esteem as well. The view of sexuality as something base and sinful, which made women feel degraded and vilified by sexuality, also did much to instill in her a low opinion of herself. Both of these are consequences of social constraints.

The relevance of Horney's theory for our argument is that (1) it is an objective reply to Freud's androcentric theory;

and (2) it challenged Freudian orthodoxy on its own grounds. The revision of psychoanalytic theory wrought deep changes in its proponents' view of the effects of society on the individual, men as well as women. Thus Horney's contribution, which offered a new perspective on neuroses,[26] has been of inestimable value to psychologists, psychoanalysts, psychiatrists, sociologists, and anthropologists alike.

Another woman who contributed to the critical revision of Freudian concepts was Clara Thompson.[27] In dealing with the question of femininity, she, like Horney, stressed the role of culture in woman's behavior. Thompson saw woman's lack of self-esteem as the product of her upbringing in a world apart from the world of men, and in a climate marked by insincerity with regard to her interests and her sexuality. If spheres as vital as these are denied by society, what is actually demanded is the negation of the whole of the female self. Instead of being a natural corollary of envy of the virile member, narcissism is linked to woman's economic dependency. In societies where women are marginalized from economic life, the attention they give to their physical attractiveness serves the end of procuring or preserving the means of subsistence and social position that are theirs by virtue of their union with males. "One sees," wrote Thompson, "that woman's alleged narcissistic pursuits and greater need to be loved may be entirely the result of economic necessity."[28]

The revision of psychoanalysis reflected the increasing comprehension by social scientists of woman's place and function in competitive societies. However, the ideal of a domestic life still persisted: a woman's functions were still seen as having essentially to do with family life, the management of the household, education of the children, and the life of the community. Of course, this ideal is a plausible one for social strata in which the man's occupational status is high enough, and his job well paid enough, to realize these aspirations, or for those strata in which the possibilities of social advancement are so remote that, in the end, whatever a woman may do is disparaged as useless, and the ideal nourished by the leisured classes is adopted to maintain the illusion of upward mobility. The feminine ideal of a domestic life thus operates in both the upper and lower classes, although it is legitimated in the two in different ways. In the middle classes, although this ideal remains it is of less importance, at least in immediate terms, than the aspiration of upward social mobility, especially among the lower layers of these classes. Thus, middle-class families aspire to move upward, and to do this they draw on female labor if necessary. Moreover, their state of social and economic insecurity drives the families of these strata to capitalize on their resources, primarily through the acquisition of formal education, and secondly by putting all their adult members to work. The combination of these two factors results in inordinate value being placed on institutionalized means for creating skilled labor.[29]

The economic changes wrought in capitalist societies by the transition from the liberal phase to the monopolistic phase broke down resistance to the single woman's working outside the home. For the married woman, such change came more slowly. Moreover, as the economy becomes more complex and hence requires more highly skilled labor, the ideal marrying age is pushed back, and this lengthens considerably the period spent as an unmarried family member. This means not only that young girls must use this time productively; it also means that they have greater chances for marriage by virtue of the contacts they make at work. So although marriage still maintains its place at the top of the list of aspirations for the majority of women, its postponement gives rise to new motivations: professional achievement prior to marriage, the social advancement of the entire family by means of the occupational positions of its unmarried members, or even procuring a permanent means of earning one's living in the event the individual should not marry. Although marriage may still be the most highly valued career for women, not only is it not incompatible with prior employment, it is even, up to a certain point, contingent on it.

If Freud's "binomial equations"—*passive-feminine* and *active-masculine*—were an accurate reflection of the way things were, one could truly say that women are becoming more masculine and men more feminine. Actually, economic and cultural change has given rise to new patterns of behavior for both sexes, and profound changes have taken place in our ideas of masculinity and femininity at both the scientific and popular levels. In urban industrial societies, more and more women, at least those who are unmarried, are becoming economically independent. The times themselves have undertaken to destroy "feminine rigidity," supposedly determined by woman's biological makeup.

Although woman has acquired a new image in the popular mind, she is still far from realizing the potential implied in advances of science—physical, biological, and social. Even in countries where science has become an institutionalized means for effecting social change, there is still some lag between scientific discoveries and the point at which they become practically useful. There are many factors which influence the way the results of scientific research are incorporated into everyday life and, moreover, hold that process back, and among these is surely the esoteric terminology of certain sciences, which acts as a real barrier between scientists and the public at large. As a consequence, other channels serve the function of communicating scientific knowledge, representing one more possibility of that knowledge suffering a reinterpretation. In addition, then, to the social reelaboration that scientific knowledge undergoes, the discoveries of science suffer a further reinterpretation in the very process of their being made public. The large-scale use of the mass communications media provides vast numbers of people with predigested scientific material which in some cases is less objective than it is mystifying. The reinterpretation of scientific knowledge becomes a factor of key significance in mass societies inasmuch as the functions it fulfills lie outside the domain of social consciousness. Just as the ideology of personal success in the United States can no longer be upheld in the monopolistic structure of that nation's economy, yet persists as a means of diverting people's attention from society's limitations, so too scientific knowledge pertaining to the psychology and social roles of women is reinterpreted with similar consequences, related to the structural limitations the system imposes upon women. These latent functions which the feminine press and propaganda perform in the end create a situation in which the results of science in general, and the discoveries of the social sciences in particular, are permanently underutilized. Since to be applied, the knowledge attained by the social sciences requires the cooperation or at least the acceptance of the people involved—such application itself being a sociocultural process—society has so far been much more successful in putting to use the results of the natural sciences.

Under these conditions, scientific analyses which reveal the restrictive nature of certain social structures are put to antithetical use in the name of certain ethical principles or traditions to conceal these structural limitations and thereby obtain, by means of nonrational mechanisms of social control, the minimum of conformist behavior any social system requires to survive. As we shall see in the next chapter, in many cases this has been the social fate of theories which have done much, however tentatively, to clarify the way the social roles of women are understood in modern life.

CHAPTER 11

Margaret Mead
and Cultural Relativism

The last chapter noted some of the consequences of the work of Margaret Mead on psychoanalytic theory, as its proponents were forced to try to distinguish the effects on the personality of cultural as well as biological inheritance. Mead's work is important not only because of this, but also because some of its practical consequences have been quite contradictory. It broadened our understanding of certain problems never before dealt with in satisfactory terms, and first formulated conclusions in terms of scientific explanations supported by a wealth of empirical material. The notion of cultural relativism, grounded in empirical facts, freed women from biological definitions alone, and opened new vistas to human thought. However, her work also had a negative influence on thousands of women, especially Americans, by virtue of the social reelaboration it underwent, which in part may have been due to the way Mead herself dealt with these problems.

With an impressive richness of detail, Mead demonstrated the enormous malleability of human nature.[1] She showed that the psychological characteristics Western societies are accustomed to regard as masculine and feminine are actually independent of sex in primitive societies. Among the Arapesh she found that the ideal personality for both men and women was docile, nonaggressive, and helpful; among the Mundugumor, that violence and aggressiveness were personality traits held in high esteem for both husband and wife; and that among the Tchambuli, women were dominant, impersonal, and leaders, while the men were emotionally dependent.

Two things stand out immediately from these interpretations. First, ethnographic data from the Tchambuli show that a total reversal of the traditional Western sex roles is possible: here it is women who are free and dominant. Second, the three studies as a whole indicate that the same sex-specific attitudes are found in every society. In the Mundugumor and Arapesh societies, cultural energies have been directed toward "the creation of a single human type regardless of class, age, or sex."[2] Is this not sufficient indication that the characteristics labeled masculine and feminine in Western society are the result of sociohistorical conditioning? Of course, Mead did not suggest that civilized societies should adopt a pattern in which no social distinctions are made between the sexes. According to her, to eliminate sexual distinctions in personality would be a step backward: "A sacrifice of distinctions in sex personality may mean a sacrifice in complexity."[3] What she was trying to show is that it is impossible to equate the psychological traits that society has carved out for men and women with presumed biological predispositions. Thus she concluded:

> If those temperamental attitudes which we have traditionally regarded as feminine—such as passivity, responsiveness and willingness to cherish children—can so easily be set up as the masculine pattern in one tribe, and in another be outlawed for the majority of men, we no longer have any basis for regarding such aspects of behavior as sex-linked. And this conclusion becomes even stronger when we consider the actual reversal in Tchambuli of the position of dominance of the two sexes, in spite of the existence of formal patrilineal institutions. The material suggests

that we may say that many, if not all, of the personality traits which we have called masculine or feminine are as lightly linked to sex as are the clothing, the manners, and the form of head-dress that a society at a given period assigns to either sex."[4]

Margaret Mead's work is highly important in that it gives us a cultural perspective on diverse societies. A cultural analysis, however, is insufficient to identify social relations and the structures determining them, the dynamics of these particular structures and the way they interact to form a complex whole, or the means available for breaking down the old structures and constructing new ones. But Mead thought she had gone beyond the limitations of the cultural approach in seeking the causes of sexual inequality in a society's system of stratification. She denounced stratification patterns in which, regardless of the contents, the women always occupied inferior positions. She tried to bring to light the link between occupations and the prestige invested in them by virtue of their being masculine and or feminine. She found that the same activity, held in low esteem socially when performed by the women of a society, enjoyed a high level of prestige when practiced by the men. She thus concluded that prestige accompanies maleness, or more precisely, that being a male is the condition for acquiring prestige. The biological diversity between men and women is in the last instance reflected socially in a stratification based on sex. All societies accord men the right, through culturally elaborated forms of expression, to realize their capacities through the quest for prestige and social recognition, and to that extent they provide men with the indispensable means for shaping a truly human life that goes far beyond their mere capacity to beget children. Thus, maleness has two basic and complementary aspects: the possibility of fatherhood, and the possibility of constructive activity from which men derive, and on which they bestow, prestige.

On the other hand, few societies create in women the

aspirations necessary to seek satisfactions beyond mother-hood,[5] and even those that do, do so within rather modest limits. Under these circumstances social stratification based on sex greatly limits the development of women's capacities, so that social activity itself, which is to say society (and even men, who are a part of it) suffers. But if society stands to lose when there is no differentiation, that is to say, if the process of social differentiation which makes society richer and more complex, is the *sine qua non* of its development, seen from another angle, differentiation based on sex is a drawback to social evolution because it does not permit the two sexes to develop at the same pace or to achieve in the same way. To put it another way, societies grade a man's achievements differently from a woman's. Mead thus thinks that both the individual and society as a whole would stand to gain much if it were left to individual abilities to regulate competition among human beings, since human qualities are distributed along a normal curve for both sexes.

Although Mead was highly critical of the limitations that society in general, and the North American society in particular,[6] places on the "humanization" of woman, and saw that in one way or another this affects men, and hence the whole of society, she was unable to get to the root of the problem. Her understanding faltered because the class structure beneath the pattern of social stratification remained hidden. As a result, her attitude, so open to social change, and the solutions she proposes, might better be called wishful thinking than reformist or revolutionary. Leaving aside for the moment the revolutionary position, which aims for total breakdown of the social structure, a reformist position requires that one always keep in mind the limits within which the reform is defined, that is, the extent of compatibility with the structure to be reformed. Mead, with all her insight into the role of competition in the North American society, did not analyze the implications of the change she desired: the replacement of social discrimination based on sex by a situation which would give free rein to the abilities of each to unfold independently on natural factors. She attributed to sexual status an importance which, in reality, it does not have, compared with the polar and antagonistic positions created by a class structure. Finally, she did not expose the nature of the phenomena concealed beneath and within social stratification. In a sense one could say that Mead became the victim of her own anthropology; in failing to look at the sociohistoric determinants of a social reality she invested that reality with a permanence it does not have.[7]

It becomes evident that Mead did not consider the limits within which it would be possible to reform North American society so as to change the social condition of women. Her method, although not strictly cultural, did not succeed in probing fully into the depths of social phenomena; her concentration primarily on sex as a category rather than on social class, to some extent vitiates her proposed solutions. On the other hand, because she did not fully appreciate the role of human *praxis,* she did not see that structural change might be achieved through collective action. Indeed, she asserted:

> Here is a vicious circle, to which it is not possible to assign either a beginning or an end, in which men's overestimation of men's roles leads one sex or the other to arrogate, to neglect, or even to relinquish part of our so dearly won humanity. Those who would break the circle are themselves a product of it, express some of its defects in their every gesture, may be only strong enough to challenge it, not able actually to break it. Yet once identified, once analyzed, it should be possible to create a climate of opinion in which others, a little less the product of the dark past because they have been reared with a light in their hand that can shine backwards as well as forwards, may in turn take the next step. Only by recognizing that each change in human society must be made by those who carry in every cell of their bodies the very reason why the change is necessary can we school our hearts to the patience to build truly and well, recognizing that it is not only the price, but also the glory, of our humanity, that civilization must be built by human beings.[8]

Mead's insight stopped short of the basic contradictions of her society. However much she protested that the social division of tasks between the two sexes was arbitrary, her view of social life remained at the perceptible surface of things. Despite the wealth of descriptive anthropological material she adduced in testimony to the impressive malleability of human nature, she remained a stranger to the idea that aside from the differing functions of men and women in reproduction, sex neither limits nor channels the activities of human beings. As a consequence of her reliance on certain psychoanalytic concepts, the opportunity to build up an entirely new perspective on the woman problem slipped from her grasp. For example, she remained bound to the assumption that an individual's view of the world initially was shaped by anatomy.[9]

Some of Lévi-Strauss's criticisms of Robert Frazer in the *Elementary Structures of Kinship* could be levied at Mead as well. She attempted to apply the same psychological theory, which holds that personality traits are the products of human anatomy, to primitive societies and North American society alike, although the latter is highly differentiated. Although she recognized differences between the way people perceive their bodies in the two societies, for example, she did not consider that these might only be differences of degree.[10] In primitive societies, too, culture provides the terms in which the individual perceives his or her body, although the compass of these cultural mediations is much greater in complex civilizations. Even admitting, therefore, that anatomy plays a role in shaping human personality, it is also true that this role has different dimensions in primitive societies and differentiated societies, which is to say that body perception does not mold human behavior directly and invariably.

Moreover, whereas Mead concluded from ethnographic data that personality traits are socially determined, she also stated that they derive from anatomy. Two passages from her books will serve to illustrate this contradiction:

When we consider the behavior of the typical Arapesh man or woman as contrasted with the behavior of the typical Mundugumor man or woman, the evidence is overwhelmingly in favor of the strength of social conditioning.[11]

If we accept the premise that we can build a better world by using the different gifts of each sex, we shall have two kinds of freedom, freedom to use untapped gifts of each sex, and freedom to admit freely and cultivate in each sex their special superiorities. We may well find that there are certain fields, such as the physical sciences, mathematics, and instrumental music, in which men by virtue of their sex, as well as by virtue of their qualities as specially gifted human beings, will always have that razor-edge of extra gift which makes all the difference, and that while women may easily follow where men lead, men will always make the discoveries. We may equally well find that women, through the learning involved in maternity, which once experienced can be taught more easily to all women, even childless women, than to men, have a special superiority in those human sciences which involve that type of understanding which until it is analyzed is called intuition.[12]

If we compare these two passages from the vantage point of Mead's own methodological position we would have to ask: (1) is it the male sex or social life which determines the appearance of gifted men in the natural sciences, in mathematics, and in instrumental music? and (2) do the intuitive abilities displayed by Western women derive from their experience of, or even merely from their capacity for, maternity, or do they stem from the type of lives women have been obliged to lead?

When sex is made responsible for the personality differences between men and women in such a sweeping manner as is done in the second quotation, there is little room left for the play of social factors, and, moreover, the limitations on the latter are defined by sex itself. This is tantamount to saying that in the last instance sociocultural factors do not play the decisive role in determining the structures of the diverse personality types of men and women. The inference is, of course, that sex is this decisive factor.

Obviously I am not trying to deny either women or men the opportunity of realizing any inherent potentials they have by virtue of their sex. If, aside from the capacities for maternity and paternity, men and women potentially have other different capacities as well, society could then guide the two sexes into activities that were particularly suited to them. It could only thereby be enriched, not impoverished. But the question remains, to continue Mead's line of thinking, does science have the means to carry out an exhaustive investigation of all the existing situations of human life so as to be able to assert with confidence that the discoveries and inventions of physics and mathematics *will always be the achievements of men,* and that women show more talent in fields where *intuition* plays a major role? Even if we employed the inductive method of science, which would obviate the need for an exhaustive study of all the facts of human existence, it is valid to ask if the diversity of male and female roles that is evident from the wealth of accumulated ethnographic material does, after all, exhibit certain invariants and recurrent patterns, i.e., certain traits which are common to most women and certain others which are common to most men. If investigation were able to answer the question affirmatively, then sex would have to be regarded as the source of specific female and specific male psychological traits; otherwise, apart from the universality of the biological functions which men and women exercise at all times and places, Mead has shown only that patterns of behavior are different for the two sexes.

Mead's own data fail to demonstrate the existence of empirical regularities that would warrant the inference that woman has a greater intuitive capacity just because she is able to conceive. The lifestyle of the inhabitants of the Marquesas Islands shows how the material conditions of existence and the way people are required to adjust to them leave deep marks on the male and female personalities. The precariousness of the material bases of existence on these islands (ever-present threat of famine) and the sex distribution of the population (100 women to 250 men) have molded a female personality characterized by severity, coldness, and lack of tenderness which is sometimes terrifying.[13] It is the father who is gentle with the children, raises them, and displays what Western societies have become accustomed to calling a maternal instinct. This contradiction is insurmountable. This contradictory work provided the feminine mystique with arguments which it then reelaborated to justify woman's economic and social dependence to just the extent that dependence was required by the social system.

CHAPTER 12

Linkages Between the Occupational Structure and the Kinship Structure

To review and summarize the major theoretical points put forward in Part I and developed in the analysis of Brazilian society in Part II, we saw, first, that once the phase of labor intensive capitalist accumulation has passed, a woman's opportunities for work are regulated in a different way and henceforth serve as a barometer of the dynamics proper to each phase of development of the capitalist socioeconomic formation. The second point, in a certain sense implicit in the first, is that with the large-scale development of technology and hence the steady improvement in the productivity of human labor, class society no longer requires the participation of all its adult members to create its wealth. A permanent contingent of unemployed, varying in size according to economic cycles, has proved historically to be an inherent feature of the capitalist mode of production. True, it has been possible to attenuate the negative effects of the periodic crises—which endanger, sometimes profoundly, the stability of competitive societies—by recourse to economic and social planning. But it is also true that during lull periods of economic growth, when the system is undergoing structural expansion, economic and social planning is concerned only with reducing unemployment, not with eliminating it entirely.[1] Moreover, this social problem becomes even graver as capitalist society matures. In certain periods, when the growth rate remains stable or declines, unemployment has assumed contours and proportions of real gravity. The accumulation and concentration of capital and the benefits of technology have brought about a new combination of production factors in which the role of manual labor has been greatly reduced.[2] Capitalist society thus appears to be inherently unable to provide useful employment for all of its potential workforce.

If, then, a competitive society is incapable of assimilating all its working-age members into its economic system, the continued existence of that system requires: (1) that criteria be found to select the individuals who are to occupy the existing positions—that is, means must be found to meet one of the *structural* requirements of the system; and (2) the development of motivating forces capable of adapting individuals to their several statuses in such a way as to achieve optimum effectiveness in the performance of their roles—that is, the development of means to meet a *functional* requirement of the system.

Social Status and Competition

To analyze the first requirement we must consider the degree of relevance in a competitive social order to the different ways social status is achieved, to ascription and acquisition. For the individual, the emergence of class society has unquestionably meant broader opportunities for occupying social positions independent of the qualities ascribed to the individual as a social actor. On the other hand, even if the criteria for status ascription are partially replaced by the mechanisms of acquisition, they will still continue to operate to prevent competition from assuming such forms and reaching such an intensity that it would imperil the stability of the social system and undermine the personality structures of its members.

As a rule, these basically different stratificatory criteria will operate at different structural levels within a society. In the kinship structure, status ascription predominates, while in the occupational structure, status is mainly acquired. This separation of functional domains is an important factor in keeping the two structures segregated. In this respect, the functional units of the occupational structure are essentially competitive in nature, whereas those of the kinship structure serve as cohesive factors. For society as a whole, as well as the individual, the cohesiveness of the family group serves to replenish the energy expended in the competitive sector and alleviate social and psychological tensions. But this does not mean that the separation of these two parts of the social structure is total, nor that, because status in the family is mainly ascriptive, competition does not exist among its members. Sociologists have not been alone in making this observation. Freud defined some of his concepts (e.g., the Oedipal complex) in the light of his perception of the role rivalry plays in the family. The difference is that whereas Freud saw rivalry as a fact of biology, sociology (and post-Freudian psychoanalysis, for that matter) sees it as a phenomenon that is itself conditioned by circumstances inherent to the competitive social order.

In any case, both the stability of the individual personality and the stability of society as a whole require a certain degree of segregation of stratificatory principles that are fundamentally different, and the result of this has been the segregation of the respective structures in which the two predominate. This relative segregation serves to regulate competition between individuals in two different but equally important areas so as to keep society in a state of dynamic equilibrium. Within the occupational structure, competition may be extremely intense, but it must remain within limits compatible with the biological and psychological equilibrium of the individual. All the same, these limits are frequently surpassed, and when that happens, periodic or permanent maladjustments result. In the family, the permissible level of competition is much lower. Solidarity, at least ideally, has always been one of the major ends of the family unit, a precondition, that is, for its existence as the group which will give issue to and raise the next generation. This is why positions within the kinship structure, with the exception of those ensuing from the individual's free choice of a marriage partner (and these too within certain limits), are defined independently of the individual's capacity for self-realization (which plays a decisive role in the competitive process) and are ascribed on the basis of classificatory and relational characteristics.[3]

Of course, these irrational criteria of status ascription—sex, age, color, beauty, etc.—are at work throughout society as a whole and influence, sometimes quite profoundly, the formation, development, and functioning of the class structure. They function, as it were, as primary selection mechanisms. The final screening of individuals in the occupational structure then takes place on the basis of leadership capacity, in the instrumental sense, and technical competence. Thus, ascriptive criteria predominate in the family while acquisitive criteria are paramount in the occupational structure; this becomes especially important in light of the fact that those domains of the human personality which seek satisfaction and recognition in these two structures are delimited in such a way that sex itself becomes a factor in determining the degree to which males and females are assimilated into these structures.

Structural segregation does not operate at the sexual level alone; that is, not only does it fix the positions of individuals more or less rigidly in terms of sex, it also provides effective social justifications to maintain and explain why these two types of criteria carry different weight for the two sexes. The harmony of social life becomes contingent on the efficacy with which the system legitimates and controls the unequal participation of men and women in these two structures. In other words, not only are functional solutions to the problems of social existence indispensable for maintaining the structure of the system, but they also serve to reinforce the established order by furnishing its legitimacy, and in this way constitute a real barrier to sociocultural change. On the other hand, the ineffectiveness of these solutions serves to generate tensions that may touch off processes of far-reaching structural change.

Socialization and the Category of Sex

In analyzing the second requirement of a competitive social system we must consider the role played by the sex factor in the socialization process, and the levels at which the motivating mechanisms of which that process makes use enter into play.

Whatever its structure, every social system subjects its members to a process of socialization, through which individuals introject the prevailing cultural patterns and acquire the necessary skills for satisfactorily performing the roles society has ascribed to them. Thus, all societies develop mechanisms of motivation which are capable of bringing the socialization process to a successful completion, and which are of incontestable functional importance for social interaction.

In capitalist urban-industrial societies, sex categories serve to regulate occupational competition, and accordingly, the goals of the socializing process and the motivational mechanisms of which it makes use differ for the two sexes. The male ideal is oriented toward family values; but above all it subserves values whose primacy in the occupational structure ensures that an intense process of competition will be the primary determinant of that structure. The female ideal, on the other hand, is dominated by values on the basis of which the family is organized. For these two structures (family and occupational) to coexist harmoniously, the socialization of males must be directed primarily toward adapting them to the occupational roles they must fulfill. There are no necessary inconsistencies, therefore, in the diverse types of roles men must perform. The competitive aspects are counterbalanced by a noncompetitive side, manifested principally in the family, where his dominant role comes into conflict with the roles he must fulfill in his occupation. For males, the criteria for status and role ascription operate parallel to the mechanisms of status acquisition. Indeed, this is so much so in class societies that laziness, that is, noncompetitiveness in work, is not socially admissible even for a wealthy man since it would be incompatible with his position as head of a family.

Of course, as we have seen, other qualities ascribed to men alter the rules of competition which is not completely free. But for our present purposes, it is sufficient to recall that these factors affect the process of social stratification in a way that men seem not to be privileged by virtue of their sex. Thus, men enter the ranks of the unemployed either because of their color or race, or because they lack skills. Women are discriminated against, however, on the basis of their sex, regardless of other factors, to keep them out of the occupational structure or to channel them into positions which do not compromise the power structure already occupied by men. Under these circumstances, woman's socialization is guided by values which invest her with the role of upholder of the status quo and defender of a family structure and moral order in which a boy is expected to grow up to be like his father and a girl like her mother. Brought up in this way, it is not surprising that domestic life represents a woman's major aspiration, just as creating a financial situation that will permit the realization of this "domestic ideal" for their wives is a major goal for men.

The female ideal, therefore, has no place for paid labor, even when it is done at home. The latter is more acceptable than working outside the home, because it is less incompatible with traditional female roles, and less incompatible also—at least outwardly—with the man's authority in the home. Working for wages is not a recognized means of self-expression for women, and hence does not fit into the female ideal; it remains an abstract possibility, therefore, to be realized only in the case of some degree of economic need. That is, a family's economic situation is not defined in absolute terms, but relative to the aspirations of its adult members: higher education for the children, a higher standard of living, the acquisition of material goods, etc. It is at this point that the first inconsistencies in feminine roles emerge, reflecting incongruities in the social system. Thus, a woman enters the occupational structure and finds employment to ensure survival or to satisfy aspirations instilled in her by her cultural environment. But this economic role is not matched by a corresponding function in the family, where the woman remains subordinate, nor in society at large, where female labor continues to be viewed as subsidiary.

Thus as female labor enters the occupational structure to meet needs this structure itself creates, and as women accordingly become economically more independent, the inconsistency in female roles can be fully eliminated only if appropriate changes also take place in the kinship structure and in social valuations which compare women with men. Such changes would place the stability of the social system itself in jeopardy, for a number of reasons, the most basic of which is that they would undermine the foundations of status ascription based on sex. Other ascriptive criteria could be made to perform the same role, namely, to eliminate superfluous persons from the occupational structure,[4] but what would happen to the kinship structure once it became competitive? The family would cease to function as a cohesive unit that helps alleviate tensions generated in the man's occupational activity. The kinship structure of Western urban societies works together with the occupational structure to restrict female employment, and to that extent demonstrates the impossibility of eliminating the sex factor as a stratificatory principle. Women are impelled by economic conditions to break down barriers and enter the working world. As they do so, however, they continue to bear the brand of inferiority in relation to men. Women "resolve" or relieve tensions generated by the inconsistency in their roles by occupying lower positions, accepting lower salaries, and forgoing any ambitions toward stepping into positions of authority. These are the kinds of solutions the stable social system permits and encourages through its motivational mechanisms. For any particular economic structure, it is only within narrow limits that the family structure may vary, yet still sustain a compatibility between the kinship structure and the occupational structure. Thus, the conjugal family, which is the most isolated of all of cohesive social structures, has proven to be the type of family which is compatible with industrial economies.

However, there is this important detail: the compatibility of the conjugal family unit with the occupational structure has been achieved through the establishment of a family hierarchy in which the members are ranked by age and sex. It is highly doubtful whether class society could be based on an egalitarian type of family, that is, whether it could radically transform the power structure within the family organization without at the same time profoundly altering the occupational and hence the entire social structure. An analysis of history shows that male domination follows upon private property, not vice-versa. Private property, not stratification by sex, is the determining factor (despite societies with collective economies which, because of tenacious cultural traditions, continue the age-old discrimination, albeit in milder form).

The central issue concerns the limits within which woman's social condition may vary without threatening the stability of capitalist societies. Since these limits are not very broad, and since the solutions that have been found all involve to some extent an inconsistency in women's roles, the social system itself develops mechanisms for reducing or alleviating tensions to avoid undermining the stability of the female personality and of the system itself. It is in this context, of course, that we must place the development of psychoanalytic and anthropological theory and the purposes they serve in capitalist society.

CHAPTER 13

The Position of Women
in Dialectical Perspective

Analyzing the links between the occupational structure and the kinship structure from another perspective, we find that these links are of two types in capitalist urban-industrial society. One of these regards the opportunities available to both sexes, as integral elements in the family, to take positions in the class structure. The roles the sexes assume do not have the same significance for society, as we saw in the last chapter. For example, as we have seen, the category of sex acts as a restraint on competition, to prevent it from exceeding bounds still compatible with a stable human personality and to keep it from penetrating the family group, where solidarity is of paramount importance in both conjugal relations and in the rearing of the young. Although female employment is considered subsidiary and is justified socially in terms of increasing the family income, the privileged component of *praxis*—labor—has the same form for both the sexes. However the activities exercised by the two may differ, the three basic constitutive elements of the labor process—the object, the medium, and concrete labor itself—are effectively the same for both. Further, the real income of a family—a cohesive unit par excellence—should not be confused with the nominal incomes of each of its gainfully employed members. First, the objects necessary to human life, such as food, are obtained by a family in semi-finished form, and hence require a final touch before being consumed. Second, certain services, such as caring for the young, are indispensable to the family's continued existence. These services may be provided for in several ways: either the society takes care of them through a system of public facilities set up for such purpose, such as we find to a certain extent in Western societies; or they are performed by individuals who are hired and paid especially to do the job; or, finally, the married couple (in most cases effectively only the woman), whose collective remunerated labor is the source of the family income, assumes the responsibility. Thus, at one stage in their development capitalist societies require, in addition to the exercise of remunerated activities, the performance of services which have not yet been fully defined as occupational specialties and hence do not yet have a fully constituted role within the dominant system of production. As housework acquires more and more of the organized features of capitalist enterprise, the relations between it and the family income take on more explicit form. A person may be hired to do the housework, or organizations specializing in this type of service may be called upon to take care of it; when this is the case, a portion of the family income is used to pay for the services performed, and the economic nature, albeit indirect, of the housewife's work becomes manifest.

The second type of link between the occupational structure and the kinship structure therefore involves the purely household labor of the woman and the paid labor of the husband. A housewife's nonpaid labor actually increases the family's real income since it adds to the husband's wages an amount of labor that could be transformed into wages. Obviously, the monetary equivalent of this household labor does not equal the wages the wife would receive if she herself were gainfully employed in the dominant system of production.

The explanation often presented to justify the role of the housewife—that the woman's wages are consumed in the payment of domestic services—is incorrect. The role of housewife can be explained only in terms of the coexistence of different modes of production, with this coexistence determining how the dominant system of production operates in the particular case. The mass of individuals taken up in modes of production left over from outmoded structures where they themselves had been dominant at one time may be regarded as unemployed labor power insofar as they can be effectively mobilized during times of capitalist upswing. Thus, not only those who are actually unemployed, but also those who are not employed directly in the dominant system of production are part of the reserve army of labor in modern capitalist economies. From this standpoint, the housewife too may be regarded as part of the reserve army, which, because it is not directly engaged in the dominant system of production, is not part of any class.

The situation of the married woman is more complicated than this, however, as other variables are at work. In effect, her husband's class situation is mirrored in her and her children, so that, in a certain sense, the class unit is the family rather than the individual (although to view it as such is valid only within well-defined limits). The husband's class situation has implications for the family, for example, in that it determines the family's income. This has consequences for social stratification as far as social status is concerned, inasmuch as the type of occupation, and the economic benefits accruing from it (each class is stratified with respect to income and prestige), give rise to a corresponding way of thinking and lifestyle and are hence evaluated and ranked in terms of a scale of values held by the society. Since in capitalist societies, however, economic status (class situation seen in terms of social stratification) is the most definitive of all the various kinds of status occupied by individuals, and since in the family only the husband takes direct part in the productive system and hence is the only family member with an economic status, that status is extended to the entire family. Assuming economic status to be not a passive reflexion, as it were, of a class situation on the level of social stratification, we can say that the social status of woman is reflexive in a double sense: it is the reflexion of her husband's economic status, which is itself the *active reflexion* of his class situation.

Since in concrete terms social stratification determines prestige, and since a housewife does not participate in the occupational structure, one, if not the principal, source of prestige for a woman, namely, her social status, accrues to her by virtue of her husband's class situation. The sex factor is thus not directly responsible for the lesser prestige women enjoy in capitalist societies. It functions rather to limit competition in the occupational sphere, which in turn augments the prestige conferred on men. Since it is in the occupational sphere that the principles of competition are most actively at play, and since there are no apparent mediating links between sex, as a stratificatory factor, and a woman's social position, the view is fostered that she is a creature incapable of acquiring status.

In general, the content of social consciousness is determined by a society's stratification schema, not by the infrastructural factors that define that schema at any particular moment and are outlived by it. This is why social consciousness of woman's situation has several different levels to it. Myths, common sense knowledge, and scientific knowledge are but different levels of perception, and in them social phenomena appear in different forms. Within science itself, considered as a form of social consciousness, the perception of social phenomena takes place at diverse levels, and this for two reasons: (1) because of the diversity of methodological approaches, and (2) because of "the process of abstraction and hence the isolation of whole elements and concepts in the special disciplines and in whole areas of study."[1]

Science's division of labor is itself responsible for this breakdown into isolated and circumscribed fields of inquiry; the result is that the scientist will abstract phenomena from the historical totality of which they are a part and place them in a position he or she feels is expedient for discovery. This accounts for the different perspectives, legitimate in themselves, among the human sciences. In this respect, the perspectives of modern psychoanalysis, anthropology (even as the strictly cultural science it has formerly been), and sociology are meaningful and valid. The danger resides in ascribing to any one of these perspectives or to the set of problems with which they deal an autonomy which none of them inherently possesses. The particular domains of enquiry are part of a dialectical totality within which alone they have meaning, and it is precisely because of this larger context that the various perspectives are not autonomous with respect to each other. Only by keeping in mind that the problems selected are parts of a dialectical whole will the scientist be able to grasp society as a totality. That is why a rigorous delimitation of the fields of science is of negative significance for the dialectic perspective.

The two ways in which women are defined, therefore, as housewife and as working (i.e., gainfully employed) woman, should be viewed as aspects of capitalist society, seen as a dialectical totality. The dialectical relations existing between social stratification and class structure reflect at functional and structural levels the inconsistency in woman's position and in women's roles, and in their movement tend toward the supersession of that inconsistency.

The Social Division of Labor

The statement that the housewife is, as a type, the most fully integrated into class society now takes on an added dimension. For many women, domestic life is an aspiration, because their socialization took place with that goal in mind; in other words, society inculcates in them certain values, the realization of which requires that they conduct their lives in accordance with this role. The feminine mystique, then, not only meets a need of the social system, but it also smoothes women's adjustment to domestic life, itself still defined by the system. From a syncretic view of society, one may indeed say that the housewife is integrated into society; if on the other hand, one goes further, and views society as a totality, then one can assert only that the economically inactive woman appears outwardly to be the most integrated into class society at the level of social stratification.

But as the capitalist system also requires the opposite type, the working woman, women find themselves shunted back and forth between two domains of prestige ascription: one which holds up the value of the "idle mother" of a family (idle, that is, with regard to the dominant system of production), whose status is a reflection of her husband's; and another which values the working woman. Since the latter has not yet been institutionalized, however, a woman who chooses to stick it out in this role will encounter obstacles that are not easily surmounted. In many cases, women do not feel courageous enough to undertake as much, nor indeed are they emotionally or occupationally prepared. One may discern, however, two opposing trends operating here: one steering women into a life in the home, the other pushing them into employment. From the compromise between these two social tendencies results the defense of the part-time job as ideal for women, since with such a job she can attend to two sets of needs imposed by capitalist society at once. Some

European countries have shortened the working day to attend to the needs of mothers with families, and in certain economic phases these function in a very special way. The increase in part-time work is one of the main factors responsible for the mass influx of women into the Brazilian civil service.

In times of economic crisis, the category of sex operates to sift workers selectively, expelling far more women than men from the occupational structure. Regarding the family as the unit of consumption, the family budget suffers much less with the woman than with the man out of work, a woman's wages usually being lower than a man's. Commodities are overproduced, and businesses are forced to cut back on production while maintaining the productivity of human labor at a given level. The result is mass unemployment. Sometimes, however, there is an attempt to effect a partial solution—for example, by reducing the length of the working day with a corresponding reduction in wages, in order to keep employment at a certain level or at least prevent it from falling too drastically.

It is worth noting that for capitalist production enterprises, it would be more expedient to dismiss their male workers and keep their women workers because of the wage differential which often exists between them. Because of the subsidiary status of female labor, however, society finds itself sustaining a set of pressures that tend more to promote female unemployment. Since a woman's working is generally justified in terms of supplementing the family income, society finds nothing essentially amiss in curtailing female employment to protect male jobs, the principal source of a family income. If unemployment affected married women only, it would represent an adequate, although not ideal, means of adjusting to crisis situations in capitalist society. But it happens that the unemployment caused by economic crisis also affects the single woman,[2] creating extremely grave social problems for which capitalism has not found satisfactory solutions.

Two sets of issues emerge from the foregoing discussion. In the first place, the situation of women in class society is a social problem. The woman who is not gainfully employed is from a functional viewpoint the most thoroughly integrated of all into society; her roles suffer from no major inconsistencies. She is at once economically dependent and a member of a group (the family) in which the man is the head, at least nominally. The inconsistencies in the role of an unemployed woman rise to the surface only when they begin to affect the relations between class structure and social stratification. The single woman is defenseless in a society in which economic stability is increasingly premised on an individual's technical competence. Quite often, women do not attain this technical competence, which is the result not only of formal schooling but of practical training acquired on the job. In those cases where a woman actually has acquired professional skills through formal schooling for the exercise of a specific activity and has also obtained practical training in it, it is harder for her to leave her job when she marries or has children. Yet if she does leave it for a few years, when she later prepares to return to gainful employment, she might find that the technical training she has has in the meantime become outmoded due to new technology. When that happens, she will find herself ill-adjusted to class society in a double sense. In the first place, her technical qualifications are not sufficient to permit her to compete on the labor market; in the second, she may have components to her personality which earmark her as a worker alienated (which she was) from the capitalist system of production.

> If we regard the concrete individual, it is the alienation (and reification) of labor, of the worker, and of the individual which is at the basis of the training of labor to specific skills in the capitalist socio-economic formation. Accordingly, the acquisition

of a skill, in the broadest and deepest sense of the term, consists in a process of putting together all the various components typifying man (as a worker) in capitalist society. . . . Thus, the formation of a worker is at once an economic, cultural, and political process and must be viewed as such, i.e., as the mediated realization of the multidimensionality of *social praxis* in the *praxis* of the individual.[3]

The modes and degrees of alienation thus constitute the second set of questions concerning woman's roles in class societies.

We noted earlier that the work a woman performs in a paying job contains the three elementary components of this process, just as does a man's work: namely, the object, its medium, and the labor itself. We also found that, even so, a woman's paid labor has a different social significance from that given to a man's labor. Let us consider: the training of labor power is more than just the acquisition of a technical skill, it is a multidimensional process which for that very reason involves a political and cultural dimension in addition to its mere technical and economic dimensions. The function of these two added dimensions is to adapt human beings in all their aspects—biological, psychological, and social—to class society. If this is so, the formation of the male worker must differ from the formation of the female worker. Woman as housewife and the gainfully employed woman must be considered separately, but since the role of the working woman has not been institutionalized, even in the most advanced capitalist countries, we can leave out of account for the present those women who, whether as capitalist entrepreneurs or as wage earners, have wholly adjusted to the competitive social order and hence display personality components required in an urban industrial capitalist society. In these cases, the process and degree of alienation are the same for male and female workers alike, and will depend for both sexes on the sociohistorical circumstances in which the capitalist system of production unfolds in each particular case.

Yet the problem of alienation must be dealt with in a special way when it pertains to the housewife or the woman who takes a job only during certain periods of her life. If we say that *praxis* is multidimensional, then, seen as a total process, alienation will have an economic aspect, a religious aspect, a political aspect, etc. Its economic dimension is only one aspect, albeit in competitive societies a special one, that is part of a broader and more general process.

In capitalist society, the alienation of labor has two dimensions, one subjective, the other objective. The division of labor is imposed by society; it is not voluntary, that is, does not derive from a free act of each individual's will. Each individual is restricted by it to one sphere of activity in which he or she can secure his or her means of subsistence.[4] Labor, humanity's privileged franchise as a means to objective expression when one may move freely from one activity to another, becomes a burdensome activity when it must be performed not as a means for self-externalization, but as a means to satisfy needs acquired outside work.

The social division of labor is not peculiar to the capitalist socioeconomic formation. But the latter differs from all previous social formations in that it ushered in for the first time in history a new form of division of labor, namely, a technical division.[5] The more labor is fragmented, the more the worker's dissatisfaction mounts, until finally labor itself becomes a source of displeasure and discomfort to the worker. This subjective dimension of alienation, however, is not just an aspect of technically fragmented labor; it is actually experienced as a form through which the individual's humanity attains objective expression. It is also present in some form or other in socially divided labor. The technical division of labor merely renders more acute the subjective alienation that is already inherent in the social division of labor; further, in the form the latter assumes in capitalist society (social production and private appropriation), it also carries with it an objective aspect of alienation, in which the product of labor, and labor itself, divided technically, assume an autonomous existence over against their producer and executor. The social division of labor exists in all societies, but the specific form it assumes in capitalist societies is distinguished by the fact that it is combined with and compounded by the technical division of labor. The division of labor that occurs within production units is only the social division of labor in its extreme form, designed to promote the concentration of private property by engineering a rise in the rate of surplus value. Its sole purpose is to increase the productivity of labor, with no regard for the person of the worker.[6] In the end, then, the two forms of division of labor, the social and the technical, converge around one objective, and it is this union which gives capitalist society its distinctive markings: the contradiction, namely, between the social nature of production and the private nature of appropriation. Rationality within an enterprise (technical division of labor) is counterpoised to the irrationality of the system as a whole (social division of labor).

The "division of labor and private property are, moreover, identical expressions; in the one the same thing is affirmed with reference to activity as is affirmed in the other with reference to the product of the activity."[7] From this it follows that wage labor does not belong to the worker, but remains external. Hence, as an activity labor affirms the capitalist system, but only by negating individuals. For them labor is not a means of self-objectification that exists *in itself and for itself;* it is a means, only, which enables them to obtain gratification elsewhere, outside the workplace, and something alien in which they cannot recognize their own natures. Labor acquires an autonomy as something apart from human beings, yet it is from them that it originally flows, and upon them that it ultimately depends. It is impossible, therefore, to dissociate completely subjective alienation from objective alienation; in capitalist societies they are but two aspects of the same process, the worker's labor, at one and the same time disagreeable to him or her as an activity of which he or she is the executor, and external to him or her as the product of that activity. Objective alienation gives rise to subjective alienation and is commingled with it. These two dimensions of alienation come together as fundamental personality components in the constitution of a particular type of human being—the worker in competitive societies—adjusted to the capitalist way of life. Considering, then, that these two aspects of economic alienation, as well as the other dimensions of alienation in all its forms, are prerequisites of a personality adjusted to competitive society, only individuals who actually participate in the dominant system of production may be said to be truly adjusted to this type of society, to a greater or lesser degree, depending on the extent of their alienation.

Since the capitalist socioeconomic formation at once sustains two different types of female personality, or more accurately, combines components of both into a single type, work as an aspect of individual *praxis* and an element of self-enrichment takes on a particular significance for women which is different from that which it has for men.

A housewife's work is nonproductive in that it does not create surplus value.[8] Of course, as we have said, it is because women do the domestic work that men can devote themselves to jobs that are directly productive. So here, too, women's work is indirectly productive in that it is necessary to men's productive work. However, the mere fact that it is necessary does not tell us anything about its potential for alienation. Rather, it is the unproductive nature of women's work that defines how it appears to women and their attitude toward such work in the process of executing it. Housework is fragmentary by its very nature in capitalist societies. A woman obtains an industrial product completely ready to use and employs it in the home as she sees fit, within the limitations imposed by the household and the objects themselves; or she gets them in semi-finished form, and must add a few finishing touches before they are ready to be consumed. The monotonous nature of housework (even preparing meals, the least monotonous of all household chores, considering that variations are only possible within the limits of the family budget, which are sometimes very narrow indeed) makes it a disagreeable and unpopular task. On the other hand, however, the need it fulfills is an immediate one; there are no mediating links that would make the work seem to be something other than a necessity. For the person performing it, housework is certainly not experienced as a means of self-externalization, because the work itself is a necessity. The work becomes, so to speak, a mediating link between the subject and the realm of necessity. Nevertheless, it is also not a means for giving objective form to something that is *other;* the subjects do not recognize themselves again in their labor.

Housework is surely alienated labor in its subjective dimension, but not in its objective dimension. It is not productive work, and hence does not directly negate the activity that produces its results; in other words, it does not transcend labor as a pure process by acquiring an autonomous existence. Of all domestic chores, only the preparation of meals may be viewed directly as a moment in production in the broad sense, immediately preceding consumption.

There is another detail which further complicates a housewife's situation with regard to her work: the implements she uses and the objects upon which she performs her work impart to the objective products of labor (i.e., of her husband's labor) a doubly—both subjectively and objectively—alienated form. The vacuum cleaner and the refrigerator, manufactured clothing and foods, embody the value created by the objectively alienated labor of her husband, and in these things the housewife herself is alienated, although only indirectly, without experiencing the typical situation of objective alienation. In this context, the words of Simmel acquire their full significance:

> Women do not extend their activity beyond activity itself in order to achieve an object situated outside it. The flood of female vitality is reabsorbed by the same source from whence it springs. On the one hand, there is the absolutely masculine, which being more than masculine signifies objectivity, a normative aloofness from all subjectivity and opposition; heights which can only be attained along the path of dualism; on the other, there is the absolutely feminine, immobile, closed in within its own essence, representing the unity of being prior to the distinction between subject and object.[9]

Between these polar extremes circumscribing the female personality stands real woman, preparing in the first place for marriage, and secondarily for a vocation. A woman can always, therefore, take on a paying job when the family's economic situation requires it. But just because to have a job is not a value in itself, but merely a means to which one has recourse in special family situations, the occupational training of the female workforce has been quite spotty. Indeed, women are not actually fully prepared for the exercise of a trade or profession, if by this we also mean embarking on a career. They prepare themselves for employment of a provisional nature, and for just this reason their training is partial and deficient not only in technical terms, but also in all those other dimensions we have delineated as factors shaping the personality of the worker in competitive societies.

Women develop other typical personality components, however, which define them as workers both subjectively and objectively alienated from capitalist society, when they give up their jobs to marry or have children, and thereby enter into a permanent state of maladjustment. Their labor power sometimes appears as a commodity, and therefore with an exchange value, but sometimes it has only a use value. In fact, female labor power is a special type of commodity with no continuity, that is, it is not continually replaced to sustain objective alienation. The state of alienation is interrupted in all its fullness, so to speak, and whether it will be restored or not is one possibility among others whose realization the future will decide. Thus, women are cut off from the possibility of conferring on the economic aspect of their *praxis* the reiterative quality that is fundamental to a human being's condition as seller of labor power since her consumption is not directly determined by her own actions—the commodity quality of her labor power—but by the value of the labor power of the head of the family. In this respect, the alienation of the housewife who is simultaneously a wage laborer is partially maintained in its objective dimensions. Though she may stop working, a woman will maintain some ties with the objective market situation through her own consumption. However, these ties are sustained by the buying power of another's wages. In addition, therefore, to all the mediating links between consumption and need, there is, for the housewife, yet another: it is through the value represented by her husband's labor that she procures the consumer articles she needs. Two points emerge from this discussion: first, the value represented by a worker's wages must be sufficient to produce and reproduce his or her existence, and second, with woman's labor being a nonpermanent complement to this value, its transitoriness entails certain consequences for the personality of the working woman and for the system of production as a whole.

The new form assumed by alienation under neocapitalism (lessening of subjective alienation through humanization of the work place, at the same time as objective alienation grows) may be a necessary stage in its own abolition, raising as it does the possibilities of self-realization to a higher level. Still, the fact remains that by its very essence capitalism offers far more practical opportunities for self-fulfillment to men than to women. If, however, alienation developed under neocapitalism, which represents an extreme form of false consciousness, and hence a conservative force in capitalist society, it is at least conceivable that "single women," who are sacrificed far more frequently than men when the maintenance of the class structure requires it, and married women, who work irregularly (and hence shuttle back and forth from a relatively more alienated to a relatively less alienated state) are potentially not as conservative as has up to now been generally assumed. Yet it must be borne in mind that social class is neither masculine nor feminine; if as a human grouping it is partially coextensive with gender, it is not because it is more general but because it is of a different nature. The categories of sex have no historical tasks to fulfill. A distinction, therefore, between male *praxis* and female *praxis* is legitimate only in a general sense, and then only in measure as the class structure marginalizes women more than men. If the male and female worlds were completely separate, the scientist's task would be easy. However, that is not the case: relations between men and women are complementary in nature. Our inquiry, therefore, must go deeper, and try to discern among the structural contradictions of the social system those essential features of the system of production that will suffice to explain at once the roles of men, the roles of women, and the complementary functions they fulfill within each particular social formation.

Conclusion

Although tentative conclusions have been drawn throughout the three parts of this book, it is useful to try to sum up
in a more systematic fashion some of the points which have
been affirmed or rejected more or less explicitly in the course
of the analysis.

The guiding assumption throughout this study has been
that women's situation in capitalist society can be elucidated
by analyzing the relations existing between the sex factor and
the essential characteristics of the capitalist mode of production. This has enabled us to bring to light the mechanisms
with which market economies regulate the activities of the
two sexes so as to mitigate the conflicts generated by the
competitive social order. Society uses gender to restrict the
number of persons who are able to participate legitimately in
the process of competition. Since the capitalist system is
unable to absorb the total labor potential represented by all
normal adult members in class society, it seeks to eliminate
labor power from the market. To preserve itself without
excessively exposing its internal contradictions, it uses biological and/or racial and ethnic categories for this purpose;
to justify the marginalization of large numbers of women
from the class structure, for example, it stresses their traditional childbearing and childraising functions.

We found that, contrary to common assumptions made both by those affirming and those negating the capitalist status quo, class society did not put women to work, nor did it give her broader chances to become an economically productive being. In fact, even more than preceding societies, competitive society has given women fewer and fewer directly economic functions. This marginalization of women grows as the productive forces of private enterprise societies develop. As material technology advances, the economic entrepreneur is obliged more and more to substitute machinery for human labor in order to appropriate a greater portion of surplus value created by the increase in labor productivity. Since the physiological limits to increasing the work pace and the length of the working day are narrow, the way that industrial capitalism established itself and expanded was to replace people by machinery. Granting that an increase in labor productivity is a socially desirable goal, we must look to the totality of which this goal is a part to determine if it represents the goal of society as a whole or only the goal of a particular social class.

It follows from the inherent ethic of social and economic democracy that nothing can be more desirable than an increase in the productivity of labor to such an extent that people may leave the realm of necessity to enter the realm of plenty. Yet when the product of social labor is distributed unequally, and when the opportunities for self-fulfillment available to human beings depend on factors over which they have no control, then as the productive forces of class society develop the possibilities of achieving real democracy in the social and economic spheres diminish proportionately. At this point competitive societies find a solution, albeit precarious and temporary, to the problem of structural unemployment by not making use of labor-saving technology. Indeed, there are no more stable and satisfactory solutions which are viable within the framework provided by the logic of the capitalist system of production. In class societies, therefore, attempts to solve the problem of unemployment are always only palliatives, aimed specifically at sectors that are in the process of developing socially unacceptable features, such as is the case with male unemployment.

For women, however, whose unemployment is justified in the light of her childbearing and childrearing functions, economic inactivity is not even considered unemployment in the strict sense. It would be illusory to think that the problem could be solved by creating the conditions by which she could function in occupations having to do with child care, food preparation, or other public services. Although capitalist societies have encouraged the transformation of former household chores into gainful employment categories, they have effectively prevented other activities from undergoing the same transformation process, since it is upon the maintenance of these distinctions that social stability to a large measure depends. Class society would be working against itself if it were to offer women conditions that were ideal, or almost ideal, for reconciling her childbearing and child-raising functions with her occupational activities. Since the system of production in market economies is unable to absorb all the potential labor force, relieving women of their traditional functions would mean a substantial increase in the available workforce, and that, aside from aggravating the problem of unemployment, would also expose the social structure to the watchful eyes of its critics.

The situation of women exemplifies quite well the impasse reached by class society, and some of capitalism's inherent contradictions may be laid bare by a careful analysis of this problem. Free-enterprise (competitive) society claims to be a society without classes—or at least without antagonistic classes—whose members enjoy sufficient freedom to acquire a social status commensurate with their personal abilities, a society in which birth, sex, and color factors are not exploited by rigidly stratified social formations (i.e., castes or status groups) to determine the destinies of individuals and groups. Actually, they merely invert the order of such factors and rearrange them to facilitate achievement of their objectives. Whereas in precapitalist societies ethnic origins and sex categories lay at the roots of the inferior social status of the slave, the servant, and woman, in competitive societies the situation is the reverse: as social and economic development proceeds, natural characteristics come to interfere less and less with the competitive order and its rational organization. Thus, all men and all women are free to acquire any and every social status that exists in society, provided they have the necessary qualifications. Behind this camouflage, however, ethnic affiliation and sex category still operate to promote or restrict opportunities for the various ethnic groups and the two sexes.

As it evolves, free-enterprise society continues to refine the social techniques it employs to induce its members to act in consonance with its overall needs, relying less and less on biological or ethnic factors and more and more on social distinctions, especially regarding the functions each person must perform to ensure the smooth functioning of the whole of which he or she is a part. Whereas in some cases the nature of the human body itself provides arguments in support of woman's remaining in the home; in others it is social factors which estrange large numbers of women from the class structure. Ultimately, however, what happens is that natural factors get worked and reworked so that society itself can no longer keep these arguments distinct. For most people, this ambiguity enables perception of the structural and functional demands of the class structure. On the contrary, it has created a similar ambiguity in the attitudes of men and women, and indeed, contains a potential means for satisfying the structural and functional demands of the market economy.

The upholding of two contradictory ideals—the goal of

social advancement and the aspiration (which is both male and female) to ensure women the financial means necessary for her to become an economically inactive woman—are striking testimony to the social contradictions inherent in a system which seeks to maintain itself by two opposing mechanisms: by preselecting the individuals who are permitted to enter the process of competition with their satisfaction mediated through the family and by guaranteeing the consumption of goods, even if only on a subsistence level, among all its members. Basically, therefore, this ambiguity has proven to be a highly rational mechanism with regard to its aims, since it permits the establishment of different types of personality, and hence behavioral patterns, for the single woman and for the married woman. Since society cannot neglect the basic consumer needs if its members are to survive, and claims that wages do not represent remuneration for the labor of an individual worker, but of the entire family, the solution found in the long process of replacing manual labor by machines is to raise children to believe in both conflicting ideals. By shaping attitudes favorable or disfavorable to female labor according to a woman's civil status (whether she has small children), financial need, and level of the family's aspirations, society regulates the occupational activities of its female members in such a way as to preserve its social equilibrium.

In any case, capitalist society does not see work as a way toward self-fulfillment for women, nor does it intend to define her labor power permanently as a commodity. When work is indicated as therapy for female neuroses, which often derive from loss of functions in the home (i.e., when the children leave the nest), or from the monotony of housework, it is often regarded as a provisional solution, not a definitive one, nor is remuneration usually considered. Quite frequently, work therapy consists of philanthropic tasks which grant neither the economic independence necessary to emotional stability in competitive societies nor the status of exploited laborer. By giving the female worker a special status, class society appears to offer freedom for individual self-realization while at the same time reinforcing biological distinctions which, in their socially elaborated forms, serve to limit the full development of the female personality.

Although male consciousness often seems to articulate the contrary, the marginalization of women from the class structures does not confer an unmixed blessing upon men, since the family has less income for its consumer needs. Not only is feminine consciousness mystified, but men, too, let themselves be duped into believing that the disadvantages of unequal distribution of the products of social labor are offset by their continued dominance over women. Since mystification of consciousness affects men and women alike, these questions do not often acquire the dimensions of a social problem. Nevertheless, social phenomena need not disrupt the consciousness of the vaious groups and strata of society to be recognized as problems. The situation of women in competitive societies may become clearer by examining it in the light of the inconsistencies present in their social roles, inasmuch as these inconsistencies are potentially capable of affecting the stability of the female personality, the functioning of institutions, and the social behavior of individuals.

The intense social changes taking place in today's world cannot alone explain woman's situation. Consequently, any effort to cope with the problem must go straight to the sources of tension, which are located in the very dynamics of social organization. But because the problematic nature of woman's situation in class society is not transitory, but stems from permanent sources of tension, social scientists may expect to encounter serious obstacles to their practical efforts. Since social scientists do not totally determine the direction of their essence, it is not surprising that they should meet with considerable resistance wherever they attempt to view the woman problem as a permanent product of the structure of class societies and not as a phenomenon of social pathology.

This is not to propose that a holistic approach is the only one; nor even that it be given preference in every particular case. As regards the control of social phenomena and their dynamics at the micro level, once a process of thoughtful intervention into social life is set into motion, an "exclusive concern with providing a synthetic description of the broad contours of social development may indeed be important as a subjective element in predicting and steering organized group action; but it is inadequate for ensuring that each step of a rational intervention will be carried out effectively."[1] Still, a holistic approach provides a broader frame of reference within which to fit these descriptive studies of particular areas of empirical fact, and in so doing creates the possibility of rational intervention into the existing social reality on behalf of a historical agent which society's division into classes has reduced to an underprivileged state. A holistic approach can be enriched by the descriptions of particular phenomena; it is, after all, important to keep under scrutiny the changes they undergo during the course of a conscious intervention into social reality. On the other hand, an extension of the viewpoint taken in studies of social pathology is viable only in periods of social revolution. At any other time, attempts to apply the knowledge of the social sciences amount to no more than treating symptoms rather than the sources of friction in competitive society. The upshot is that, in the long run, science itself becomes a source of social tension in class society. While representing a higher level of consciousness of social problems, at the same time it is prevented from acting to eliminate the contradictions which generate them.[2]

Any attempt to deal with the problem of women in class societies, therefore, must take into account the fact that the capitalist system of production imposes insurmountable structural limitations on any deliberate intervention into social life with a view toward getting to the roots of such problems. In socialist societies, the conditions for surmounting these problems exist potentially, and can be made a reality once the society of abundance becomes a historical fact, through equal distribution of the products of social labor, with material technology being put to use to reduce the working day of both men and women. Yet the belief that the institution of socialism would automatically bring about the demolition of the cultural factors responsible for woman's inferior social standing undercut the chances of finding a satisfactory solution to the woman problem. We now know that it is not enough merely to channel the collective will into revolutionary action if the structure of class societies is to be demolished. It is also necessary to analyze and predict the behavior of crucial sociocultural factors so that the process of radical change can be steered to successful completion.

Since the categories of sex are not autonomous, and since they are not essential characteristics of the capitalist system of production, a consciousness which totally negates capitalism only touches the surface of the woman problem without really entering into all its intricacies. It will directly attack the essential properties of a class society, believing that such an attitude is sufficient to solve all the system's contradictions. The socialist perspective has not been able to come up with solutions to feminist questions, on either the theoretical or practical levels. Theoretically, the shortcoming is due to its equating relations between the sexes with relations between social classes. Some socialists have put forward the idea that feminism is valid only as a limited perspective and is dependent on points of view that are structurally determined, that is, by the consciousness of diametrically opposed classes, yet none has been able to come up with a convincing explanation of women's situation in capitalist society based on a thorough examination of the relations between the value systems that shape the stratificatory schema and the class structure. On the practical side, although the socialist experience by no means represents a definitive solution to feminist issues, it has seen to it that the progress of women's emancipation at the social level was matched by guarantees of economic security. In this respect the socioeconomic development of socialist societies could in the not too distant future establish a real social equality between the sexes. In class societies, on the other hand, women's sexual and reproductive liberation, and their growing social equality, tend to be accompanied by their increasing marginalization from productive and decision-making functions. Thus, "the overcoming of the age-old antagonism, that is, the overcoming of masculinity and femininity as real things, existing together in amicable discord, as it were, must wait until later. It still depends on the utopian exploration of the possible, and of the impossible."[3]

Notes

Notes to Introduction

1. Aside from descriptive studies dealing with very limited aspects of the life of the Brazilian woman, there exist only two historical works: Luiz Pereira, *O Magistério Primário na Sociedade de Classes,* and Manoel Tosta Berlinck, *"Algumas percepções sôbre a mudança do papel ocupacional da mulher, na cidade de São Paulo."* Pereira is concerned with a specific occupation filled mainly by women, not with woman's condition in general, and therefore does not go into the main areas in which women are active and how they are dependent on the Brazilian social structure. Berlinck concentrates on the city of São Paulo, and although he tries to go beyond this rather restricted empirical field of enquiry, he provides no new theoretical insights into the problems which directly or indirectly affect the female condition in class societies in general, or the Brazilian society in particular.
2. See Jean-Paul Sartre, *Search for a Method.*
3. To speak of demystifying science might at first glance seem to imply an attempt to invalidate Marx's thesis that "the mode of production of material life conditions the general process of social, political and intellectual life." (*A Contribution to the Critique of Political Economy,* pp. 20-21.) The real issue is not to dispute Marx, however, but to discern in science not a moment of false consciousness but a posterior moment of falseness of consciousness. See Georg Lukacs, "Class Consciousness," in *History and Class Consciousness.*

4. "Every piece of historical knowledge is an act of self-knowledge." Lukacs, "The Changing Function of Historical Materialism," in ibid., p. 223.
5. Lukacs, "Reification and the Consciousness of the Proletariat," in ibid., p. 83.
6. Lucien Goldmann, *The Human Sciences and Philosophy*.
7. As Marx pointed out, "The question whether objective truth is an attribute of human thought—is not a theoretical but a practical question," which individuals must work out. "The dispute over the reality or nonreality of thinking that is isolated from practice is a purely *scholastic* question. See Marx and Engels, *The German Ideology*, p. 197.
8. "Many have erred for different reasons, distorting and disparaging the Negro, who could not have benefited less from such treatment." Florestan Fernandes, *A Integração do Negro à Sociedade de Classes*, p. v.

Notes to Chapter 1:
Class and Status in Stratified Society

1. The social aspect of the division of labor between classes has a very specific meaning here and should not be confused with the notion of the social division of labor that refers to the three major branches of the overall system of production of goods and services: the primary sector, the secondary sector, and the tertiary sector. As it is used in the present context the term implies that in class society labor is divided in such a way that the class of wage laborers produces surplus value directly or contributes to its production. This surplus value is appropriated by the capitalist as profit, whether that be regarded as payment for the capitalist's present labor, or for past labor congealed in capital.
2. "Even the most abstract categories, despite their validity in all epochs—precisely because they are abstractions—are equally a product of historical conditions even in the specific form of abstractions, and they retain their full validity only for and within the framework of these conditions." Karl Marx, *A Contribution to the Critique of Political Economy*, p. 210.
3. Georg Lukacs, *History and Class Consciousness*, p. 57.
4. Although my methodological approach is obviously quite close to Weber's, it is not identical. I do agree with Weber, however, when he states:

Very frequently a status group is instrumental in the production of a thoroughbred anthropological type. Certainly status groups are to a high degree effective in producing extreme types, for they select personally qualified individuals (e.g., the knighthood selects those who are fit for warfare, physically and psychically). But individual selection is far from being the only, or the predominant, way in which status groups are formed: political membership or class situation has at all times been at least as frequently decisive. And today the class situation is by far the predominant factor. After all, the possibility of a style of life expected for members of a status group is usually conditioned economically. . . .

For all practical purposes, stratification by status goes hand in hand with a monopolization of ideal and material goods or opportunities, in a manner we have come to know as typical. Besides the specific status honor, which always rests upon distance and exclusiveness, honorific preferences may consist of the privilege of wearing special costumes, of eating special dishes taboo to others, of carrying arms—which is most obvious in its consequences—the right to be a dilettante, for example, to play certain musical instruments. However, material monopolies provide the most effective motives for the exclusiveness of a status group; although, in themselves, they are rarely sufficient, almost always they come into play to some extent. Within a status circle there is the question of intermarriage: the interest of the families in the monopolization of potential bridegrooms is at least of equal importance and is parallel to the interest in the monopolization of daughters . . . With an increased closure of the status group, the conventional preferential opportunities for special employment grow into a legal monopoly of special offices for the members. Certain goods become objects for monopolization by status groups, typically, entailed estates, and frequently also the possession of serfs or bondsmen and, finally, special trades. This monopolization occurs positively when the status group is exclusively entitled to own and to manage them; and negatively when, in order to maintain its specific way of life, the status group must *not* own and manage them. For the decisive role of a style of life in status honor means that status groups are the specific bearers of all conventions. (Max Weber, *Economy and Society*, vol. 2, pp. 935-36.)

5. Lukacs, *History and Class Consciousness*, p. 56.
6. Stanislaw Ossowski, *Estrutura de Classes na Consciência Social*. The inherent difficulties in trying to work out a schema of composite rank in a class structure are avoided here inasmuch as a privileged economic position corresponds to a privileged position in

the political and social spheres. Moreover, the same type of correspondence is observable with regard to underprivileged positions among the lower layers. The stratification pattern of the societies under discussion could also be called a functional pattern. Since the two terms are not incompatible, I chose the term composite rank in consonance with the aims of this study.

7. Weber explained that the differentiation of property classes is not dynamic because it does not necessarily result in class struggle and revolution. Slave owners, for example, may coexist with peasants, "frequently without any class antagonism and sometimes in solidarity (against the unfree)," as was true with the alliance between plantation owners and "poor white trash" in the pre-Civil War U.S. South. He added that the juxtaposition of property classes may lead to revolutionary conflict between landowners and the declassed, or creditors and debtors (often urban patricians versus peasants or small urban craftsmen). Weber, *Economy and Society*, vol. 1, pp. 303-4.

8. Weber made this point explicitly: "the notion of honor peculiar to status absolutely abhors that which is essential to the market: hard bargaining." Ibid., vol. 2, p. 937.

9. Ibid., vol. 1, p. 25.

10. The term *rationalization* is used here in the sense of an action that is rational relative to its ends, as Weber defined it. Ibid., p. 26. The Weberian concept of an instrumentally rational action corresponds to Mannheim's notion of functionally rational.

11. Lukacs, *History and Class Consciousness*, p. 57.

12. Marx, *A Contribution to the Critique of Political Economy*, p. 21.

13. Ibid., p. 212.

14. Ibid.

15. This is clear in Marx's *A Contribution to the Critique of Political Economy:*

> It would be inexpedient and wrong therefore to present the economic categories successively in the order in which they have played the dominant role in history. On the contrary, their order of succession is determined by their mutual relation in modern bourgeois society and this is quite the reverse of what appears to be natural to them or in accordance with the sequence of historical development. . . . It is precisely the predominance of agricultural peoples in the ancient world which caused the merchant nations— Phoenicians, Carthaginians—to develop in such purity (abstract precision).

(Ibid., p. 213.)

16. Lukacs, *History and Class Consciousness*, p. 58.
17. Weber identified the social actions that determine the class situation of the worker and the entrepreneur as the labor market, the commodities market, and the capitalistic enterprise:

> But, in its turn, the existence of a capitalistic enterprise presupposes that a very specific kind of social action exists to protect the possession of goods *per se*, and especially the power of individuals to dispose, in principle freely, over the means of production: a certain kind of legal order. Each kind of class situation, and above all when it rests upon the power of property *per se*, will become most clearly efficacious when all other determinants of reciprocal relations are, as far as possible, eliminated in their significance. It is in this way that the use of the power of property in the market obtains its most sovereign importance.

Before examining how status groups hinder the strict operation of the market principle, he summarized the changing forms of class antagonism:

> the struggle in which class situations are effective has progressively shifted from consumption credit toward, first, competitive struggles in the commodity market and then toward wage disputes on the labor market. . . .
>
> The propertyless of Antiquity and of the Middle Ages protested against monopolies, pre-emption, forestalling, and the withholding of goods from the market in order to raise prices. Today the central issue is determination of the price of labor. The transition is represented by the fight for access to the market and for the determination of the price of products. Such fights went on between merchants and workers in the putting-out system of domestic handicraft during the transition to modern times. Since it is quite a general phenomenon we must mention here that the class antagonisms that are conditioned through the market situations are usually most bitter between those who actually and directly participate as opponents in price wars. It is not the rentier, the share-holder, and the banker who suffer the ill will of the worker, but almost exclusively the manufacturer and the business executives who are the direct opponents of workers in wage conflicts.

(Weber, *Economy and Society*, vol. 2, pp. 930-31.)
18. Rodolfo Stavenhagen, "Estraficação social e estrutura de classes," *Ciencias Politicas y Sociales*. This is reproduced in *Estrutura de Classes e Estratificação Social*, pp. 136-37.

19. John Eaton, *Marx Against Keynes.*

20. This useful distinction is made by Stavenhagen:

> If a social category is not in structural opposition to a class, but rather occupies an intermediate position in all respects, then it is not a class, but only a fraction, a layer, or simply an intermediate category. If, therefore, one wishes to be consistent with this conception of classes, one cannot speak of "middle classes." ... The intermediate categories or layers are not structurally independent elements in society; they are shaped by particular economic circumstances and their members gravitate toward one or the other of the classes in opposition.

(Stavenhagen, "Estratificação social," reproduced in *Estrutura de Classes,* p. 141.)

21. Weber, for example, made clear that "whereas the genuine place of classes is within the economic order, the place of status groups is within the social order, that is within the sphere of the distribution of honor. From within these spheres, classes and status groups influence one another and the legal order and are in turn influenced by it. *'Parties'* reside in the sphere of power." He noted that one might say that "classes are stratified according to their relations to the production and acquisition of goods; whereas status groups are stratified according to the principles of their *consumption* of goods as represented by special styles of life." (Weber, *Economy and Society,* vol. 2, pp. 937, 938.) The fact that Marx distinguished three, four, and even more classes in his analyses of concrete sociohistorical situations does not invalidate the concept of social classes defined as groupings occupying diametrically opposed positions in the productive system, nor the two-class model. Although every society has its dominant mode of production, vestiges of former modes of production exist side by side along with it, and it is the existence of these forms of production that are marginal to the dominant one that is responsible for the existence of secondary social classes.

22. Ralf Dahrendorf, *Las clases sociales y su conflicto en la sociedad industrial.* (In English as *Class and Conflict in Industrial Society.*)

23. Fernando Henrique Cardoso, *Capitalismo e Escravidão no Brasil Meridional,* p. 135.

24. Weber pointed out the consequences of these differences:

> When the bases of the acquisition and distribution of goods are relatively stable, stratification by status is favored. Every

technological repercussion and economic transformation threatens stratification by status and pushes the class situation into the foreground. Epochs and countries in which the naked class situation is of predominant significance are regularly the periods of technical and economic transformations. And every slowing down of the change in economic stratification leads, in due course, to the growth of status structures and makes for a resuscitation of the important role of social honor.

(Weber, *Economy and Society*, vol. 2, p. 938.)

25. In a letter to Joseph Bloch, September 21, 1890, after Marx's death, Engels tried to formulate the precise terms in which dialectical materialism views the relationship between the economic infrastructure and the ideological superstructure, rejecting the distortions to which the materialist conception of history had been subjected. He wrote:

The economic situation is the basis, but the various elements of the superstructure—political forms of the class struggle and its results ... the juridical forms, and especially the reflections of all these real struggles in the brains of the participants, political, legal, philosophical theories, religious views ... also exercise their influence upon the course of the historical struggles and in many cases determine their form.

(Karl Marx, *Selected Correspondence*, p. 394.)

26. Social mobility studies are in effect, whether consciously or not, attempts to demonstrate that the class system is open and permits its members a broad range of mobility from one "class" to another. What is actually at issue is mobility between strata, or just mobility from one status to another. In fact, mobility rarely exists between classes. Even Dahrendorf, who distinguishes social class from sector (stratum) falls into the error of placing the bureaucracy among the ruling classes, although he acknowledges its heteronomy. The case of Dahrendorf is a good illustration of the extent of the confusion reigning as regards the concepts of social class and stratum, although for him domination, not ownership of the means of production, is the criterion marking the division of society into social classes. See Dahrendorf, *Las Clases Sociales*, pp. 323-24.

27. This is why functionalist analyses are unable to explain interstructural changes. Even in making use of the concept of dysfunction, they still remain at the functional level, which is only one (apparent) aspect of social phenomena. The recourse to the notion

of functional equivalent shows that the structural oppositions, which are what explanations of structural change are based on, have been put out of the picture.

From another perspective, Florestan Fernandes shows that the way they deal with the *time* factor is the most important logical limitation of functionalist analyses, dealing as they do with the "period of functioning" of societies. Such analyses look at "already constituted societies, with a view toward determining how at a given moment (or for the period of time under consideration) human collectivities exercise the activities vital to their existence. Although time is a variable, it is necessary to manipulate it, considering that the functional links have some interpretative value." While choosing a sufficiently long period may not be a problem in societies where the pace of change is slow, in those "experiencing relatively rapid structural transformations the functional connections that help to explain certain phenomena within a particular social configuration may be inadequate or even irrelevant for explaining the same phenomena in later social configurations." He illustrates this with a study of prejudices against blacks and mulattos in the city of São Paulo: "a full explanation of this phenomenon required a study of the functional connections obtaining in each phase of the structural development of São Paulo society. . . ." See Florestan Fernandes, *Fundamentos Empíricos da Explicaçao Sociológica*, pp. 272-74.

28. Marx, *A Contribution to the Critique of Political Economy*, p. 207.
29. See Lukacs, "What Is Orthodox Marxism?" in *History and Class Consciousness*, pp. 25-26.
30. Stavenhagen does not view social stratifications solely as "fossils of class relations on which those relations had originally rested"; he also sees them as forces that affect the functioning of the system of production, providing it with a justification, and reducing or attenuating the conflicts generated in the relations of production. Nevertheless, the question must still be seen from the opposite perspective which would mean to view social stratification as a requirement of the system of production, a necessary form of phenomenal manifestation." Stavenhagen, "Estratificaçao social," reproduced in *Estrutura de Classes*.
31. Ibid., p. 144.

Notes to Chapter 2:
Levels of Consciousness of the Woman Problem

1. Georg Simmel, *Cultura Femenina y otros ensayos*, p. 53.
2. The fact that an individual's worldview will tend to correspond to his or her place in the social structure does not mean that certain individuals cannot assume the perspective of other persons belonging to a different social class. On this point see Robert K. Merton, "Contributions to the Theory of Reference Group Behavior" and "Continuities in the Theory of Reference Groups and Social Structure," in Robert K. Merton, *Social Theory and Social Structure.*
3. "The distinctive character of social science discourse is to be sought in the fact that every assertion, no matter how objective it may be, has ramifications extending beyond the limits of science itself. Since every assertion of a fact about the social world touches the interests of some individual or group, one cannot even call attention to the existence of certain facts without courting the objections of those whose very *raison d'être* in society rests upon a divergent interpretation of the factual situation." Louis Wirth, preface to Karl Mannheim, *Ideology and Utopia*, p. xv.

Notes to Chapter 3:
The Rise of Capitalism and the Social Position of Women

1. Weber distinguished the two terms as follows:

> We may speak of a "class" when (1) a number of people have in common a specific causal component of their life chances, insofar as (2) this component is represented exclusively by economic interests in the possession of goods and opportunities for income, and (3) is represented under the conditions of the commodity or labor markets. This is "class situation."
>
> It is the most elemental economic fact that the way in which the disposition over material property is distributed among a plurality of people, meeting competitively in the market for the purpose of exchange, in itself creates specific life chances. . . . "Property" and the "lack of property" are, therefore, the basic categories of all class situations. It does not matter whether these two categories become effective in the competitive struggles of the consumers or of the producers. . . . But always this is the generic connotation of the

concept of class: that the kind of chance in the *market* is the decisive moment which presents a common condition for the individual's fate. Class situation is, in this sense, ultimately market situation.

(Max Weber, *Economy and Society*, vol. 2, pp. 927 and 928.)

2. Karl Marx, *A Contribution to the Critique of Political Economy*, p. 204.

3. Ibid., pp. 204-5.

4. Marx stated this clearly in *Capital*. "The capitalist epoch is therefore characterized by this, that labor power takes in the eyes of the laborer himself the form of a commodity which is his property; his labor consequently becomes wage labor. On the other hand, it is only from this moment that the produce of labor universally becomes a commodity." Karl Marx, *Capital*, vol. 1, p. 120, fn. 1.

5. Ibid., p. 568.

6. "The essential difference between the various economic forms of society, between for instance a society based on slave labor and a society based on wage labor, lies only in the mode in which the surplus labor is in each case extracted from the actual producer, the laborer." Ibid., p. 217. The capitalist mode of production is characterized by the appropriation, by the capitalist, of the surplus labor of the actual producer in the form of relative surplus value.

7. Bernhard J. Stern, "Woman, Position in Society," in *Encyclopedia of the Social Sciences*.

8. Marx stated this explicitly in *A Contribution to Critique of Political Economy*:

> In the social production of their existence, inevitably men enter into definite relations, which are independent of their will, namely relations of production appropriate to a given stage in the development of their material forces of production. The totality of these relations of production constitutes the economic structure of society, the real foundation, on which arises a legal and political superstructure and to which correspond different forms of social consciousness . . . It is not the consciousness of men that determines their existence, but their social existence which determines their consciousness (pp. 20-21).

9. Ibid., p. 21.

10. Jean Freville, for example, has noted that wages for working women in the Middle Ages were extremely low. "The guilds opposed female labor, and tried to eliminate a dangerous competition

which they considered disloyal. Some forced women to join, but prohibited them access to master's status; others refused to admit them at all, claiming the arduousness of the tasks." As a result, he concludes, women, barred from the guilds, "were subject to the trying conditions and low wages of work in the home." Jean Freville, *La Femme et le communisme*, p. 24.

In medieval France, a master's widow was permitted the status of master, but she lost this right if she remarried. In both female and mixed guilds, the representative functions were performed by men. The former were few in number and inconspicuous; in the latter, the women often did the work while their husbands held the status of master. Women's wages were lower, being estimated at 75 percent of men's wages for the fourteenth century. See Madeleine Guilbert, *Les Fonctions des femmes dans l'industrie*, pp. 23-25.

11. Marx, *Capital*, vol. 1, p. 394.
12. Ibid., p. 395.
13. Mary van Kleeck, "Women in Industry," in *Encyclopedia of the Social Sciences.*
14. Ten Hours' Factory Bill, The speech of Lord Ashley, March 15, 1844, cited in Marx, *Capital*, vol. 1, p. 402, fn. 2.
15. Ibid., p. 499.
16. Simone de Beauvoir, *The Second Sex.*
17. Kleeck, "Women in Industry."
18. Bernard Muldworf, "La Femme à la recherche de sa personne," in *La Femme à la recherche d'elle même*, p. 199.
19. Fédération nationale de l'alimentation. IIe Congrès, Lyon, 1903. Agenda presented by the Lille delegation, in Guilbert, *Les Fonctions des femmes*, pp. 51-52.
20. Ibid., p. 44.
21. Marguerite Thibert, "L'évolution du travail féminin," p. 735.
22. Alva Myrdal and Viola Klein, *Women's Two Roles*, p. 46.
23. Guilbert, *Les Fonctions des femmes*, pp. 60-61.
24. Myrdal and Klein, *Women's Two Roles*, p. 52.
25. Survey carried out by the Amalgamated Engineering Union in 228 factories in 1945; in ibid., p. 53.
26. Thibert, "L'évolution du travail féminin," p. 736.
27. Ralph E. Smith, "Sources of Growth of the Female Labor Force, 1971-75," pp. 27-29.
28. Harry Braverman, *Labor and Monopoly Capital*, p. 85.
29. Smith, "Sources of Growth of Female Labor Force," p. 28.
30. Betty Friedan, *The Feminine Mystique.*

31. Takashi Koyama, *The Changing Social Position of Women in Japan,* pp. 105-6.

32. Thibert, "L'évolution du travail féminin," p. 737. For more details on France see: Andrée Michel and Geneviève Texier, *La condition de la française d'aujourd'hui,* p. 133; on Japanese women, see: Koyama, *Changing Social Position;* on Arab women, see Renée Rochefort, "La femme dans les pays sous-developpés," in *La femme à la recherche d'elle-même,* 1966. On the United States, England, France, and Sweden see Myrdal and Klein, *Women's Two Roles.* The figure on Britain is quoted in Sheila Rowbotham, *Woman's Consciousness, Man's World.*

33. The role of education as an economic elevator and as a phenomenon correlated with the expropriation of the petty bourgeois property owner by monopoly capitalism has been analyzed in exhaustive detail for American society by C. Wright Mills, in *White Collar,* especially chs. 8, 9, and 12.

34. A survey carried out by the Observation Center at Vitry shows that working women are less nervous than those who do not work; they scold their children less, and have less tension at home. Other studies have shown that the mother's full-time presence in the home during a child's first years is not necessary. Children's problems seem to arise much more from insufficient affective relations between mother and child than from the mother's temporary absence. The children of working mothers show a distinct advantage over other children in school. Generally speaking, therefore, the excess attention a mother gives her children when she remains home all day long is much more detrimental to the child than attention given by a working mother when she has the time available. Conjugal relations are more harmonious when the wife works, and family stability is not threatened when the wife holds down a job, according to a study by F. Paris. Adultery is rarer among working wives than among those who do not work. Receiving an income of her own promotes a woman's self-confidence and stability, and undermines her fatalistic self-conception. See Menie Grégoire, "Mythes et réalités."

35. The rate of abenteeism for single women is much higher than for men, while that of married women is double that of men. See Myrdal and Klein, *Women's Two Roles,* ch. 6.

36. These four points are always present in modern Marxist sociological literature, although the space devoted to each will vary, with most weight being given to the productive sector. The following are

a few of the studies that take up the question from this perspective: *Femmes du XXe siècle* (Semaine de la Pensée Marxiste); *La femme à la recherche d'elle-même* (Semaine de la Pensée Marxiste de Lyon); Michel and Texier, *La condition de la française d'aujourd'hui;* Evelyne Sullerot, *La vie des femmes* and *Demain les femmes.* An article by Juliet Mitchell, entitled "Women: The Longest Revolution," follows this same line of thought and ventures to suggest some daring solutions to the woman problem. Her use of Louis Althusser's notion of overdetermination enables her to gain an overall perspective of woman's condition on the basis of her four basic roles: worker, reproducer, sexual being, and socializer of children. What is innovative in the concept of overdetermination is the notion that the contradictions between the different partial structures of society may cancel or reinforce each other. The term *unité de rupture* refers to "the moment when the conditions so reinforce each other as to coalesce into the conditions for a revolutionary change." The notion may have a heuristic value, but Mitchell's use of it is questionable: "It is only in the highly developed societies of the West that an authentic liberation of women can be envisaged today. But for this to occur there must be a transformation of all the structures in which they are integrated, and a *unité de rupture.* A revolutionary movement must base its analysis on the uneven development of each, and attack the weakest link in the combination. This may then become the point of departure for a general transformation." (p. 30)

37. Raymonde Noireaut-Blanc, *Tous les droits de la femme,* ch. 7.
38. Myrdal and Klein, *Women's Two Roles,* p. 59. The figures are for women between 15 and 60 years of age. The percentage of women workers among the total number of employed has risen in recent years in countries whose capitalist structure has undergone an accelerated growth.
39. Thibert, "L'évolution du travail féminin," p. 737.
40. Madeleine Guilbert and Viviane Isambert-Jamati, *Travail féminin et travail à domicile,* p. 43.
41. Ibid., p. 40. Actually, according to these authors the percentage of women working at home in the women's clothing industry may be almost 80 percent, although it is practically impossible to ascertain the exact numbers because many are kept secret by firms. The figures given refer to the period from August 1952 to April 1953, when the survey was carried out.

42. Ibid., p. 182.

43. A "single wage subsidy" is given to families in which only one of the spouses works and which have at least one child. Noireaut-Blanc, *Tout les droits*, p. 79. Thus once again it is the married woman with children who is the most exploited in the case of work taken on in the home.

44. Unless another source is specifically mentioned, the figures on female union membership are taken from Elsie Glück, "Women in Industry—Problems of Organization," in *Encyclopedia of the Social Sciences*.

45. Pierrette Sartin, *La Promotion des femmes*, pp. 210-11. Eleanor Flexner notes, however, that one of the bills they successfully supported was that of a Congress-financed investigation into the condition of women workers. See *Century of Struggle*, p. 213.

46. The statistics for France are taken from Francine Dumas, "La femme dans la vie sociale," in *Femmes du XXe siecle*, p. 51.

47. Up until 1930, in every industrial country the proportion of workers under 21 and in the age group 21-30 was far greater for women than for men. In the United States in 1930, 60 percent of the women workers ranged from 16 to 34 years as against 46 percent for men. The increasing proportion of married women among these workers (in 1890 one of seven was married, and in 1930 one of three) produced a more mature group of working women; but the position of the married woman created other difficulties for the union movement. Glück, "Women in Industry."

48. The figures on male-female wage differences are taken from ibid. See also Myrdal and Klein, *Women's Two Roles*, p. 107.

49. Guilbert, *Les Fonctions des femmes*, p. 69.

50. Koyama, *Changing Social Position*, p. 112.

51. Glück, "Women in Industry."

52. Gilbert Maire, *L'homme et la femme*, p. 196.

Notes to Chapter 4: The Socialist Perspective

1. Although Saint-Simon offered no more than a bare outline of an ideology for liberation, it was certainly a source of renewed inspiration for women. In 1832, the first issue of the newspaper *La Femme Libre* put out a call that was far bolder than a document issued at the end of the eighteenth century, "La Pétition des femmes du tiers état au Roi," describing the conditions of exis-

tence of French women. This document concluded with a request to the king to prohibit men the exercise of those activities which naturally belonged to the female sex, namely, sewing and weaving. At that time women had no designs on male occupations. Their claims, in fact, were modest; they wished merely to retain those activities which were theirs traditionally, and in a wholly conformist frame of mind were quite willing to accept sexual segregation over sexual equality. *La Femme Libre* took the opposite tack: it denounced the subjugation of women to men, arguing that both were born free, and assailed women's passivity in a historical period when upheaval of the body politic was justified in the name of liberty, and the proletariat was demanding release from bondage. For further discussion of the influence of Saint-Simon's writings on women, see Edith Thomas, *Les Femmes en 1848*, pp. 6-8.

2. Friedrich Engels, *Socialism, Utopian and Scientific*, pp. 73-74.
3. After declaring that "the degree of emancipation of woman is the natural measure of general emancipation," Fourier wrote:

> The humiliation of the female sex is an essential feature of civilization as well as of barbarism. The only difference is that the civilized system raises every vice that barbarism practices in a simple form to a compound, equivocal, ambiguous, hypocritical mode of existence.... No one is punished more severely for keeping woman in slavery than man himself.

(Quoted by Karl Marx and Friedrich Engels in *The Holy Family*, p. 230.)
4. Karl Mannheim, *Ideology and Utopia*, ch. 4, "The Utopian Mentality."
5. *Rheinische Zeitung*, November 15, 1842.
6. Karl Marx, *Capital*, vol. 1, p. 489.
7. See, for example, *The Economic and Philosophical Manuscripts of 1844*, pp. 133-34, where he states:

> In negating the *personality* of man in every sphere, this type of communism is really nothing but the logical expression of private property which is this negation. . . . In the approach to *woman* as the spoil and handmaid of communal lust is expressed the infinite degradation in which man exists for himself, for the secret of this approach has its *unambiguous*, decisive, *plain* and undisguised expression in the relation of *man* to *woman* and in the manner in which the *direct* and *natural* species relationship is conceived. This

direct, natural, and necessary relation of person to person is the *relation of man to woman*. . . . From this relationship one can therefore judge man's whole level of development.

8. See, for example, Marx and Engels, *The Holy Family*, p. 224.
9. Marx and Engels explained this fully in *The Communist Manifesto:*

> Bourgeois marriage is in reality a system of wives in common and thus, at the most, what the communists might possibly be reproached with, is that they desire to introduce, in substitution for a hypocritically concealed, an openly legalized community of women. For the rest, it is self-evident that the abolition of the present system of production must bring with it the abolition of the community of women springing from that system, i.e., of prostitution both public and private (p. 35).

10. See, for example, Karl Marx, *A Contribution to the Critique of Political Economy*, p. 20. The mode of production does not refer merely to the reproduction of the physical existence of individuals; "rather it is a definite form of activity of these individuals, a definite form of expressing their life, a definite *mode of life* on their part." Karl Marx and Friedrich Engels, *The German Ideology*, p. 31.
11. Friedrich Engels, *The Origin of the Family, Private Property and the State*, p. 55.
12. "It is the practice of slavery by the side of monogamy, the presence of young, beautiful slaves belonging unreservedly to the man that stamps monogamy from the very beginning with its specific character of monogamy *for the women only*, but not for the man. And that is the character it still has today." Ibid., p. 56.
13. Marx and Engels, *The German Ideology*, p. 44. In this work also, Marx and Engels saw the family as containing the beginnings of the division of society into classes, albeit only in embryonic form.
14. Engels, *The Origin of the Family*, p. 58.
15. "Within the family he is the bourgeois; and the wife represents the proletariat." Ibid., pp. 65-66.
16. "If in all ideology men and their circumstances appear upside down as in a camera obscura, this phenomenon arises just as much from the historical life process as the inversion of objects on the retina does from the physical life process." Marx and Engels, *The German Ideology*, p. 37.
17. See, for example, Simone de Beauvoir, *The Second Sex*.

18. Betty Friedan noted, with regard to "labor-saving" appliances: "The more a woman is deprived of function in society at the level of her own ability, the more her housework, mother-work, wife-work, will expand—and the more she will resist finishing her house-work and mother-work and being without any function at all. . . . The time required to do housework for any given woman varies inversely with the challenge of the other work to which she is committed." She found that American housewives were spending as many or more hours on housework as women thirty years earlier, despite smaller, easier-to-care-for homes, and various appli-ances; women who worked outside the home did the same house-keeping activities as women who did not, "but even with a thirty-five hour work week on the job, their workweek was only an hour and a half a day longer than the housewives." *The Feminine Mystique*, pp. 239-41.

19. Ibid., ch. 1.

20. A recent incident in Soviet Lithuania is a case in point. Anna Vikentyevna, unmarried teacher over thirty years old, expected a child. When her pregnancy became obvious, and there was no chance of interrupting it, Anna was advised to reveal the name of the child's father. In the meetings called by the teacher's union, the party, and the heads of the school to discuss the problem, it was decided that Anna should have a month's leave of absence to "hide her shame." Since Anna still refused to follow the advice given her, she was dismissed when the month's leave was up and her request for an apartment where she planned to live with her child was refused. Published in *O Estado de S. Paulo*, August 21, 1966.

21. Engels, *The Origin of the Family*, p. 67.

22. In the mountainous regions of the Caucasus, it is still the custom for men to abduct and violate young girls whom they intend to marry. About thirty girls are abducted every year in this region; according to custom, they then resign themselves to marrying their seducers, even when they have no amorous feelings toward them. Recently a young girl who was abducted and ravished in this way refused to marry her seducer, who was then convicted along with his accomplices, three other youths, by a court in Alagir where the incident occurred. The Soviet newspaper that reported the story praised the girl for her courage, reproved the passivity of the eyewitnesses who did nothing to prevent the abduction, and de-plored the attitude of an official who had aided the abductor in his undertaking. Published in *O Estado de S. Paulo*, January 12, 1967.

23. Juliet Mitchell considers this *unité de rupture* to be possible only in highly developed societies of the West because economic development was achieved there in an antithetical form (capitalism), which in the last instance determines all the other contradictions present in the female condition. Juliet Mitchell, "Women: The Longest Revolution," p. 30.

24. In *The Condition of the Working Class in England,* pp. 173-75, he states:

> In many cases the family is not wholly dissolved by the employment of the wife but turned upside down. The wife supports the family, the husband sits at home, tends the children, sweeps the room, and cooks. This case happens very frequently; in Manchester alone, many hundred such men could be cited, condemned to domestic occupations. It is easy to imagine the wrath aroused among the working men by this reversal of all relations within the family, while the other social conditions remain unchanged. If the family of our present society is being thus dissolved, this dissolution merely shows that at bottom the binding tie of this family was not family affection but private interest, lurking under the cloak of a pretended community of possessions.

25. Auguste Bebel, *Women and Socialism,* p. 100.

26. Ibid.

27. Ibid., p. 131.

28. "Girls and women of the petty bourgeoisie as well as of the working class thus compete with their fathers, brothers, and husbands." Paul Lafargue, "La Question de la femme," in *La Femme et le communisme,* p. 124. The use of the expression *partial competition* should be clear from the foregoing analysis.

29. "Motherhood, a sacred labor, the highest of the social functions, in capitalistic society turns into the cause of horrible economic and physiological miseries. The intolerable condition of women endangers the reproduction of the species." Ibid., p. 128.

30. Rudolf Schlesinger, *The Family in the USSR,* pp. 44 and 251. In 1937, the birth rate was 20 percent higher than in 1936; T. Serebrennikov, *La Mujer en la Union Soviética,* p. 34.

31. Schlesinger, ibid., p. 401, suggests that since motherhood is an occupation like any other, it is remunerated by the state, but this is misleading.

32. Clara Zetkin, "From My Memorandum Book," in V. I. Lenin, *The Emancipation of Women,* pp. 106-7.

33. Central Statistical Office, Moscow, *Women and Children in the USSR*, p. 126. In Denmark statistics show that 9 percent of women refuse any kind of help from men with the household chores. Menie, Grégoire, "Mythes et Réalités," p. 758. From casual observation it would seem that this figure is considerably higher in other Western countries, where women may receive occasional help from men, but refuse it on a regular basis. Given the massive proportion of working women in the Soviet Union it seems likely that opposition to men helping with household chores does not come from them, at least, not in the large urban centers, where women have not only made inroads into all occupations but are assuming more and more managerial and administrative posts as well. However, only a detailed survey will give a clear idea of women's attitudes toward this question.

34. In the Soviet Union, female participation in the economic structure of the nation is almost on a par with men's. In 1959, when women comprised 55 percent of the population of the USSR, they represented 48 percent of the nation's employed workforce. In this same year women made up 54 percent of persons with a completed or incomplete higher or specialized secondary education. In 1961 women made up the following percentages of persons with higher education employed in the national economy: engineers, 31 percent; agronomists, animal husbanders, veterinaries, 41 percent; economists, statisticians, market specialists, 59 percent; jurists, 32 percent; doctors (not including dentists), 74 percent; teachers, specialists with university education, librarians, etc., 67 percent. These figures are taken from *Women and Children in the USSR.*

Evelyne Sullerot has analyzed the progress made by women in certain professional sectors and shows that often they lower the status of an occupation because they entered into it through the civil service and are poorly paid. She gives this as a reason why the majority of school doctors in France are women. In fact this devaluation of professions that become "invaded" by civil servants is quite common in societies with private enterprise economies. However, Sullerot would seem to be mistaken when she applies the same line of reasoning to the Soviet Union. In a collective economy, such as exists in the USSR, professionals are perforce "civil servants." See Evelyne Sullerot, *Demain les femmes,* p. 187.

Notes to Chapter 5:
Some Aspects of the Development of the Brazilian Economy

1. Criticisms of these interpretations can be found in Caio Prado Jr., *A Revolução Brasileira*, and Luiz Pereira, *Trabalho e Desenvolvimento no Brasil*, especially ch. 3.

2. The following passage is typical of her approach:

> The situation of women in the underdeveloped countries may be described in terms of a scale of values proper to an emerging society that has been kept at a stage of development already surpassed by the capitalist metropolises. We could simplify the point by likening it to women's situation in medieval society, but by stating the problem in these terms we lose sight of everything that is novel to the historical condition of peripheral societies, namely, that which is fundamental to underdevelopment. What distinguishes underdeveloped countries is their dependency—the distortion and obstruction of their development as the metropolitan economy constantly grows stronger. In them, we will be able to find a wide range of relations, from the most primitive to pure capitalist relations. . . . We shall find even that one of the characteristic features of underdeveloped countries is just this overlapping of social structures, in different stages, which then come into conflict with one another as the contradictions grow more acute. In Brazil, for example, one can easily find one area where feudal and semifeudal relations still persist, and another where capitalist relations are already developing.

3. The fact that the cited article "suffers by being taken out of a context of a larger study aimed at capturing woman's shifting situation throughout the course of history" (p. 331), does not invalidate this criticism. On the contrary, it leads one to suspect that the larger study of which the article was a part interprets the situation of Brazilian women in terms of a purported feudal structure that was in the process of being replaced by a capitalist structure.

4. Karl Marx, *A Contribution to the Critique of Political Economy*, p. 21.

5. Max Weber, *Economy and Society*, vol. 3, p. 1099. He explains this opposition fully in the pages that follow:

> The feudal association and also the related patrimonial forms that have a stereotyped status structure constitute a concrete synthesis of purely concrete rights and duties. . . . Instead of a

system of abstract rules, compliance with which permits everybody the free use of his economic resources, we find a congerie of acquired rights, which impede the freedom of acquisition and provide opportunities for capitalist acquisition only through the granting of further concrete privileges, as they were generally the basis of the oldest manufactories. . . . Capitalist development is handicapped even more by the economic foundations and consequences of feudalism. . . . In general the feudal stratum tends to restrict the accumulation of wealth in bourgeois hands or at least to "declass" the *nouveaux riches*. . . . The social prestige of the manorial lords also motivates the *nouveaux riches* to invest their acquired wealth not in a capitalist venture but in land, in order to rise into the nobility if it be possible.

6. Celso Furtado, *Formação Econômica do Brasil*, 1963; Caio Prado Jr., *História Econômica do Brasil; Formação do Brasil Contemporâneo; Evolução Política do Brasil e Outros Estudos.*

7. Weber, *Economy and Society*, vol. 3, p. 1100.

8. The term *rational* is here used to mean an action relative to ends, or to a choice of means appropriate to the achievement of some predefined ends. See ibid., p. 25.

9. In discussing the differences between ancient and modern slavery Marx wrote:

But as soon as people whose production still moves within the lower forms of slave labor, corvée labor, etc., are drawn into the whirlpool of an international market dominated by the capitalistic mode of production, the sale of their products for export becoming their principal interest, the civilized horrors of overwork are grafted on the barbaric horrors of slavery, serfdom, etc. Hence the Negro labor in the Southern States of the American Union preserved something of a patriarchal character, so long as production was chiefly directed to immediate local consumption. But in proportion as the export of cotton became of vital interest to these states, the over-working of the Negro and sometimes the using up of his life in seven years of labor became a factor in a calculated and calculating system. It was no longer a question of obtaining from him a certain quantity of useful products. It was *now a question of production of surplus-labor itself.* (Author's italics)
(Karl Marx, *Capital*, vol. 1, p. 236.)

10. Actually, surplus value is appropriate at the point of production,

and is first converted into money through the circulation of commodities.

11. Marx, *Capital*, vol. 2, p. 478.

12. "It is in the tropical culture, where annual profits often equal the whole capital of plantations, that Negro life is most recklessly sacrificed." Ibid., vol. 1, p. 266.

The cultivation of sugar in Brazil yielded enormous profits during the best periods as Furtado has pointed out:

> Taking a figure of 1.5 million pounds for gross proceeds in the sugar sector, and figuring that roughly 10 percent of these proceeds goes to pay wages, purchase cattle, firewood, etc., and that the costs of replacing imported factors was on the order of 120 thousand pounds, we arrive at a figure of about 1.2 million pounds net profits for this sector. Subtracting 600 thousand pounds for imported consumer goods, that leaves us with 600 thousand pounds, as the total amount invested in this sector. Since the value of fixed capital ran to 1.8 million pounds and at least one third of this was in the form of buildings and facilities built by the slaves themselves, it follows that this capital was able to double its value in two years.

(Furtado, *Formação Econômica do Brasil*, p. 60.) The fact that a large part of the profits generated by the sugar-growing industry was appropriated by middlemen in no way alters the industrial character of these profits.

13. Ibid., p. 43. Although the importation of European labor under conditions of temporary indenture was less of a business risk in the case of the worker's death, and in the short term cheaper in that it immobilized less capital, a large-scale exporting agricultural economy could not be based on it, and indeed was not. According to Celso Furtado, the productivity of the economies of colonies relying on this imported labor was perceptibly inferior to that of colonies which employed slave labor on a massive scale.

14. "It was hence as a part of one system that this original, primitive mercantile capitalism evolved and was transformed under identical circumstances (although operating in different ways at the center and the periphery) into the major dominant economic powers of the imperialist system, on the one hand, and the dependent nations of Latin America on the other." Prado, *A Revolução Brasileira*, pp. 101-2.

15. Pereira, *Trabalho e Desenvolvimento no Brasil*, p. 80.

16. Although England did not succeed in renewing the treaty of 1827, which permitted British officials to board Brazilian ships suspected of carrying slaves, and although the United States was by the time it expired (in 1844) Brazil's largest market for exports, the fifty sugar factories built between 1875 and 1885 in Brazil were financed mostly with English capital, with its profits guaranteed by the Brazilian government. See Furtado, *Formação Econômica do Brasil*, p. 164. When Brazil refused to renew the treaty, England countered by placing heavy tariffs on the importation of products originating in slave-owning nations. Thus, Brazilian sugar paid 63 shillings duty while sugar imported from British colonies paid only 43 shillings. Brazil responded to this measure with the Alves Branco Tariff Bill, which provided that "the English cotton mills, whose imports to Brazil are equivalent to a loss annually of a million and a half pounds sterling, shall henceforth be required to pay a sum equivalent to that which Great Britain levies on our sugar in its ports." The Alves Branco tariff was approved in 1844, and England responded with the Aberdeen Bill, a unilateral measure which claimed the right of investiture, compounded by the right of capture and jurisdiction on the British high seas. England's repressive measures, however, served only to stimulate the slave trade. In the years prior to the Aberdeen Bill, the number of Africans entering the country ranged from 20 to 30 thousand; in 1846, this number had risen to 50,000, in 1847 to 56,000, and in 1848 to 60,000; a decline set in in 1849, when 54,000 slaves entered Brazil. This demonstrates the clearly political character of Brazil's resistance to the abolition of the slave trade, since no repressive measure was really effective in controlling it. In this respect, Furtado's observation that abolition was more a political than an economic measure is justified, though not precisely what he meant. See ibid., p. 166. (Figures taken from Nelson Werneck Sodré, *História da Burguesia Brasileira*, pp. 71 and 127.)

17. Florestan Fernandes, "Côr e estrutura social em mundanca," in: Roger Bastide and Florestan Fernandes, *Brancos e Negros em São Paulo*, p. 115.

18. See on this point the work cited in note 17 above and Fernando Henrique Cardoso, *Capitalismo e Escravidão no Brasil Meridional*, ch. 5; and Octávio Ianni, *As Metamorfoses do Escravo*, ch. 5.

19. Ianni, *As Metamorfoses*, p. 235.

20. Quite apart from the contradictions inherent in the slavocratic system, and even in the "capitalist-slavocratic" system, which were

already at work undermining the foundations of the Brazilian system of production, the emancipation of the blacks at the purely legal level began almost sixty years before abolition. The laws of 1831, 1871, and 1885 formally proclaimed the freedom of, respectively: Africans imported after 1831; children born from that time onward of a slave mother; and slaves who were over seventy years old at the time.

21. See Cardoso, *Capitalismo e Escravidão*, p. 204.

22. Paula Beiguelman, "O encaminhamento político do problema da escravidão no Império," in *Pequenos Estudos de Ciência Política*, p. 29, fn. 2.

23. The fact that the orientation of the groups that were directly or indirectly involved in the struggle for abolition or contributed to it by omission was much more economic than social is attested to by the position taken by the São Paulo delegates Prudente de Morais and Campos Salles on the government bill (presented to the Chamber of Deputies on July 15, 1884) providing for the automatic freedom of every slave who had reached the age of sixty before or after the law entered into force without any indemnification to his owner. These deputies, who represented the vital core of the Brazilian economy of that time (coffee-growing region) "declared themselves indifferent to the question of slavery and interested exclusively in immigration." Ibid., p. 42.

24. Nícia Vilela Luz, *A Luta Pela Industrialização do Brasil*, ch. 4.

25. The number of workers grew from 150,841 in 1907 to 275,512 in 1929; in ibid., p. 146.

26. In the 1930s, state subsidies to the coffee industry increased prices on imported goods as a consequence of foreign exchange policy; "idle production capacity in some industries supplying the domestic market," and "a small nucleus of capital goods industries existing within the country," together explain "the rapid increase in industrial production, which then became the principal dynamic factor in creating the national income." Furtado, *Formação Econômica do Brasil*, p. 233.

27. The average annual exchange rate in London decreased from 26.38 dollars per thousand réis in 1889 to 7.13 dollars per thousand réis in 1898. In 1925 the exchange rate fluctuated between a maximum of 7.63 and 4.88 dollars per thousand réis. Luz, *A Luta pela Industrialização*, pp. 153 and 172. In August 1961, one dollar fetched 220 cruzeiros; in April 1964, 1850 cruzeiros were necessary to buy one dollar, and in February 1967 the dollar had risen

to 2,710 cruzeiros. As had almost always been the case in preceding periods, this last measure was accompanied by a decree which reduced customs tariffs by 20 percent in an effort to offset the effects of the declining value of the cruzeiro on the costs of imported goods. By not applying differential tariff rates to the different categories of goods imported, the decree stimulated the importation of consumer goods to the detriment of the nation's industry.

28. Although the survey done by the Brazilian Institute of Social Sciences in 1962 gave only a partial picture, since it covered only the state of São Paulo, it did determine that 35 percent of the nation's economic groups owned agricultural enterprises (crop growing, animal raising, truck-farming, industrial crops), often with no relationship whatsoever to the principal activities of the group. Large sugarmill firms which dominate the sugar industry in the Northeast, for example, are linked with the principal industrial, commercial, or financial enterprises of the region, and frequently even have branches in other centers of the country. Prado Jr., *A Revolução Brasileira*, pp. 107-8.

29. According to Caio Prado Jr.:

> In the sugar-growing areas of the Northeast, the rural worker today lives in poorer conditions than in the past, and the fact directly responsible for this was the development and consolidation of capitalist relations of labor and production. A similar process is taking place in the state of São Paulo where the tenant farmer of old on coffee plantations is rapidly being replaced by the day laborer, i.e., the wage laborer in pure form. This day laborer has material standards which are unquestionably much poorer than those of the former tenant farmer.

(Ibid., p. 153.)

30. Pereira, *Trabalho e Desenvolvimiento*, p. 126.

31. Statistics on the number of persons employed in the various sectors of the nation's economy will be drawn on elsewhere in this work.

32. See Celso Furtado, *Subdesenvolvimento e Estagnação na América Latina*, chs. 3 and 4.

33. The United States is considered a highly developed country, despite the fact that 35 percent of its population, or 41.5 million Americans, were in 1958 living with "demonstrably substandard incomes." Michael Harrington, *The Other America*, p. 180.

Notes to Chapter 6: The Social Position of Women

1. The patrimonial structure resides in a decentralization of the household "when the lord settles dependents (including young men regarded as family members) on plots within his extended land-holdings, with a house and family of their own, and provides them with animals and equipment." Max Weber, *Economy and Society*, vol. 3, p. 1010. Patrimonial domination derives originally from organized power over the household; patriarchal domination is "essentially based not on the official's commitment to an impersonal purpose and not on obedience to abstract norms, but on a strict personal loyalty. The roots of patriarchal domination grow out of the master's authority over his household." Ibid., p. 1006.

2. See Caio Prado Jr., *Formação do Brasil Contemporâneo*, p. 362.

3. Although it is not my intention to classify Brazilian society according to Weber's typology, which rests on a specific interpretation of history, it is useful to employ his concepts in their political dimension insofar as it is possible to separate them from their economic dimension.

4. See Fernando Henrique Cardoso, *Capitalismo e Escravidão no Brasil Meridional*, p. 108.

5. Weber, *Economy and Society*, vol. 3, p. 1070.

6. Weber discusses this point more fully:

   > Patrimonialism is compatible with household and market economy, petty bourgeois and manorial agriculture, and the absence and presence of capitalist economy.... In general we can say about capitalism only that, since its opportunities for expansion are limited under feudalism and patrimonialism, its champions usually attempt to substitute bureaucratization or a plutocratic domination by *honoratioren*. This, too, however, is only true of production-oriented modern capitalism, based on the rational enterprise, the division of labor and fixed capital, whereas politically oriented capitalism, just as capitalist wholesale trade, is very much compatible with patrimonialism.... In contrast to feudalism, *trade* has often been a historically important factor in the development of strong, centralized patrimonial bureaucracies.

   (Ibid., pp. 1091-92.)

7. Roger Bastide and Florestan Fernandes, *Brancos e Negros em São Paulo*, p. 83.

8. The question here is one of a correspondence between interethnic

and racial stratification and socioeconomic stratification, according to Florestan Fernandes. (Ibid., p. 79) In my opinion, the question is rather one of a correspondence between social stratification and class structure, although in slavocratic Brazil the classes only partially tested on caste stratification.

9. Prado Jr., *Formação do Brasil Contemporâneo*, p. 342.

10. The belief in the authority of the lord is "rooted in filial piety, in the close and permanent living together of all dependents of the household which results in an external and spiritual community of fate. The woman is dependent because of the normal superiority of the physical and intellectual energies of the male." Weber, *Economy and Society*, p. 1007.

11. See, inter alia, Charles Expilly, *Mulheres e Costumes do Brasil.*

12. In a letter dated June 19, 1881, in which Ina von Binzer describes her life as a tutoress in Brazil, she says: "Dona Gabriela, Dona Olímpia, and Dona Emília are already nineteen, twenty-one, and twenty-two years old, respectively, which means for Brazilians they are almost old maids." Ina von Binzer, *Alegrias e Tristezas de uma Educadora Alemã no Brasil*, p. 23.

13. See inter alia, Domingos do Loreto Couto, *Desagravos do Brasil e Glórias de Pernambuco*, vol. 24; and Afonso de E. Taunay, *Sob el-Rei Nosso Senhor*, cited by Gilbert Freyre, *Casa-Grande e Senzala*, vol. 2, p. 588.

14. Ibid., p. 592.

15. A. Alcântara Machado, *Vida e Morte do Bandeirante*, chapter entitled "A Família." This author claims that vast legions of bastards grew "alongside and in the shadow of the legitimate family. Few were the homes in which they were not present" (p. 158).

16. "Our most humble poor display a most shameful lustfulness with an impudence that finds no counterpart in the most corrupt cities of Europe." Auguste de Saint-Hilaire, *Voyages aux sources du Rio São Francisco et dans la province de Goyaz*, vol. 1, p. 127.

17. See Antônio Cândido Mello e Souza, "The Brazilian Family," in Smith, *Brazil—Portrait of Half a Continent*, p. 296.

18. In a letter dated July 11, 1882, written in the province of São Paulo, Ina von Binzer refers to the activity of Dona Maria Luisa, the woman of the household where the German tutoress was teaching:

> She is everywhere, she always has her eye on the blacks; she herself is an excellent white master. . . . She makes the butter

herself, despite the considerable difficulties involved, using a cream separator as a churn; she sews on and on without tiring at her Singer, making underclothing and dresses for the children and huge winter coats for the house servants. In short, she is busier than any of those celebrated German Hausfrauen in a much more trying situation, and she demands and receives the consideration and respect of all. . . . Dona Maria Luisa, unlike the majority of Brazilian mistresses of the house, has literally everything under control.

(Binzer, *Alegrias e Tristezas,* pp. 99-100.)

19. Gilberto Freyre, *Casa-Grande e Senzala,* vol. 2, p. 587.
20. Mello e Souza, "The Brazilian Family," p. 303.
21. Gilberto Freyre, *Sobrados e Mocambos,* vol. 1, p. 102.
22. Property, "the source of all political rights, assumes, so to speak, the traits of sovereignty. It is the privilege of free men. Women in principle shall not be permitted sway over it." Machado, *Vida e Morte do Bandeirante,* p. 41.
23. The dowry made by Garcia Rodrigues Velho for his daughter included "first, two silk dresses, one of satin, and a third of camel's hair." Ibid., p. 155.
24. The economic consequences of the full establishment of the capitalist system of production in Brazil with regard to female roles will be analyzed later.
25. Blacks began to constitute legal families about the middle of the nineteenth century. In areas with a high concentration of blacks, such as Bahia and Maranhão, there was a hybrid between legal, Christian monogamous marriage and certain primitive customs with regard to the organization of sexual and domestic life, and a marked polygynous tendency. See Mello e Souza, "The Brazilian Family," p. 305.
26. Even the members of the Catholic clergy recognized that the roles society ascribed to the Brazilian married woman were incompatible with the indissoluble Christian family. In various pronouncements Father Charbonneau indicated a favorable attitude toward a transformation of woman's roles within the family so that the woman would be able to act as her husband's lover alongside of her other functions.
27. Emílio Willems, "A estrutura da família brasileira," p. 332.
28. Even at the end of the empire the number of persons who were legally married was infinitesimally small. "The family as a bureaucratic privilege, within the means of 27 percent of the population,

is not a public institution; it is an immoral disgrace." Tito Lívio de Castro, *A Mulher e a Sociogenia.*

29. Antônio Cândido Mello e Souza, "A vida familial do caipira," p. 350.

30. Cited in ibid., p. 352.

31. Antônio Cândido has summarized this as follows:

> In theory, the purpose of selecting a godfather is his function as a replacement for the father; in practice, the godchild functions almost always as merely an occasion for establishing some sort of cross-familial bonds. But in principle, the function of the godfather is so clear and so important that very often grandchildren refer to their grandfathers by this name, regardless of whether they are real godchildren or not, thus demonstrating the semi-paternal character of that institution.

(Ibid., p. 358.) See also Donald Pierson, "Família e compadrio numa comunidade rural paulista."

32. A recent event shows not only that female roles are undergoing a redefinition within urban industrial centers, but also that certain taboos are vanishing. The January issue of the journal *Realidade*, devoted entirely to the woman question, was widely read in the large cities. Half of the issue of 300,000 copies was sold in little more than one day, even though it was confiscated as soon as it appeared. (A statement by the first curator of minors of Guanabara, Newton de Barros Vasconcelos, published in *Fôlha de São Paulo*, January 5, 1967, read in part: "in neither the press nor in any other human activity ... shall different situations be blended together indiscriminately with the manifest intent of perverting aims, confusing minds, and upsetting the social order.")

Notes to Chapter 7:
Education for Women in Brazil
from the Colonial Period to the Present

1. On the instruction of parents in their religious tasks, see Serafim Leite, *História da Companhia de Jesus no Brasil.*

2. Fernando de Azevedo, *A Cultura Brasileira*, pp. 512-13.

3. According to Gilberto Freyre, for example:

> In the sixteenth century, priests and brothers of the more flexible orders, that is, with the exception of the Jesuits who

were intransigent celibates, cohabited on a broad scale with Indian and Negro women. For Father Nóbrega, the clergy of Pernambuco and Bahia were simply a disgrace. The clergy continued through the seventeenth, eighteenth, and a large part of the nineteenth century to freely tuck up their cassocks to exercise quasi-patriarchal functions, if not to engage in lustful excesses with Negro and mulatto women. A number of chroniclers relate how, very often under the camouflage of the most seraphic names in the world—Divine Love, Assumption, Mount Carmel, Immaculate Conception, and Rosary—thrived some doughty stallions instead of tormented ascetics harried by their vows of celibacy.

(Gilberto Freyre, *Casa-Grande e Senzala*, vol. 1, p. 619.)

4. Affonso de E. Taunay, *História de Villa de São Paulo, no século XVIII*, p. 178.

5. Sérgio Buarque de Holanda, *Raízes do Brasil*, pp. 180-81.

6. Alcântara A. Machado, *Vida o Morte*, p. 101.

7. Dona Isabel Pires Monteiro, a wealthy widow with one daughter, remarried João Fernandes, a widower himself, with a son and no money or other possessions. Taking advantages of his wife's ignorance, João Fernandes had a document drawn up without her consent and signed by a priest which divested her of her fortune to the benefit of the son of his first marriage. See Pedro Taques de Almeida Paes Leme, *Nobiliarchia Paulistana Histórica e Genealógica*, vol. 2, p. 191.

8. Jean Baptiste Debret, *Viagem Pitoresca e Histórica ao Brasil*, vol. 2, p. 17. The term *colégio* is used very broadly in Brazil, in much the same way as the word *school* is used in this country. During the period that this account covers, *colégio* most generally referred to a seven-year course of study, following four years of elementary school. During the final two years students could specialize in either science and math (*científico*) or arts and humanities (*clássico*), if they were going on to university, or in vocational training if they were not. *Colégios* were thus less advanced than colleges or universities but more inclusive than high school. The terms *ginásio* and *liceu*, loosely, junior high school, referred to four-year courses, following elementary school, which could be chosen instead. *Colégio* thus was also used to refer to the additional three years, which would have to be taken before going on to university. Since all of these programs have been periodically redefined, the Portuguese terms will be used when it is necessary to distinguish among

the three, while in general usage they will be referred to as secondary schools.

9. Letters written by the German tutor in Rio de Janeiro contain numerous references to the lack of interest shown by her pupils. Because of the apathy of her three wards she nicknamed them "the Holy Inquisition." With regard to girls' *colégios*, she said:

> The best families categorically refuse to send their daughters to *colégios*, and for this reason that social grouping is in general the most poorly educated or the most uncivilized to be found; the little girls carry on, scream, not infrequently until their faces are as red as cherries. On such occasions, our youngest French tutoress, Mlle. Serôt, puts them in a closet until they calm down. We rarely see the lady of the house other than at mealtimes. She is the only one who enjoys any authority over this wild bunch, perhaps because she appears so rarely.

(Ina von Binzer, *Alegrías e Tristezas de uma Educadora Alemã no Brasil*, pp. 65-66.)

10. *Annaes do Parlamento Brasileiro*, Constituent Assembly, Session of August 11, 1823.

11. Items 32 and 33, respectively, of Paragraph 7, of the general provisions and guarantees of the civil and political rights of Brazilian citizens.

12. *Annaes do Parlamento Brasileiro*, Chamber of Deputies, Sessions of June 16, 1826.

13. In defense of a bill providing identical primary education for girls and boys, Lino Coutinho stated: "Women, in particular, need education inasmuch as it is they who provide the first elements of education to their children. It is they who make men good or bad." He defended the equality of the sexes at another level when he objected to a proposal of Diogo Antônio Feijó to exempt women schoolteachers from examination (to qualify for teaching in the primary schools) because it required ample self-assurance. Finally, he proposed that the convents teach young girls reading, writing, and arithmetic, catechism, sewing, and other feminine arts. However, neither the ecclesiastical commission nor the commission of public education concurred with this proposal, which they considered contrary to the canonical regulations for the cloisters.

14. In the 1848 report, Minister Visconde de Macahé referred to the general competence of teachers as follows: "With rare exceptions, our teachers, both male and female, lack the indispensible knowl-

edge for carrying out fully the major tasks with which we are faced, the result being the poor showing of education and instruction in the early years." In Primitivo Moacyr, *A Instrução e o Império*, vol. 1, p. 215. Similar reports from provincial presidents as well as government ministers, repeatedly pointed to the calamity of basic education, especially the incompetence of the teachers.

15. Afrânio Peixoto, *Martha e Maria*, p. 56.

16. Leda Maria Pereira Rodrigues, *A Instrução Feminina em São Paulo*, p. 83.

17. Peixoto, *Martha e Maria*, p. 56. One century later, Peixoto had this to say about primary school instruction:

> Male elementary school teachers are indeed anomalies. Other than it being a calling, a decision which is always late in men, I cannot see why they would choose this profession except because of an inability to compete with other men in the male careers. . . . At an age when one dares all and has an ambition to get somewhere, they cast their anchors in an occupation with neither renown nor good pay. It is a psychological and economic test of male inferiority. In a country that pays other masculine activities so well, to take refuge parsimoniously in elementary school teaching is tantamount to throwing in the towel.

(Ibid., pp. 360-61.)

18. Actually, the 1934 constitutional amendment empowered the government to enact its own legislation on higher education. Yet following tradition, it also enacted legislation on secondary education, and indeed had an effective monopoly in this area after it had thwarted attempts to give the provincial *colégios* equal status with the Pedro II Imperial Colégio. R. S. M. de Barros defended the position that the solution to the problem of Brazilian education lay in the creation of an educational system from above, since "the illustrious ideal does not grow out of popular demand." This would have assisted the workings of the central government in that it would have created in Brazil an elite capable of provoking and stimulating popular desires for the acquisition of knowledge. This educational process, imposed from the top down, was a hallmark of the empire from 1870 onward and of the Republic up to World War I; in fact, it had a highly constructive function in this sense since integration at the level of the indigenous or African culture was inconceivable for Brazil, whereas in a Euro-American community it was indeed even a necessity. Roque Spencer Maciel de

Barros, *A Ilustração Brasileira e a Idéia de Universidade*, p. 25ff. On the constructive functions of laws in new nations see Roger Bastide and Florestan Fernandes, *Brancos e Negros em São Paulo*, chapter entitled "Côr e estrutura em mudança."

19. Law No. 9, March 24, 1935, in *Anais da Assembléia Legislativa Provincial*, 1835-1861. Official publication compiled by Eugênio Egas and Oscar Motta Mello, 1926.

20. Statistical data taken from Moacyr, *A Instrução e o Império*, vol. 2, pp. 72, 75, 84, 91, and 95.

21. Celso Furtado, referring to the inability of Brazilian intellectuals to understand the difficulties the Brazilian economy experienced in achieving stability while maintaining the gold standard in the second half of the past century, has the following comments:

> Since the Brazilian economy was dependent on the industrial centers it was difficult to avoid the tendency to "interpret" the country's economic problems on the basis of analogies with what was taking place in Europe. In Europe the science of economics had made its way through the law schools and had a tendency to become a "body of doctrine" in its own right without any attempt to test it against reality. Wherever reality took leave of the ideal world of doctrine, it was supposed that at that point commenced social pathology.

(Furtado, *Formação Econômica do Brasil*, p. 187.)

22. In 1930, 113 girls enrolled in the primary course and 9 were doing their vocational training. *Estatística Escolar de 1930.*

23. In an opinion handed down in 1883, Ruy Barbosa denounced the perversity of a normal school that met at night, neglecting its primary functions, that is, practical teaching skills. It was not just the society in general that reacted to the coeducation practiced in the teacher-training schools; public figures came out squarely against it. Ruy commented:

> The school is mixed on the pretext of economizing. Male and female teachers are trained by the same methods, the same instructors, and in the same classrooms—and this in a country where the two sexes live completely divorced from one another as regards their respective ideas and customs, the consequence of a traditional education. The result has been as interesting as it was unexpected. A depressing imbalance has developed in the attendance of the two sexes. Male attendance has declined in proportion as the attendance of the female students has risen, so that the first impression a

visitor to the school gets is that it is solely for women. Despite this majority, one could say that the female students do not feel themselves in a secure place since the halls of the school are packed chaotically with "chaperones" who accompany the girls and wait for them there until the end of the day's lessons.

(In Moacyr, *A Instrução e o Império*, vol. 3, pp. 221-22.) Ruy proposed a system of basic education with four types of schools: kindergarten and primary elementary schools, middle schools, and high schools. The kindergartens were to be coordinated with followup courses for girls between the ages of sixteen and twenty-five who had already learned the elements of literacy to prepare them for their roles as mothers. These complementary courses did not qualify the girl students for the position of kindergarten teacher, but were intended exclusively to round out their training as mothers of families. Their object was not to provide women with gainful occupations.

24. The Leôncio de Carvalho reform, instituted by Decree 7247, April 19, 1879, legally established coeducation in primary schools, although certain precautionary measures were taken to prevent contact between the sexes after a certain age. The reform's position on coeducation reads as follows:

> Another provision of broad import, advisable for many reasons, is the abolition of boys schools and girls schools, and their conversion into mixed schools. Experience has demonstrated the baselessness of the fears aroused by the idea of coeducation, and the most unbiased witnesses are united in their acclaim of the uncontestable results of the U.S. system, in which coeducation is universal. Initially, only primary schools shall be mixed, for the time being, and staffed preferentially by female teachers, with no boys over the age of ten being admitted.

(Ibid., vol. 2, p. 186.)

25. The baccalaureate was for a long time conferred only by the Pedro II Imperial Colégio; later, the general and provincial *liceus* were raised to an equal status. Persons who did their secondary studies in a private institution or a lower ranking public institution had to pass examinations at designated public *colégios* to obtain the school-leaving or baccalaureate degree. The records mention not even one case of a girl who completed her secondary studies in a private secondary school and qualified for the baccalaureate by

examination in a public *colégio* in the nineteenth century.

26. Francisco Venâncio Filho, cited in de Azevedo, *A Cultura Brasileira*, p. 630.
27. Tobias Barreto, *Estudos de Sociologia*, pp. 59-67.
28. Dona Ambrozina de Megalhães was the first woman to enter the College of Medicine at Rio de Janeiro. At the time the report was given, she had attended "conscientiously and to good advantage" the first three years of the course of study. In 1882 Elisa Borges Ribeiro and Generosa Estrella entered the College of Medicine as full-time students, while Josefa Mercedes de Oliveira attended as an auditor. Of these four women, two attended the college accompanied, one by her father, the other by an elderly woman; the other two were unaccompanied. Report of the director of the College of Medicine of Rio de Janeiro from 1883, in *Realtório do Ministério do Império*, appendix B., p. 20, cited by Barros, *A Ilustração Brasileira*, note 253, p. 185.
29. de Azevedo, *A Cultura Brasileira*, note 19, p. 639.
30. "Women must play no part in the electoral assemblies, in the parliaments, in the supreme councils of the state, or in public office of any kind, for moral and social reasons." José Maria Correa de Sáe Benevides, *Filosofia Elementar de Direito Público, Interno, Temporal e Universal*, p. 19.
31. Tito Lívio de Castro, *A Mulher en Sociogenia*, p. 320. The author adds:

> Either education for women leads to the break-up of the family, in which case women must be educated specifically to destroy this institution, which depends for its existence on ignorance, servitude, and deceit in mutual agreements, and is therefore harmful and immoral; or else the education of women does *not* lead to the break-up of the family because the family is not based on the ignorance of women, in which case women must be educated because it is a useful thing which causes no harm.

32. Ibid., p. 204. On this page and the following one, the author gives figures to back up his argument that the so-called Christian family is no more prevalent than the nonfamily:

> In the Neutro Municipality there are 2,954 legitimate male baptisms as against 1,444 illegitimate male baptisms and 116 foundlings, 2,879 legitimate female baptisms as against 1,488 illegitimate births and 117 foundlings; in Rio de Janeiro: 6,494 legitimate male births as against 5,152 illegiti-

mate, 6,344 legitimate female births as against 5,088 illegitimate. In Pará: 429 legitimate males and 421 illegitimate, 326 legitimate females and 379 illegitimate. If extramarital liaisons are immoral, is it not obvious that the present organization of the family in Brazil is a disgrace?

33. Roque Spencer Maciel de Barros, *Diretrizes e Bases da Educação*, p. 311.

34. Antônio de Almeida Oliveira, *O Ensino Público*, quoted in ibid., p. 181.

35. In the section relating to primary schooling we find the following statements: "Girls shall receive, in addition to the general courses, special classes in needlework and washing and other things which are the preserve of women," and "Women may enroll in any school and receive from them diplomas and certificates. In all educational establishments there shall be separate places for girls, and wherever possible, a separate entrance and exit." See Moacyr, *A Instrução e o Império*, vol. 2, pp. 410 and 418.

36. Raimundo Teixeira Mendes, *A Mulher*, p. 68.

37. A passage from Teixeira Mendes illustrates this conclusion:

> And now you see the absurdity of mixed schools; it is impossible to teach men and women, and boys and girls at the same time. To learn is to be innovative; teaching means putting the mind of the listener, the learner, in a situation where it can make discoveries on its own. There are therefore no invariable rules for teaching everyone; each case is a special case; the true teacher is the mother. The public school is a transitory institution [which in the West should last] twelve years—just long enough for all women to learn enough to carry out their functions as mothers, as educators of men, instead of being in competition with men.

(Teixeira Mendes, *A Mulher*, pp. 65-66.)

38. Again, Teixeira Mendes is illustrative:

> Women are morally and socially preeminent and yet at the same time extremely dependent. In fact, it is precisely because they are the most noble and the most delicate of beings, both biologically and socially, that they have so many more needs, and therefore are in a greater degree of dependence than others. Woman's greater purity, that is, the relative weakness of her body and her admirable superiority in altruistic pursuits are natural counterparts to that complexity of constitution which makes her dependent on

the support of active thinkers, and therefore cause her much more than men to live her life for others. It would therefore be no more fitting for woman to assert her dignity by refusing to recognize man's supremacy in industry and politics than by refusing to recognize the material supremacy of the Earth.... For both sexes, true nobility consists in voluntary submission to Destiny, and through this, to evolve an ever greater degree of altruism.

(Ibid., pp. 82-83.)

39. Ibid., p. 136.

40. Tobias Barreto, as we have seen, was opposed to the political emancipation of women, judging it to be inopportune at that moment in time. This left women worse off than the freed slave, who was, for electoral purposes, a Brazilian citizen.

41. de Castro argued that while it might seem natural at first sight for the education of children to be in the hands of women,

this, however, is an evil thing, a danger, and disastrously lacking in forethought.... Education by women can only be compared to education by the clergy. Both prepare for the past creatures who will have to act in the present or in the future; both shape a creature who has to live in the real world of today in the ways of the outdated world of the past which they represent.... There is only one possible conclusion. The woman of today must not be entrusted with any role in the intellectual guidance of our progeny.

(de Castro, *A Mulher*, pp. 280, 281, 285, 287.)

42. Ibid., p. 235. The author does not give the precise year to which the figures refer, but we do know that the book was written during the 1880s.

43. Ibid., p. 252.

44. In 1882, Rodolfo Dantas introduced a bill proposing the establishment of a *liceu* for women, in the Côrte municipality. The next year M. J. Alves Nogueira proposed four more: one in Côrte, one in São Paulo, one in Bahia, and one in Pernambuco.

At the Education Congress on the subject of the "Organization of Secondary Education for Women," he said:

Our teacher-training schools have only just begun their mission, and our primary school still provides a very poor basis for secondary education.... The state must regulate the education of women by legislative measures; it must prepare the foundations of public education before it is in a

position to compete. People do not disregard the education
of women. The proof of this is to be found in the private
schools which are springing up everywhere; the proof is to be
found in the heavy monthly fees. . . . Secondary schooling
for girls is urgently needed as soon as possible in Brazil.

(Moacyr, *A Instrução e o Império*, pp. 517, 557-58.)

45. Respectively Paragraph 6 of Article 72, subsection 30 of Article 34
and subsection 2 of Article 65 of the 1891 Constitution of the
Republic.

46. de Azevedo, *A Cultura Brasileira*, p. 626.

47. Pandiá Calógeras, in a speech made in 1912 criticizing the 1911
Comprehensive Law on Education, quoted in Primitivo Moacyr, *A
Instrução e a República*, vol. 4, p. 62. Calógeras adds:

In abandoning this area to free competition among those
interested in it, successive governments forgot that they were
thus giving indirect protection to that institution which,
through centuries-old privilege, had the means to act, the
experience, and an elite cadre in the service of a social ideal
that had been clearly spelled out by the Syllabus, and more
recently by the encyclicals on modern life. Under the
Republic, insufficient attention was paid to the educational
work of the Church; without persecuting the Church and
indeed even endeavoring to give it the greatest possible
measure of freedom, the state should at the same time have
provided secular education as a counterweight.

48. In 1940 only 43.1 percent of Brazilians over the age of 10 could
read and write. Of men above 10 years of age, 48.3 percent could
read and write, against 38 percent of women in the same age group.
The proportion of literate women in the other age groups was even
lower: 30 percent in the 50–59 age group and 27.5 percent in the
60-69 age group. Figures from Lynn Smith, *Brazil: People and
Institutions*, p. 551.

49. The need for a certificate of completion of a course of study at a
teacher training or secondary school as a condition of entry to
nursing schools was one of the obstacles to rapid occupational
training in this essentially female profession. See Glete Alcântara,
*A Enfermagen Moderna como Categoria Profissional: Obstáculos
à sua Expansão na Sociedade Brasileira*, pp. 19-20.

50. In addition to schools founded during the imperial period in Juiz
de Fora, Porto Alegre, and Piracicaba, various girls' schools
appeared in the early years of the Republic, although some were
short-lived. These included: the Escola do Alto, in Rio de Janeiro,

in 1892; the Colégio Mineiro, in Juiz de Fora, in 1891; the Colégio Americano Fluminense, in 1892; the Colégio Americano de Petrópolis, in 1895 (all of which were closed, in 1895, 1914, 1915, and 1920 respectively); and the Colégio Metodista, established in 1899 in Ribeirão Preto. The Methodist Church founded three other girls' schools in the first three decades of this century: the Colégio Isabela Hendrix (1904) in Belo Horizonte; the Colégio Bennett in 1921 in Rio de Janeiro with which the Colégio Americano Fluminense and the Colégio Americano Petrópolis were merged; and the Colégio Centenário, in 1922, in Santa Maria, in Rio Grande do Sul. See James Kennedy, *Cincoenta Anos de Metodismo no Brasil*, quoted in de Azevedo, *A Cultura Brasileira*, p. 620, note 13.

51. The ability of the Catholic Church to defend its lucrative Brazilian school empire is shown by the bitter controversy that raged between its representatives and the supporters of the public school, less than a decade ago, in connection with the bill which established the guidelines and foundations for State education. Detailed information on the campaign for public schooling is available in *Diretrizes e Bases da Educação*, a collection of writings edited by Barros. See especially "Análise e crítica do projeto de lei sôbre diretrizes e bases," by Florestan Fernandes, pp. 217-306; and "Análise dos fundamentos do projeto," by R. S. M. de Barros, pp. 307-48.

52. The 1929 figure of 167 men completing pharmacy courses had increased to 463 in 1964; the 1929 figure of 62 women increased to 167 in 1964; that is, there was an increase of 277 percent for men and 269 percent for women. Statistics on those completing the course at the end of 1964 taken from *Sinopse Estatística de Ensino Superior, 1965*, IBGE, 1966.

53. Figures taken from Moacyr, *A Instrução e o Império*, vol. 3, pp. 487, 493-94, 496, 499.

54. In 1930, the state of São Paulo had ten public teacher-training schools: two in São Paulo city and eight in the interior. In the same year, there were only five *ginásios* in the state. From *Estatística Escolar de 1930*, previously quoted.

55. Figures from *Anuário Estatístico do Brasil*, IBGE, 1966.

56. Afrânio Peixoto, "Discurso de colação de grau" (Graduation Speech) to the women about to receive their teaching certificates in 1935 from the Instituto de Educação, Rio, December 12, 1935, in *Ensinar a Ensinar*, p. 260.

57. *Anuário do Ensino de São Paulo*, 1935-1936.

58. The number of independent normal schools increased to forty-nine in 1930. See *Anuário do Ensino de São Paulo,* 1935–1936.

   A more detailed analysis of the role of independent normal schools is offered by Tirsa Regazzini Peres, "Advento da Escola Normal Livre e seus resultados comparados com os da Escola Normal Oficial" (1927–1930), unpublished manuscript.

59. In 1930, 137 and 43 men and 1,066 and 891 women graduated from public and private normal schools, respectively. See *Estatística Escolar de 1930.*

60. Report of Professor E. de Azevedo as director of education for São Paulo, in *Anuário do Ensino do Estado de São Paulo,* 1935–1936.

61 See Tirsa Regazzini Peres, "Ensino Secundário no Estado de São Paulo (1920–1933)," unpublished manuscript.

62. Until 1920 the normal schools of São Paulo were divided into primary and secondary schools, turning out primary and secondary school teachers, respectively.

63. Article 165 of Decree 2,367, dated April 14, 1913, reads: "Students qualifying from secondary normal schools shall be able to obtain a baccalaureate degree in Science and Arts from the state *ginásios* or to study in them without taking a degree, if they take an examination in those subjects which are not included in the course of study offered by normal schools."

64. Article 38 of Law 1,750, dated August 12, 1920, modified by Decree 3,356, dated May 31, 1921.

65. Law 374, Article 2, paragraph 3: "Students with degrees from state *ginásios* who teach for one year in any experimental school will be eligible for certification according to law as primary school or follow-up course teachers."

66. Law 1,341, Article 11: "Those with baccalaureate degrees in Science and Art from the state *ginásios* and those who attended the latter without receiving such a degree shall be eligible to receive teaching certificates for the secondary normal schools if they take an examination in those institutions in subjects which they did not study in them without prejudice to the prerogatives offered under Article 2, paragraph 3 of Law 374, dated September 9, 1895, to obtain which they shall have to take an examination in education theory."

67. At the São Paulo Municipal Ginásio seven normal school graduates (six boys and a girl) passed the necessary additional qualifying examination in 1921. In 1922, seventeen (15 boys and 2 girls) qualified in the same way. See the *Relatório do Secretário do*

Interior (Report of the Secretary for the Interior), Alarico Silveira, to the president of the state of São Paulo, Dr. Washington Luis Pereira de Sousa, the "Diário Oficial," Report for 1921, published 1922, p. 40, and the 1922 Report, published 1923, p. 134.

68. Chapter I, Article 5, subsection XIV, of the 1934 Constitution; Article 150, subsection (a) of the Constitutional Charter of 1937; and Article 15, subsection IX of the 1937 Constitution. See also Article 16, subsection XXIV in the 1937 Constitutional Charter.

69. The number of secondary school pupils in Brazil quadrupled between 1930 and 1936 from 40,000 to 160,000. The number of girls in secondary schools increased considerably following the reforms described above. See de Azevedo, *A Cultura Brasileira*, pp. 684-85.

70. Under Title III, "Do ensino secundário feminino" (On secondary education for women), Article 25 of Law 4,244, we read: "The following special provisions shall be observed in secondary education for women: (1) Secondary education for women should preferably be offered in institutions attended only by women. (2) In establishments of secondary education attended by both men and women, the education of women should as far as possible be taught in all-women classes. (3) Home economics should be included in the 3rd and 4th years of *ginásio* courses. (4) In its methodological aspects the syllabus shall keep in view the nature of the female personality and pay special attention to women's calling in the home. (The wording for items 1,2, and 3 was taken from Decree 8,347, of December 10, 1945.)

71. Decree 1,190, Article 31, provides that applicants as full-time students must in the first year:

> (1) Present in a formal application to the dean of the faculty: (a) evidence of having successfully completed the basic and follow-up courses, or one of the courses of the *colégio*.
>
> §1. The requirement of subsection (a) of this article may also be met, for purposes of registering in the competition for final degree by presenting a duly certified diploma from any recognized course of higher education. The following will also be exempt in conformity with the terms of the preceding paragraph and with the following restrictions: (b) teachers with normal school diplomas who have completed the regular course of at least six years and who have teaching experience in their chosen field from the courses in educational theory, Romance literature, Anglo-

Germanic literature, Classics, geography and history; (c) teachers already certified with the National Education Department with effective experience of at least three years in the fields covered by the course in which they wish to enroll.

72. Decree 8,530, of January 2, 1946, Chapter IV, Article 6, subsection 3: "Students who have completed the second part of a teacher training course will be guaranteed the right of entry to courses in the Faculties of Arts, except where there are special conditions for registration."

73. Law 1,821, of March 12, 1953, Article I provided that classics or science matriculates also had to complete a regional teacher training course or equivalent, which was defined in Decree 8,530 as follows: Article 8: "The training course for primary school teachers shall comprise three one-year curricula." Article 9: "The course referred to in Article 8 may also be completed in two years of intensive study."

74. Paragraph 1, Article 2, of Law 1,821 states: "Aside from those exceptions permitted by law, a candidate with only one or neither of the secondary school courses will be required to undergo examination in as many subjects as may be necessary to complete the secondary course."

75. Of the number of students completing their studies in 1964, the distribution of male and female students in the Colleges of Arts and Sciences throughout the country was as follows: in the social sciences, 719 men and 502 women; in education, 1,454 men and 1,141 women; and in the humanities 2,259 men and 1,619 women. See *Sinopse Estatística do Ensino Superior*, 1965, IBGE, 1966.

76. In 1964, 20,282 men and 6,890 women completed higher courses, with 3,699 of these women graduating from Colleges of Arts and Sciences. Ibid.

77. The canonesses of Santo Agostinho founded the Instituto Superior de Pedagogia, Ciências e Lêtras "Sedes Sapientiae" in São Paulo, which obtained temporary certification by Decree 157, December 13, 1934, and permanent certification by Decree 1,668, June 4, 1937. Until the end of 1940, it offered courses in philosophy, classical literature, romance literature, Anglo-German literature, geography and history, and educational theory and practice. To qualify as secondary school teachers, its students were expected to attend (simultaneously if they wished) the three-year course of the Institute of Education for their professional training.

78. Figures from *Anuário Estatístico do Brasil*, IBGE, 1955.
79. Figures from *Sinopse Estatística do Ensino Superior*, 1965.
80. Figures extrapolated from ibid.

Notes to Chapter 8: The Female Workforce

1. The term *rational* is used here in the sense of functional rationality described by Karl Mannheim: "a series of actions organized in such a way that it leads to a previously defined goal, every element in the series of actions receiving a functional position and role."

    The term *irrational* is used here in the Mannheimian sense of substantive irrationality: any act is substantively irrational which is "either false or not an act of thought at all (as for example, drives, impulses, wishes, and feelings, both conscious and unconscious)." See Karl Mannheim, *Man and Society in an Age of Reconstruction*, p. 53.

2. The difficulties involved in making such a survey in part derive from the absence of any systematic data on the employed labor force in slavocratic Brazil. The 1872 census employed criteria that are difficult to apply today. Moreover, different criteria were used from one census to another to classify the various types of economic activities, with categories that ought to have been kept distinct frequently lumped together under one heading.

3. Excluding persons whose profession was not known (31.6 percent of whom were women) and persons in unproductive occupations (56.6 percent of whom were women), 45.3 percent of the employed population were women. A total of 52.6 percent of all working women were in domestic services; 24.6 percent in agriculture; 14.2 percent in arts or crafts; only 4.2 percent were in manufacturing industries; and the remaining 4.4 percent were in the commercial sector and other activities. Women made up 21.1 percent of the total employed in the primary sector; 91.3 percent in the secondary sector; and 75.2 percent of the group whose occupation was not known, not clearly specified, or unproductive.

4. The number of workers in 1907 was 150,481, increasing to 275,512 in 1920. See Nícia Vilela Luz, *A Luta pela Industrialização do Brasil*, p. 146. Of this 1920 figure, 182,670 were men and 92,842 were women.

5. Although the proportion of women among the total employed population had increased slightly (from 15.3 percent in 1920 to

15.9 percent in 1940), the increase was not statistically significant, and the proportion of women in secondary jobs fell to 25.3 percent. In contrast; the proportion of women rose to 13.5 percent in the primary sector and to 22.7 percent in the tertiary sector. In the secondary sector, women made up 22.2 percent of the workers eighteen years of age or over, and 42.3 percent of the under-eighteen group. Finally, women constituted 82.3 percent of all persons taking on work at home. Since the 1940 census included housework and school activities under the same heading, it is impossible to know how many women were engaged exclusively in housework.

6. Women constituted 90.3 percent of all those engaged in unpaid housework or attending school among the population ten years of age or over, but only 14.7 percent of the total number of workers gainfully employed. The proportion of women in secondary activities (17.4 percent) also declined between 1940 and 1950, whereas the proportion of women in the tertiary sector (32.2 percent) rose considerably. During this same period, women accounted for 7.3 percent of those employed in the primary sector.

7. If we leave out domestic work, the employed female labor force represented 17.8 percent of the total, divided up in the following way: 10.8 percent in the primary sector, 16 percent in the secondary sector, and 27.4 percent in the tertiary sector. In the eastern region women accounted for 19.4 percent of the nation's total employed labor force, with figures of 10.8 percent in the primary sector, 15 percent in the secondary sector, and 32.5 percent in the tertiary sector.

8. Clearly, the marginalization of large numbers of women from the system of production favored capital accumulation, though not to the extent that the substitution of female labor for male labor would have allowed as it did in Britain in the early stages of its industrialization. In other words, the more refined the techniques of capital domination, the more subtly women are barred from gainful employment.

9. Information from a *Senai* publication, quoted in Luiz Pereira, *Trabalho e Desenvolvimento no Brasil*, p. 180, fn. 14.

10. In May 1906, 600 textile workers (mostly women) at São Bento Mill in Jundiaí went on strike for higher wages (they earned less than U.S. $1 per day for thirteen hours' work). The next year workers in predominantly or exclusively female occupational categories, such as dressmaker and weaver, were involved in the struggle for a reduction of the working day to eight hours. Whereas the

predominantly male occupational categories achieved total victory in the struggle for a shorter working day, those who were predominantly or exclusively female achieved only a partial victory: a reduction of the working day to nine and one-half hours. This partial victory was achieved both in São Paulo and in the cities of the interior. The textile workers' strike for higher wages in Bahia in September 1907 ended with an agreement between management and the workers.

Another dressmakers' strike took place in São Paulo in November of the same year. The cutters came out in sympathy but the police intervened and many people were arrested or hurt. In January 1912, 5,000 workers in the shoemaking, textile, and printing industries went on strike for higher wages. The workers in the shoemaking industry achieved a partial victory, but the other two occupational categories gained nothing. Many women were arrested following the strikes in the São Paulo textile industries in 1917, beginning in the Crespi textile mill. There was a further strike in May 1919, involving 30,000 textile workers in São Paulo and about 10,000 in São Caetano and São Bernardo, in response to the arbitrary imposition of fines, wage cuts, and poor working conditions. The ensuing police violence left one worker killed and many women and children hurt in São Bernardo. In October, there was yet another textile workers' strike, this time in sympathy with the light and power workers who had struck for higher pay. Textile workers in Santo André, São Bernardo, and São Caetano also went out in sympathy with the light and power workers. See Everardo Dias, *História das Lutas Sociais no Brasil*, pp. 257, 265, 267-68, 273, 291-97, 304-5.

11. The presence of large numbers of foreigners among the urban working class in the first quarter of this century facilitated the introduction of ideologies which were radically opposed to the capitalist status quo. Thus according to Celso Furtado:

> Europeans demanded higher wages and much better minimum conditions than were the norm in a country molded in the traditions of slavery. Those who took jobs in the manufacturing industries were individuals w o had had some prior experience in that sector in their native countries, and wages tended to be set in accordance with the conditions to which they had been accustomed. Thus, industrialization was not the result of recruitment of the labor force from the land or from previously existing crafts.

(Celso Furtado, *Desenvolvimento e Subdesenvolvimento*, p. 255.)

See also Leôncio Martins Rodrigues, *Conflito Industrial e Sindicalismo no Brasil*, p. 122. On the part played by foreigners in the process of industrialization of Brazil, either as entrepreneurs or as workers, see Manuel Diégues Júnior, *Imigração, Urbanização, Industrialização*.

12. Of the eleven points made in the report presented by the Committee for the Defense of the Proletariat of São Paulo to the representatives of management and the government in 1917, only one referred to women workers: "Night work for women should be abolished." In the first Brazilian Workers' Congress held in Rio de Janeiro in April, one of the thirteen topics discussed was concerned with women: "Regulation of work for women and apprentices in factories and offices." The Fourth Brazilian Workers' Congress, held in Rio de Janeiro in 1912, included on its agenda an item headed "Work restrictions for women and minors." At the conclusion of the Fourth Congress, the Brazilian Labor Confederation was founded as a political party, with a program that included the "establishment of associations to protect the interests of old people, women and children" and "legislation regulating work by women and minors in factories and offices, with the ultimate aim of abolishing it." Dias, *História das Lutas Sociais no Brasil*, pp. 229, 255, 278, 280, and 281.

13. According to Celso Furtado, heavy industrial investment between 1950 and 1960 did not change the occupational structure of the population.

> During that decade, although industrial production shot up at an annual rate of about 10%, jobs in the manufacturing sector increased at an annual rate of 2.8%, less than the rate of population growth (the annual rate of population growth was 3.5%), and about half the urban population growth rate. Chronic underemployment thus became worse, at a time when heavy investment was being made in industrial sectors with excess capacity, and equipment was rapidly rendered out-of-date by the introduction of labor-saving techniques.

(Furtado, *Subdesenvolvimento e Estagnação na América Latina*, pp. 98-99.)

Notes to Chapter 9: Manifestations of Feminism

1. Before 1930 Brazilian unions forced passage of labor laws on the strength of social aspirations based on the life patterns of the proletariat of industrialized countries. Since the capital accumulation that was needed in Brazil required broad reserves of manual labor, this legislation proved to be premature in that to a certain extent it inhibited that accumulation. Attempts to raise working and living conditions of the Brazilian proletariat to fit the expectations of foreign workers caused Brazilian workers to make demands which the nation could not fulfill at that historical moment (without foregoing capital accumulation). As we saw in the last chapter, this factor was largely responsible for the enormous discrepancies that existed between urban and rural wages. Since a good portion of the nation's enterprises were and are multidimensional, the greater exploitation of the rural worker made possible the "generosity" of the industrial entrepreneur in granting higher wages.

   Thus the two stages of development typical of classic capitalism—a phase of accumulation based on the appropriation of the absolute surplus value created in the industrial sector, and a phase of less unjust distribution of the national income—did not occur in two separate periods. Instead, they occurred contemporaneously (and are still in process), with the rural worker fulfilling the role of the laborer in the technologically less advanced period. This parallel existence of two phenomena which in autonomous economies usually occur at different stages is largely responsible for the regional and sectorial disparities seen in the Brazilian economy.

2. To situate means "to determine the real place of an object considered without the total process." Jean-Paul Sartre, *Questions de Méthodes*, p. 33.

3. Although the 1934 Constitution established the principle of equality of all persons before the law, without distinction as to birth, sex, race, social class, wealth, etc., the Afonso Arinos law, ratified in 1951, was intended to combat abuses. This provided penalties of fines or imprisonment for anyone who tried to restrict housing, education, jobs or recreation and entertainment facilities to anyone on the basis of race or color. See Roger Bastide and Florestan Fernandes, *Brancos e Negros em São Paulo*, p. 304. The Arinos law, while it was violated in practice, formally advanced civil rights.

4. The concept of conservatism is here utilized in the Mannheimian sense, that is, as an objective, dynamic, structural configuration,

historically developed. People experience a conservative mode, as distinct from the merely "traditionalist" mode, to the extent that they are incorporated in one of the phases of development of this mental objective structure (usually in the contemporary phase) and act in terms of it. Mannheim pointed out that traditionalist behavior is almost wholly reactive, whereas conservative behavior is meaningful in relation to the circumstances that change from epoch to epoch. See Karl Mannheim, "Conservative Thought," in *Essays on Sociology and Social Psychology*, pp. 97-98 and 101.

5. Actually, the first Brazilian feminist was Nísia Floresta Brasileira Augusta (1810-1885) who had lived for twenty-eight years in Europe and shared the emancipationist ideas current there. She translated Mary Wollstonecraft's *The Rights of Women and the Injustices of Men* into Portuguese in 1852, and wrote a book, *A Mulher*, which was published in Brazil in 1856 and later translated into English. In 1842 she wrote *Conselhos à Minha Filha*, which the bishop of Mondavi, Italy, recommended as a text for use in the schools of his diocese. Nísia Floresta's feminist position, however, remained limited to her personal efforts, as she organized no movement for the emancipation of women. She seems to have assumed a firmer position with regard to abolition, inasmuch as she arranged conferences in Rio de Janeiro in 1842 in which she preached freedom of religion, emancipation of slaves, and a federation for the Brazilian provinces. Everything indicates, however, that her ideas, whether feminist, abolitionist, or republican, were steeped in the romanticism which dominated even French socialism during the two decades following the 1830 revolution. For more on Nísia Floresta's activities see *Mulheres Brasileiras*, 1950; Lima Oliveira, "Nísia Floresta"; Adauto da Câmara, *Historia de Nísia Floresta;* Vidal Barros, *Precursoras Brasileiras*.

6. "Atividades da Federação Brasileira pelo Progresso Feminino," a mimeographed publication from 1962, prepared by Maria Sabina de Alburquerque, in cooperation with Dr. Zeia Pinho Rezende, vice president and legal consultant of the BFWP, respectively.

7. In 1917 Maria José de Castro Rebelo Mendes was granted the right to register as a candidate for a post in the Ministry of Foreign Affairs through the favorable representations of Ruy Barbosa, at that time legal advisor. The second woman to enter Brazilian public service was Bertha Lutz, who in 1919 won out over ten male candidates in a competition for a post at the National Museum.

8. Article 69. The definition of Brazilian citizen shall include:

 1. Persons born in Brazil, even of foreign parents, provided the latter do not remain in the service of their country of birth;

 Article 70. Citizens above the age of 21 who register as provided by law are eligible to vote.

 § 1. The following are not entitled to register as voters in the federal or state elections: (1) Beggars; (2) Illiterates; (3) Army privates, except for students at military schools of higher education; (4) The clergy in monastic orders, societies, congregations, or communities of any denomination who are subject to the vow of obedience, a rule, or a statute which requires the renunciation of individual liberty.

 § 2. Citizens unable to register are not eligible.

 Article 72. The Constitution ensures Brazilians and foreign residents the inviolability of their rights to liberty, individual safety, and property under the following terms:

 §1. No one may be obliged to do, or to omit to do, anything except as provided by law;

 §2. All are equal before the law.

9. The statements of both jurists are quoted in *The Opinion of the Special Commission on the Code for Women* on the draft bill for the creation of a National Women's Bureau, July 3, 1939, p. 41.

10. Despite the fact that the Legal Congress convened by the Lawyers' Institute in 1922 in the Federal District approved an earlier decision to the effect that "the Federal Constitution does not prohibit women the exercise of political rights, which shall accordingly be allowed to them" (in *O Voto Feminino perante a Justiça*, 1929, p. 35), a lower court judge in São Paulo the same year disallowed the petition of a woman wishing to exercise the right to vote declaring:

> Women may not register as voters. The social competence of women to exercise the right to vote has not yet been recognized in Brazil. The restrictions imposed on her in civil life bear on political life as well. . . . Our publicists, such as Dr. Tito Fulgêncio, who put themselves forth as such ardent proponents of woman's political emancipation, claiming that her exclusion from the right to vote is arbitrary, completely forget the conception that has always reigned in the life of our society concerning women, namely, that she is a being whose purpose is to share harmoniously with a man the responsibilities of a life together, she in the tranquility of the

home, caring for the domestic order, and he in his daily labors, earning the means to provide for his family's subsistence. It may be that sometime in the future mankind will witness the mixing of these roles. But for the present it behooves us to preserve what has been preserved until now with regard to women's competence.

(Marly A. Cardone, "A Mulher nas constituções Brasileiras," pp. 48-49.)

11. Two other draft bills granting women the right to vote, put forth as independent proposals on the incentive of Nogueira Penado and Bittencourt Filho, found their way to the Senate in the late twenties at the same time as the Justo Chermont bill. None of them, however, succeeded in getting approved in the final debate. See João Batista Cascudo Rodrigues, *A Mulher Brasileira: Direitos Políticos e Civis*, p. 52.

12. Cited in Rodrigues, *A Mulher Brasileira*, p. 57.

13. *Opinion No. 8-A*, May 18, 1928.

14. Several judgments published by the BFWP in 1929 under the title *O voto feminino perante a justiça* stipulated that it was to be legal for a woman to register in Rio de Janeiro, Ceará, Minas Gerais, Goiás, Alagoas, and Rio Grande do Norte.

15. Adalzira Bittencourt, *A Mulher Paulista na História*, p. 299.

16. From the accounts of Alzira Vargas do Amaral Peixoto, in *Getúlio Vargas Meu Pai* one can see that she was largely responsible for bringing her father's views on the social roles of women up to date.

17. Dr. Carlota Pereira de Queiroz, the first woman in the Brazilian legislative body, participated in the Constituent Assembly in 1933 as the São Paulo delegate. Dr. Bertha Lutz was named by the head of the provisional government to represent the organized feminist movement on the committee for a preliminary draft of the 1938 Constitution. After sounding out feminist opinion, Bertha Lutz prepared written suggestions, the only form of participation permitted by the bylaws. These centered on thirteen basic principles: rationalization of power, organization of the economy, humanization of work, nationalization of health services, universalization of social security, socialization of education, democratization of justice, sexual equality, guarantee of freedom, prohibition of violence, raising public morals, the flexibility of the laws, and maintenance of a dynamic legal system. In Bertha Lutz, *13 Princípios Básicos*, 1933. Each of the items in her draft bear clearly in one way or other on woman's position in society. But the generalized form in

which she formulated her suggestions showed her concern for women's participation on all levels of national and international life.

18. In 1936 she filled a post vacated by Deputy Cândido Pessoa; she was elected as an alternate, as a candidate of the Independent Voters League, feminist section of the Autonomous Party.

19. See the section entitled "Female Labor" in "Suggestions Concerning the Women's Bureau," presented by Bertha Lutz as a member of the Committee on the Statutes of Women, as an addendum to the Draft Bill 623, July 27, 1937. Under Lutz's sponsorship, this bill proposed the creation of a National Bureau and General Council for the Home, Female Labor, Social Security, and Insurance for Motherhood.

20. Similar ambivalence can be observed in the attitudes of some Brazilian feminists toward the notion of male chivalry. Daisy Pôrto, in her "As Mulheres e seus direitos," explains the feminists' aims in the struggle for reform of the Civil Code in this way:

> They say that the issue will be resolved next February (1959). The discussions are still going on. The leaders of the movement have been conscientiously trying, in a debate free of any scandal-mongering and of any unseemliness that might do damage to their objectives, to explain the reasons that have led them to struggle for this cause. They are careful to see that nothing occurs to misrepresent or distort the intended aim of this equality. It is not even admitted that women themselves may be the cause of ill-treatment their sex may have received. God save us if men, once we have gained these rights, come to feel that our constitution is henceforth as doughty as theirs and resolve to be done with the *chivalry* we expect of them, or rather, which *we need from them eternally. That would be a disaster!* (Italics mine.)

The Second International Feminist Congress, sponsored by the BFWP and held at Rio de Janeiro in 1931, passed the following resolution:

> To petition the railroad companies that run between the capital of the Republic and its suburbs, as well as others performing an analogous service in other major cities, such as São Paulo, to reserve each day special cars for women during peak hours; and, further, to call on the men who travel on these lines to cooperate in this initiative, confident as we are that the *innate chivalry of Brazilian men* will suffer them to honor from the very outset this innovation we aim to introduce. (Italics mine.)

(*O Trabalho Feminino* [A Mulher na ordem econômica e social],
Papers collected by Bertha Lutz, president of the commission for
the woman's statutes, p. 71.)

21. Bill 623, 1937, p. 11.
22. Article 141 of the 1934 Constitution states: "Assistance to
mothers and children is mandatory throughout all the nation's
territory, and for it the Union, the States, and the municipal
governments shall set aside one percent of their respective tax
proceeds."
23. Bertha Lutz, July 28, 1937, in Bill 623, p. 41.
24. Carlotta P. de Queiroz, July 28, 1937, in Bill 623, pp. 42-43.
25. However, some jurists were of the opinion that since the family
was not itself a proper juridical person, it could not be legally
represented, and that "if there is a natural representative in the
family this would much more logically be the woman." Jacob
Dolinger, *A Capacidade Civil da Mulher Casada a as Relações Conjugais de Ordem Pessoal no Código Civil e na Reforma da Lei
4,121*, p. 86.
26. Bill 3,263, the draft for which was prepared by Orlando Gomes
and discussed by a committee convened by its author, and integrated by Orosimbo Nonato e Caio Mario da Silva Pereira (see
Journal of the National Congress, Supplement no. 162, section I,
October 30, 1965), introduced some daring innovations, especially
under the paragraphs "Right of the Family" and "Laws of Inheritance." Article 119, section IV, "Annulment of Marriage," is
worth quoting: "Fundamental mistake: A marriage is also annull-
able when one of the spouses entered into it on the basis of a fundamentally mistaken judgment concerning the qualities of the
other, such that knowledge later acquired makes life together impossible." This caused a public uproar across the nation, and some
groups even mounted intense campaigns against the "divorce codi-
cil"—for example, the newspaper *O Estado de S. Paulo* and the Brazilian society for the Defense of Tradition, Family, and Property.
Others defended the bill, either because they supported divorce,
even if called by another name, or because they did not view it as
camouflaged divorce, as did the Catholic Church. *O Estado de S.
Paulo*, of July 26, 1966, contains a bitter exchange between the
Central Committee of the National Conference of Bishops of
Brazil, which supported the Orlando Gomes bill, and the Brazilian
Society for the Defense of Tradition, Family, and Property, a lay
Catholic organization, radically opposed to the "divorce bill."

Regarding the camouflaged divorce interpretation, see Teófilo Cavalcanti Filho, "Maioridade, desquite e família," an article in the series "O Projeto de Código Civil, Uma Análise," in *Fôlha de São Paulo*, July 17, 1966. The divorce law passed on December 26, 1977.

27. Movements organized by women, whether they call themselves feminist, or, as their militants prefer, "women's," whether molded in a leftist ideology or merely progressive, or finally, those which theoretically have no ideological leanings, but have come to be made up of persons inclined to negate the capitalist status quo, will be dealt with here in summary fashion, for two reasons. First, the 1964 revolution made it difficult to find any written material on these movements since such material was either confiscated by the police or destroyed by those holding it. Second, the movement of April 1 and ensuing police unease made it difficult to get oral accounts. Nevertheless, the material that I have been able to gather, mostly through personal interviews, is sufficient to trace the general direction taken by the activities of the women associated directly or indirectly with that ideology. Some facts are necessarily omitted as are names of individuals.

28. Bertha Lutz, who attended this meeting, was one of those who backed off.

29. The then president of the BFWP represented Brazilian women at the Council of the International Democratic Federation of Women; at a meeting in Prague in 1947, the BFWP joined this federation. When she returned to Brazil the president called a number of conferences at Minas Gerais, São Paulo, and in the former Federal District, in which she laid stress on the determination shown by the women of numerous countries in their struggle against the war and Nazism. She took a very active part in the peace movement, and was chosen to represent Brazil at the congresses at Paris and Mexico City, although, having been denied a passport, she was unable to attend.

Brazilian women had been represented at the First International Congress of Women sponsored by the International Democratic Federation of Women, between November 1926 and December 1, 1945, in Paris. The two Brazilian women who were permitted to speak underscored the role of men in fascism and the need to educate women politically to enable them to participate effectively in movements against war and against regimes upheld by force. See *Congrès International des Femmes*, published by the

International Democratic Federation of Women, Paris, 1946, pp. 84-86, and 182-83.

30. It seems that Juscelino Kubitschek was compelled to undertake these measures under pressure from groups of businessmen and women from the privileged strata.

31. The delegations who were to represent the BFW were not appointed by the executive board, but were chosen by elections held after a discussion of the problems by the municipal, state, and national organizations. For this reason, the Brazilian delegations which represented the BFW were always large in number, and the theses they presented reflected a variety of regional problems.

32. I am using this term as defined by Mannheim, as follows:

> By "reality level" we mean that every society develops a mental climate in which certain facts and their interrelations are considered basic and called "real," whereas other ideas fall below the level of "reasonably acceptable" statements and are called fantastic, utopian, or unrealistic. In every society there is a generally accepted interpretation of reality. In this sense every society establishes a set of respectable ideas through its conventions, and ostracizes any others as "diabolic," "subversive," or "unworthy." Being "real" or "less real" is always an *a priori* reason for ascribing more or less worth to certain facts. Whatever different schools of philosophy may think about this, and however much instrumentalism and logical positivism may consider such ontology fallacious, it is a sociological fact that public thinking unconsciously establishes such reality-levels, and a society is only integrated if its members roughly agree on a certain ontological order.

(Karl Mannheim, *Freedom, Power and Democratic Planning*, pp. 138-39.)

33. See Georges Gurvitch, *Tratado de Sociologia*, ch. 5; and Marcel Mauss, *Sociologie et Anthropologie*, pp. 273-79.

Notes to Chapter 10:
Psychoanalytic Theory and the Feminine Mystique

1. Sigmund Freud, *Three Essays on the Theory of Sexuality*, p. 107.
2. Sigmund Freud, *The Complete Introductory Lectures on Psychoanalysis*, vol. 32, p. 589.

3. Ibid., p. 593.
4. Ibid., p. 581.
5. Ibid., p. 596.
6. Ibid., p. 593.
7. Ibid., p. 594.
8. Ibid.
9. Ibid., p. 598-99.
10. An example is this passage from Henri Lefèbvre:

> One of the most evident, most "poetic"—in both senses of the word—consequences of modernity is the mature woman. Still beautiful and desirable, the youthfulness of her body still intact, and made truly human through the cultivation of feelings and sensitivity, this new Eve is no longer reduced to mere physiological or social functions; it is no longer, therefore, her alienation which determines her being. As an individual human being become an individual, who performs her functions without losing herself in them, who stands above the times, and indeed struggles against them by preparing the way to the dawn of a new era, this woman marks an extraordinary achievement, although still uncertain, restrained, and little understood (even by herself) by the modern age.

(Henri Lefèbvre, "Nature et conquêtes sur la nature," in *Introduction à la modernité*, p. 154.)

11. Robert K. Merton, *Social Theory and Social Structure*, p. 423.
12. Freud, *The Complete Introductory Lectures*, p. 595.
13. Ibid.
14. Georg Simmel, *Cultura femenina y otros ensayos*, p. 33.
15. Karen Horney, *The Neurotic Personality of Our Time*, especially ch.1, entitled "Cultural and Psychological Implications of Neuroses."
16. Florestan Fernandes, "A sociologia: Objeto e principais problemas," in *Ensaios de Sociologia Geral e Aplicada*, pp. 17-20.
17. Ibid., p. 20.
18. Durkheim considered that a "social fact is normal in relation to a given social type at a given phase of its development, when it is present in the average society of that species at the corresponding phase of its evolution." Emile Durkheim, *The Rules of Sociological Method*, p. 64.
19. Betty Friedan, *The Feminine Mystique*, ch. 8.
20. Helene Deutsch, *The Psychology of Women*, pp. 142-43.

21. Mead's works before 1944 included *Coming of Age in Samoa* (1928) and *Sex and Temperament in Three Primitive Societies* (1935).

22. Deutsch lists the psychological traits of women as "(1) greater proneness to identification, (2) stronger fantasy, (3) subjectivity, (4) inner perception, and (5) intuition . . ." In her view, these traits all stem from woman's passivity. Deutsch, *The Psychology of Women*, p. 139.

23. Karen Horney, "On the Genesis of the Castration Complex in Women," pp. 50-65, and "The Flight from Womanhood," pp. 324-39.

24. Karen Horney, *New Ways in Psychoanalysis*, pp. 112-13.

25. Ibid.

26. See Horney, *The Neurotic Personality of Our Time*.

27. Clara Thompson, "Cultural Pressures in the Psychology of Women," and "The Role of Women in this Culture," both in *A Study of Interpersonal Relations*, pp. 130-61.

28. Thompson, "Cultural Pressures in the Psychology of Women," p. 139.

29. See C. Wright Mills, *White Collar*.

Notes to Chapter 11:
Margaret Mead and Cultural Relativism

1. See especially *Male and Female*, and *Sex and Temperament in Three Primitive Societies*.

2. Margaret Mead, *Sex and Temperament*, p. 287.

3. Ibid., p. 313.

4. Ibid., p. 280.

5. Mead, *Male and Female*, pp. 159-60.

6. See Margaret Mead's analysis of North American society in part 4 Of *Male and Female*, especially ch. 11, entitled "Sex and Achievement."

7. Florestan Fernandes expresses what is meant here:

> in contrast to sociology, anthropology lacks the investigatory means to bring to light the deeper connections between types of social stratification and their corresponding cultural contents. Synchronic analysis (anthropology) unquestionably provides us with a detailed knowledge of the conduct of the members of each class, of relations between classes, etc., but as a rule it explains sociohistorical situations in terms of how the factors constitutive of these situations are integrated

within them, i.e., it interprets the present by the present, and is hence for the most part content to trace out the relations between ideal patterns and manifest behavior. Hence, the anthropologist finds himself constrained, if he sticks rigorously to the "cultural" method, to describe and rank social classes on the basis of objective, directly observable differences. Whereas the determining factors of the historicosocial situations are rendered inaccessible to anthropological analysis, sociological analysis has the isolation and explication of these factors as its principal objectives. Obviously, this shortcoming is not irremediable. On the contrary, the new trends toward a historical approach in anthropology have made some notable headway in pinpointing problems of this kind, despite the inordinate emphasis they place on cultural processes.

(Florestan Fernandes, "A análise sociológica das classes sociais," in *Ensaios de Sociologia Geral e Aplicada,* pp. 70-71.)

8. Mead, *Male and Female,* p. 384.
9. "In our own society, we have invented a therapeutic method that can laboriously deduce from the recollections of the neurotic or the untrammeled phantasies of the psychotic, how the human body, its entrances and exits, originally shaped the growing individual's view of the world." Ibid., p. 57. To be fair, it should be stated that Mead did not accept the whole of Freudian orthodoxy. She rejected, for example, the notion that the existence of a phallic stage in girls constituted a regular obstacle to complete sexual adjustment in women. But she did accept the notion of a girl's identification with her mother, if not as a permanent element in her life, at least as an intermittent process after the break that takes place at puberty. See ibid., pp. 114, 150.
10. For example, she wrote:

Living in the modern world, clothed and muffled, forced to convey our sense of our bodies in terms of remote symbols like walking sticks and umbrellas and handbags, it is easy to lose sight of the immediacy of the human body plan. But when one lives among primitive peoples, where women wear only a pair of little grass aprons, and may discard even these to insult each other or to bathe in a group, and men wear only a very lightly fastened G-string . . . and small babies wear nothing at all, the basic communications between infant, child, and adult that are conducted between bodies become very real.

(Ibid., p. 57.)

11. Mead, *Sex and Temperament*, p. 280.
12. Mead, *Male and Female*, pp. 382-83. Although the last two quotations were extracted from different books, it was not intended to point up the contradiction between the two. The contradiction is apparent enough taking *Male and Female* alone, and simply comparing the extracts.
13. See Jean-Paul Sartre, *Search for a Method*.

Notes to Chapter 12: Linkages Between the Occupational Structure and the Kinship Structure

1. This in no sense implies that planning is ineffective as a rational means of control of social problems. What is true, however, is that the full utilization of planning is unrealizable under the capitalist mode of production. Thus, in capitalist societies, efficacy of the planning techniques fall short of their actual potential, that is, they function to relieve the tensions generated by the mode of production.

2. The organic composition of capital undergoes a change as a result of the increase in the productivity of human labor: constant capital grows relative to variable capital. When we look beyond the composition of capital to the material elements, i.e., of which it is composed, "the difference between the mass of the means of production into which the constant, and the mass of the labor-power into which the variable, capital is converted" is even greater. (Karl Marx, *Capital*, vol. 1, p. 623.) Practically, all this means is that the capitalist appropriates a greater degree of surplus value with a smaller number of workers.

3. Talcott Parsons divides the criteria of role ascription into classificatory (sex, age, physical characteristics and personality traits) and relational (biological position, spatial location, temporal location, ecological situation, collectivity membership). See Talcott Parsons, *The Social System*, p. 142.

4. The segregation of women from the occupational structure has led some thinkers to equate womanhood as a sexual category with racial minorities, who have also remained relatively marginal to that structure. The two, however, are different, and have their own distinctive characteristics. As the pressures of the labor market force the absorption of some racial minority into the competitive social order, not only does this minority find itself with a new

means of access to the distribution of social wealth; the opportunities for interracial marriages may also be broadened, perhaps for that very reason. The visible racial features of the minority group, which very often brand the individual socially in a negative manner to place him at a competitive disadvantage with another racial group, may thus be lost through miscegenation. In the case of women, the quality singled out socially to regulate competition, namely, sex, can be neither diluted nor eliminated. Hence, it would be wrong to think that stratification based on sex will ever disapear from society.

Notes to Chapter 13:
The Position of Women in Dialectical Perspective

1. Georg Lukacs, *History and Class Consciousness*, p. 28.
2. This term is used to designate an unmarried woman, widow, divorced, legally or informally separated.
3. Luiz Pereira, *Trabalho e Desenvolvimento no Brasil*, pp. 51 and 53.
4. For a detailed discussion of the problems generated by the social division of labor and the technical division of labor, see Karl Marx and Friedrich Engels, *The German Ideology*. Also see chapter 14 of Karl Marx, *Capital*, vol. 1.
5. According to Marx, "While division of labour in society at large, whether such division be brought about or not by exchange of commodities, is common to economic formations of society the most diverse, division of labour in the workshop, as practised by manufacture, is a special creation of the capitalist mode of production alone." *Capital*, vol. 1, p. 359.
6. Even when capitalist enterprises attempt to make work pleasant by resorting to various techniques, this does not mean that the capitalist is concerned with the humanization of the worker. On the contrary, it is done in an effort to increase profits and thus the surplus value affirmed or negated by these profits. Even when essence and appearance coincide at an immediate level, the former must still be uncovered, so to speak, in the latter.
7. Marx and Engels, *The German Ideology*, p. 44.
8. For an analysis of productive and nonproductive labor, see Karl Marx, *Theories of Surplus-Value*, vol. 1, pp. 171-74.
9. Georg Simmel, *Cultura femenina y otros ensayos*, pp. 35, 36, 121.

Notes to Conclusion

1. Florestan Fernandes, "A Sociologia Aplicada: seu campo, objeto e pincipais problemas," in *Ensaios de Sociologia Geral e Aplicada,* p. 142.
2. Hence "the melancholy state of the practical work of social scientists, in Fernandes' terms. "For any social problem, whatever its gravity, the success of rational intervention will depend more on extraneous social influences which steer or spur on that intervention than on consciousness of ends, the availability of means, or on a combination of these two." Ibid., pp. 149-50.
3. Henri Lefèbvre, "Nature et conquêtes sur la nature," in *Introduction à la modernité,* p. 156.

Bibliography

References cited: English

Beauvoir, Simone de. *The Second Sex.* New York: Alfred A. Knopf, Inc., 1952.

Bebel, Auguste. *Women and Socialism.* New York: Socialist Literature Co., 1910.

Braverman, Harry. *Labor and Monopoly Capital.* New York: Monthly Review Press, 1974.

Central Statistical Office, Cabinet Council. *Women and Children in the USSR.* Moscow, 1963.

Chamber of Deputies, Hall of Committees. *The Opinion of the Special Commission on the Code for Women.* Brazil: National Printing Office, 1937.

Dahrendorf, Ralf. *Class and Conflict in Industrial Society.* Stanford, Cal.: Stanford University Press, 1959.

Deutsch, Helene. *The Psychology of Women,* vol. 1. New York: Grune and Stratton, 1944.

Durkheim, Emile. *The Rules of Sociological Method.* New York: Free Press of Glencoe, 1964.

Eaton, John. *Marx Against Keynes.* London: Lawrence and Wishart, 1951.

Engels, Friedrich. *The Condition of the Working Class in England.* Stanford, Calif.: Stanford University Press, 1958.

———. *The Origin of the Family, Private Property, and the State.* New York: International Publishers, 1942.

———. *Socialism: Utopian and Scientific.* New York: International Publishers, 1935.

Freud, Sigmund. *Three Essays on the Theory of Sexuality.* New York: Basic Books, 1962.

———. *Complete Introductory Lectures on Psychoanalysis.* New York: Basic Books, 1966.

Friedan, Betty. *The Feminine Mystique.* New York: Norton, 1963.

Glück, Elsie. "Women in Industry—Problems of Organization." In *Encyclopedia of the Social Sciences.* New York: Macmillan, 1935.

Goldmann, Lucien. *The Human Sciences and Philosophy.* London: Jonathan Cape, 1969.

Harrington, Michael. *The Other America.* New York: Macmillan, 1967.

Horney, Karen. *Feminine Psychology.* New York: Norton, 1967.

———. "The Flight from Womanhood." *International Journal of Psychoanalysis* (1926):324-39.

———. *New Ways in Psychoanalysis.* New York: Norton, 1939.

———. *The Neurotic Personality of Our Time.* New York: Norton, 1937.

———. "On the Genesis of the Castration Complex in Women," *International Journal of Psychoanalysis* 5 (1924):50-65.

Kleeck, Mary van. "Women in Industry." In *Encyclopedia of the Social Sciences.* New York: Macmillan, 1935.

Koyama, Takashi. *The Changing Social Position of Women in Japan.* Geneva: UNESCO, 1961.

Lenin, V. I. *The Emancipation of Women.* New York: International Publishers, 1970.

———. *Women and Society.* New York: International Publishers, 1966.

Lukacs, Georg. *History and Class Consciousness.* Cambridge, Mass.: MIT Press, 1971.

Mannheim, Karl. *Freedom, Power and Democratic Planning.* Oxford University Press, 1950.

———. *Essays on Sociology and Social Psychology.* New York: Oxford University Press, 1953.

———. *Ideology and Utopia.* New York: Harcourt, Brace and Co., 1936.

———. *Man and Society in an Age of Reconstruction.* New York: Harcourt, Brace & World, 1940.

Marx, Karl. *Capital,* vol. 1 and 2. New York: International Publishers, 1967.

———. *A Contribution to a Critique of Political Economy.* New York: International Publishers, 1970.

———. *Economic and Philosophical Manuscripts.* New York: International Publishers, 1964.

———. *Theories of Surplus-Value.* Vol. 1. Moscow: Progress Publishers, 1963.

———. *The Holy Family.* Moscow: Progress Publishers, 1975.

Marx, Karl, and Engels, Friedrich. *The Communist Manifesto.* New York: Monthly Review Press, 1964.

———. *The German Ideology.* Moscow: Progress Publishers, 1968.

———. *Selected Correspondence.* Moscow: Progress Publishers, 1975.

Mead, Margaret. *Coming of Age in Samoa.* New York: New American Library, 1951.

———. *Male and Female.* New York: William Morrow and Co., 1949.

———. *Sex and Temperament in Three Primitive Societies.* New York: William Morrow and Co., 1963.

Mello e Souza, Antônio Cândido. "The Brazilian Family." In *Brazil—Portrait of Half a Continent.* Ed. Thomas L. Smith. New York: Dryden, 1972.

Merton, Robert K. *Social Theory and Social Structure.* Glencoe, Ill.: Free Press, 1962.

Mills, C. Wright. *White Collar.* New York: Oxford University Press, 1951.

Mitchell, Juliet. "Women: The Longest Revolution," *New Left Review,* November-December, 1966.

Myrdal, Alva, and Klein, Viola. *Women's Two Roles.* London: Routledge and Kegan Paul, 1956, 1962.

Parsons, Talcott. *The Social System.* Glencoe, Ill.: Free Press, 1956.

Rowbotham, Sheila. *Woman's Consciousness, Man's World.* Baltimore, Md.: Penguin, 1973.

Sartre, Jean-Paul. *Search for a Method.* New York: Knopf, 1963.

Schlesinger, Rudolf. *Changing Attitudes in Soviet Russia.* Vol. I: *The Family in the USSR.* London: Routledge and Kegan Paul, 1949.

Smith, Ralph E. "Sources of Growth of the Female Labor Force, 1971-75," *Monthly Labor Review,* August 1977.

Smith, T. Lynn. *Brazil: People and Institutions.* Baton Rouge: Louisiana State University Press, 1954.

———. *People and Institutions.* Baton Rouge: Louisiana State University Press, 1954.

Smith, T. Lynn, and Marchant, Alexander. *Brazil: Portrait of Half a Continent.* New York: The Dryden Press, 1951.

Stern, Bernhard J. "Women, Position in Society: Historical." In *Ency-*

clopedia of the Social Sciences. New York: Macmillan, 1935.
Thompson, Clara. "Cultural Pressures in the Psychology of Women." In A Study of Interpersonal Relations. New York: Grove Press, 1949.
———. "The Role of Women in This Culture." In A Study of Interpersonal Relations. New York: Grove Press, 1949.
Weber, Max. Economy and Society. New York: Bedminster Press, 1968.
Wirth, Louis. Preface to Mannheim, Karl. Ideology and Utopia. New York: Harcourt, Brace and Co., 1936.

Portuguese, French, and Spanish

Albuquerque, Maria Sabina de, e Rezende, Zeia Pinho. "Atividades da Federação Brasileira pelo Progresso Feminino." 1962. Mimeographed.
Alcântara, Glete. A Enfermagem Moderna como Categoria Profissional: Obstáculos à sua Expansão na Sociedade Brasileira. Escola de Enfermagen de Ribeirão Prêto, Universidade de São Paulo, 1966.
Azevedo, Fernando de. A Cultura Brasileira. Ediçoes Melhoramentos, 1966.
Baretto, Tobias. Estudos de Sociologia. Instituto Nacional do Livro, Ministério da Educação e Cultura, 1962.
Barros, Roque Spencer Maciel de. Diretrizes e Bases da Educação. Livraria Pioneira Editôra, 1960.
———. A Ilustração Brasileira e a Idéia de Universidade. Bulletin 241. Faculdade de Filosofia, Ciências e Lêtras da U.S.P., 1959.
Barros, Vidal. Precursoras Brasileiras. Rio de Janeiro: A Noite Editôra, n.d.
Bastide, Roger, and Fernandes, Florestan. Brancos e Negros em São Paulo. Companhia Editôra Nacional, 1959.
Beer, Max. História do Socialismo e das Lutas Sociais. Editorial Calvino, 1944.
Beiguelman, Paula. Pequenos Estudos de Ciência Política. Editôra Centro Universitário, 1967.
Berger, Ida. Les Maternelles. Paris: Centre National de la Recherche Scientifique, 1959.
Berlinck, Manoel Tosta. "Algumas Percepções sôbre a mudança do papel ocupacional da mulher, na cidade de São Paulo." São Paulo, 1964. Mimeographed.

Binzer, Ina von. *Alegrias e Tristezas de uma Educadora Alemã no Brasil.* Editôra Anhembi, 1965.

Bittencourt, Adalzira. *A Mulher Paulista na História.* Rio de Janeiro: Livros de Portugal, 1954.

Câmara, Adauto da. *História de Nísia Floresta.* Rio de Janeiro: Irmãos Pongetti, 1941.

Cardone, Marly A. "A Mulher nas constituições Brasileiras," *Revista dos Tribunais* 360 (October 1965).

Cardoso, Fernando Henrique. *Capitalismo e Escravidão no Brasil Meridional.* Difusão Européia do Livro, 1962.

Castro, Tito Lívio de. *A Mulher e a Sociogenia.* Ed. Francisco Alves. Preface by Sílvio Romero dated 1893. Rio de Janeiro, n.d.

Cerati, Marie. *Le Club des Citoyennes Républicaines Révolutionnaires.* Paris: Editions Sociales, 1966.

Chombart de Lauwe, Paul-Henry. *Images de la Femme dans la Société.* Paris: Editions Ouvrières, 1964.

Colmeiro-Laforet, Carlos. *Orto y ocaso del feminismo.* Madrid: Tipografia Faro de Vigo, 1956.

Congrès International des Femmes. Paris: Fédération Democratique Internationale des Femmes, 1946.

Couto, Domingos Loreto. *Desagravos do Brasil e Glórias de Pernambuco.* Anais da Biblioteca Nacional do Rio de Janeiro, vol. 24.

Debret, Jean Baptiste. *Viagem Pitoresca e Histórica ao Brasil.* Livraria Martins Editôra, 1940.

Desanti, Dominique. *Visages des Femmes.* Paris: Editions Sociales, 1955.

Dias, Everardo. *História das Lutas Sociais no Brasil.* Editôra Edaglit, 1962.

Diégues Júnior, Manuel. *Imagração, Urbanização, Industrialização.* Instituto Nacional de Estudos Pedagógicos, 1964.

Dogan, Mattei, and Narbonne, Jacques. *Les Françaises face à la politique.* Paris: Librairie Armand Colin, 1955.

Dolinger, Jacob. *A Capacidade Civil da Mulher Casada e as Relações Conjugais de Ordem Pessoal, no Código Civil e na Reforma da Lei 4,121.* Edições Biblos, 1966.

Droz, Jacques. *Histoire de l'Allemagne.* Paris: Presses Universitaires de France, 1958.

Dumas, Francine. "La femme dans la vie sociale." In *Femmes du XXe siècle.* Paris: Presses Universitaires de France, 1965.

Expilly, Charles. *Mulheres e Costumes do Brasil.* Companhia Editôra Nacional, 1935.

Femmes Diplômées (Victor Duruy et l'Enseignement secondaire féminin). Edition de L'Association des Françaises Diplômées des Universités 43. Special issue, 1962.

Fernandes, Florestan. *A Integração do Negro à Sociedade de Classes.* Bulletin 301, Faculdade de Filosofia, Ciências e Lêtras da U.S.P., 1964.

———. *A Sociologia numa Era de Revolução Social.* Companhia Editôra Nacional, 1963.

———. *Ensaios de Sociologia Geral e Aplicada.* Livraria Pioneira Editôra, 1960.

———. *Fundamentos Empíricos da Explicação Sociológica.* Companhia Editôra Nacional, 1959.

Filho, Teófilo Cavalcanti. "O Projeto do Código Civil, Uma Análise." In *Fôlha de São Paulo.* 1966.

Fiorani, Mário. *Breve História do Fascismo.* Editôra Civilização Brasileira, 1963.

Freville, Jean. *La femme et le communisme.* Paris: Editions Sociales, 1951.

Freyre, Gilberto. *Casa-Grande e Senzala.* Livraria José Olympio Editôra, 1958.

———. *Sobrados e Mocambos.* Livraria José Olympio Editôra, 1961.

Furtado, Celso. *A Pré-revolução Brasileira.* Editôra Fundo de Cultura, 1962.

———. *Desenvolvimento e Subdesenvolvimento.* Editôra Fundo de Cultura, 1961.

———. *Formação Econômica do Brasil.* Editôra Fundo de Cultura, 1963.

———. *Subdesenvolvimento e Estagnação na América Latina.* Editôra Civilização Brasileira, 1966.

Girard, Allain; Petot, P.; Rouast, A., et al. *Sociologie Comparée de la Famille Contemporaine.* Paris: Colloques Internationaux du Centre National de la Recherche Scientifique, 1955.

Grégoire, Menie. "Mythes et réalités," *Esprit.* Paris (May 1961).

Guilbert, Madeleine. *Les Fonctions des femmes dans l'industrie.* The Hague: Mouton & Co., 1966.

Guilbert, Madeleine, and Isambert-Jamati, Viviane. "Statut professionnel et rôle traditionnel des femmes," *Cahiers Internationaux de Sociologie* 17 (1954).

———. *Travail féminin et travail à domicile.* Paris: Centre National de la Recherche Scientifique, 1956.

Gurvitch, Georges. *Tratado de Sociología.* Buenos Aires: Editorial Kapelusz, 1962.

Holanda, Sérgio Buarque de. *Raízes do Brasil.* Livraria José Olympio Editôra, 1948.

Hourdin, Georges. *Les Femmes célibataires vous parlent.* Paris: Editions du Cerf, 1962.

Ianni, Octávio. *As Metamorfoses do Escravo.* Difusão Européia do Livro, 1962.

Isambert-Jamati, Viviane. "Adaptation au travail et niveau de qualification des femmes salariées," *Revue Française de Sociologie* 1 (January-March 1960).

Klein, Viola. *El carácter femenino.* Buenos Aires: Editorial Paidós, 1958.

Lafargue, Paul. "La Question de la femme." In *La Femme et le communisme.* Paris: Editions Sociales, 1951.

La Femme à la recherche d'elle-même. Paris: La Palatine, 1966.

"La Politique sociale face à l'évolution des besoins de la famille, pour la vie," *Revue d'Etudes Familiales* 85-86 (July 1961).

Lefébvre, Henri. *Introduction à la modernité.* Paris: Editions de Minuit, 1961.

Leite, Serafim. *História da Companhia de Jesus no Brasil.* Livraria Portugália, 1938.

Leme, Pedro Taques de Almeida Paes. *Nobiliarchia Paulistana Histórica e Genealógica.* Livraria Martins Editôra, 1953.

Lévi-Strauss, Claude. *Les Structures élémentaires de la parenté.* Paris: Presses Universitaires de France, 1949.

"L'Homme dans son foyer," *Revue Mensuelle de l'Action Sociale et des Services Sociaux* 4 (April 1962).

Lutz, Bertha. *13 Princípios Básicos* (Sugestões ao Anteprojeto da Constituição). Rio de Janeiro: Edição da Federação Brasileira pelo Progresso Feminino, 1933.

Luz, Nícia Vilela. *A Luta pela Industrialização do Brasil.* Difusão Européia do Livro, 1961.

Machado, Alcântara A. *Vida e Morte do Bandeirante.* Livraria Martins Editôra, 1965.

Maire, Gilbert. *L'homme et la femme.* Paris: Editions du Vieux Colombier, 1952.

"Manifesto Feminista," *Educação* 3, no. 2 (May 1928). Diretoria Geral da Instrução Pública e Sociedade de Educação de São Paulo.

Marzellier, Françoise. "Une enquête sur le travail féminin," *Les Temps Modernes* 180 (April 1961).

Mauss, Marcel. *Sociologie et Anthropologie.* Paris: Presses Universitaires de France, 1960.

Maynaud, Jean. *Les Groupes de pression en France.* Paris: Librairie Armand Colin, 1962.

Mello e Sousa, Antônio Cândido. "A vida familial do caipira," *Sociologia* 16, no. 4 (October 1954).

Michel, Andrée. *Famille, Industrialisation, Logement.* Paris: Centre National de la Recherche Scientifique, 1959.

Michel, Andrée, and Texier, Geneviève. *La condition de la française d'aujourd'hui.* Geneva: Editions Gonthier, 1964.

Moacyr, Primitivo. *A Instrução e o Império.* Companhia Editôra Nacional, 1936.

———. *A Instrução e a República.* Vol. 4. Rio de Janeiro: Imprensa Nacional, 1942.

Moscovici, Marie. "Le changement social en milieu rural et le rôle des femmes," *Revue Française de Sociologie* 3 (July-September 1960).

Muldworf, Bernard. "La Femme à la recherche de sa personne." In *La Femme à la recherche d'elle-même.* Paris: La Palatine, 1965.

Mulheres Brasileiras. Rio de Janeiro: Galeria da Fundação Osório, 1950.

Noireaut-Blanc, Raymonde. *Tous les droits de la femme.* Paris: Union Générale d'Editions, 1964.

Oliveira, Lima. "Nísia Floresta," *Revista do Brasil* 12, no. 48 (December 1919).

O Voto Feminino perante a Justica. Federação Brasileira pelo Progresso Feminino, 1929.

Ossowski, Stanislaw. *Estrutura de Classes na Consciência Social.* Zahar Editôres, 1964.

Peixoto, Afrânio. *Ensinar a Ensinar.* Companhia Editôra Nacional, 1937.

———. *Martha e Maria.* Rio de Janeiro: Documentos de Acção Pública, 1930.

Peixoto, Alzira Vargas do Amaral. *Getúlio Vargas, meu Pai.* Editôra Globo, 1960.

Pereira, Luiz. *O Magistério Primário na Sociedade de Classes.* Boletin 277. Faculdade de Filosofia, Ciências e Lêtras da U.S.P., 1963.

———. *Trabalho e Desenvolvimento no Brasil.* Difusão Européia do Livro, 1965.

Peres, Tirza Regazziai. "Advento da Escola Normal Livre e seus resultados comparados com os da Escola Normal Oficial (1927-1930)." Mimeographed.

———. "Ensino Secundário no Estado de São Paulo (1920-1933)." Mimeographed.

Pierson, Donald. "Família e compadrio numa comunidade rural paulista," *Sociologia* 16, no. 4 (October 1954).

Pimentel d'Oliveira Júnior, José Pires. *A Doutrina Social da Igreja.* Dominus Editôra, 1962.

Pôrto, Daisy. "As Mulheres e seus direitos," *Suplemento Intergráfico SINGRA* 18, no. 305 (1958).

Prado Júnior, Caio. *A Revolução Brasileira.* Editôra Brasiliense, 1966.

———. *Evolução Política do Brasil e Outros Estudos.* Editôra Brasiliense, 1953.

———. *Formação do Brasil Contemporâneo.* Editôra Brasiliense, 1963.

———. *História Econômica do Brasil.* Editôra Brasiliense, 1963.

"Rapport Général de la Commission d'Etudes des Problèmes de la Famille, Pour la Vie." *Revue d'Etudes Familiales,* no. 88 (March 1962).

Rochefort, Renée. "La Femme dans les pays sous-développés." In *La Femme à la recherche d'elle-même.* Paris: La Palatine, 1966.

Rodrigues, João Batista Cascudo. *A Mulher Brasileira: Direitos Políticos e Civis.* Fortaleza: Imprensa Universitária do Ceará, 1962.

Rodrigues, Leôncio Martins. *Conflito Industrial e Sindicalismo no Brasil.* Difusão Européia do Livro, 1966.

Sá e Benevides, José Maria Corrêa de. *Filosofia Elementar do Direito Público Interno. Temporal e Universal.* São Paulo: Tipografia Baruel, 1887.

Saint-Hilaire, Auguste de. *Voyages aux sources du rio São Francisco et dans la Province de Goyaz.* Paris, 1847.

Sartin, Pierrette. *La Promotion des Femmes.* Paris: Librairie Hachette, 1964.

Sartre, Jean-Paul. *Questions de Méthodes.* New York: French and European Pubs., 1971.

Serebrennikov, T. *La Mujer en la Union Soviética.* Moscow, 1948.

Simmel, Georg. *Cultura femenina y otros ensayos.* Colección Austral, 1946.

Simonsen, Roberto C. *História Econômica do Brasil.* Companhia Editôra Nacional, 1962.

Sodré, Nelson Werneck. *A Ideologia do Colonialismo.* Editôra Civilização Brasileira, 1965.

———. *As Razões da Independência.* Editôra Civilização Brasileira, 1965.

———. *Formação Histórica do Brasil.* Editôra Civilização Brasileira, 1964.

———. *Introdução à Revolução Brasileira.* Editôra Civilização Brasileira, 1963.

Stavenhagen, Rodolfo. "Estratificação social e estrutura de classes." In *Estratificação Social e Estrutura de Classes.* Zahar Editôres, 1966; originally in *Ciencias Políticas y Sociales* 8, no. 27 (January-March 1972). Journal of Escuela Nacional de Ciencias Políticas y Sociales, Universidad Autónoma de México.

Sullerot, Evelyne. *Demain les femmes.* Geneva: Laffont & Gonthier, 1965.

———. *La pressé féminine.* Paris: Librairie Armand Colin, 1966.

———. *La vie des femmes.* Paris: Editions Gonthier, 1965.

Taunay, Affonso de E. *História da Villa de São Paulo, no século XVIII.* São Paulo: Imprensa Oficial, 1931.

Teixeira Mendes, Raimundo. *A Mulher* (A preeminência social e moral da mulher segundo os ensinos da verdadeira ciência positivista). Rio de Janeiro: Empreza Brasil Editôra, 1920.

Thibert, Marguerite. "L'évolution du travail féminin," *Esprit* (May 1961).

Thomas, Edith. *Les Femmes en 1848.* Paris: Presses Universitaires de France, 1948.

Werneck, Olga. "O subdesenvolvimento e a situação da mulher," *Revista Civilização Brasileira*, no. 4 (September 1965).

Willems, Emílio. "A estrutura da família brasileira," *Sociologia* 16, no. 4 (October 1954).

Documents

Anais da Assembléia, Legislativa Provincial, 1835-1861. 1926.

Annaes do Parlamento Brasileiro. Chamber of Deputies, sessions 1826 to 1834. Rio de Janeiro: Tipografia do Imperial Instituto Artístico.

Annaes do Parlamento Brasileiro. Constituent Assembly, 1823. Rio de Janeiro: Tipografia do Imperial Instituto Artístico, 1872.

Código Civil Brasileiro. Law 3,071, January 1, 1916. Historical and critical introduction by Dr. Paulo de Lacerda. Ed. Jacintho Ribeiro dos Santos. Rio de Janeiro, 1916.

Consolidação das Leis de Assistência e Proteção a Menores e Mulheres. São Paulo: Edições e Publicacões Brasil Editôra, n.d.

Constituicões do Brasil. São Paulo: Edição Saraiva, 1963.

Diretrizes e Bases da Educação Nacional. Imprensa Nacional, 1961.

Enciclopédia da Legislaçao do Ensino. Ed. Vandrick Londres da Nóbrega. São Paulo: Rodrigues & Cia., 1954.

O Trabalho Feminino (A Mulher na ordem econômica e social). Documents collected by Bertha Lutz. Imprensa Nacional, 1937.

Paracer da Comissão Especial do Estatuto da Mulher. Chamber of Deputies. Imprensa Nacional, July 3, 1937.

Paracer no. 8-A. Imprensa Nacional, May 18, 1928.

Projeto no. 623. Imprensa Nacional, 1937.

Projeto no. 736. Chamber of Deputies. Imprensa Nacional, October 15, 1937.

Projeto de Código do Trabalho. Comissão de Estudos Legislativos do Ministério da Justiça e Negócios Interiores, Serviço de Reforma dos Códigos, 1965.

"Projeto no. 3,263. Código Civil." Chamber of Deputies, 1965. Mimeographed. Also in "Diário do Congresso Nacional," supplement 162, sect. 1, October 30, 1965.

Relatório ao Secretário do Interior, Alarico Silveira ao Presidente do Estado de São Paulo,Washington Luis Pereira de Sousa. Office of "Diario Oficial." Those from 1921 and 1922 published in 1922 and 1923.

Sources of Portuguese Statistics

Anuário do Ensino do Estado de São Paulo, 1935-1936. Secretaria da Educação e da Saúde Pública. São Paulo: Tipografia Siqueira.

Anuário Estatístico do Brasil. Rio de Janeiro: IBGE, 1955.

Anuário Estatístico do Brasil. Rio de Janeiro: IBGE, 1960.

Anuário Estatístico do Brasil. Rio de Janeiro: IBGE, 1964.

Anuário Estatístico do Brasil. Rio de Janeiro: IBGE, 1965.

Anuário Estatístico do Brasil. Rio de Janeiro: IBGE, 1966.

Censo Agrícola (Recenseamento Geral do Brasil, 1950). Vol. 2. Rio de Janeiro: IBGE, 1956.

Censos Agrícola, Industrial, Comercial e dos Serviços. (Recenseamento Geral do Brasil, 1 de setembro de 1940). Rio de Janeiro: Serviço Gráfico do IBGE, 1950.

Censos Comercial e dos Serviços (Recenseamento Geral do Brasil, 1950). Vol. 3, bk. 2. Rio de Janeiro: IBGE, 1956.

Censo Demográfico (Recenseamento Geral do Brasil, 1960). Special series, vol. 5. Rio de Janeiro: Serviço Gráfico do IBGE, 1965.

Censo Demográfico (Recenseamento Geral do Brasil, 1 de setembro de 1940). Rio de Janeiro: Serviço Gráfico do IBGE, 1950.

Censo Demográfico (Recenseamento Geral do Brasil, 1 de julho de 1950). Rio de Janeiro: IBGE, 1956.

Estatística Escolar de 1930. São Paulo: Secção de Estatística e Archivo, 1931.

Estatística Intelectual do Brasil. Departamento Nacional de Estatística, Ministério do Trabalho, Indústria e Comércio. Rio de Janeiro: Tipografia do Departamento Nacional de Estatística, 1931.

Salários. (Recenseamento do Brasil, 1 de setembro de 1920). Ministério da Agricultura, Indústria e Comércio, Diretoria Geral de Estatística. Tipografia da Estatística, 1928.

Sinopse do Recenseamento realizado em 1 de setembro de 1920 (contains data for 1872, 1890, 1900, and 1920). Rio de Janeiro: Tipografia da Estatística, 1924.

Sinopse do Recenseamento realizado em 1 de setembro de 1920 (contains data for 1872, 1890, 1900, and 1920). Rio de Janeiro: Tipografia da Estatística, 1925.

Sinopse do Recenseamento realizado em 1 de setembro de 1920 (contains data for 1872, 1900, and 1920). Ministério da Agricultura, Indústria e Comércio, Diretoria Geral de Estatística. Rio de Janeiro: Tipografia da Estatística, 1926.

Sinopse Estatística do Ensino Superior, 1965. Rio de Janeiro: IBGE, 1966.